CHRISTIAN CELEBRATION
Understanding the Sacraments

ERSIT

CHRISTIAN CELEBRATION:

Understanding the Mass
Understanding the Sacraments
Understanding the Prayer of the Church

CHRISTIAN CELEBRATION

Understanding the Sacraments

J.D. Crichton

**GEOFFREY
CHAPMAN**

Geoffrey Chapman
An imprint of Cassell Publishers Limited
Villiers House, 41/47 Strand, London WC2N 5JE
387 Park Avenue South, New York, NY 10016–9910

First published 1973 as *Christian Celebration: The Sacraments*
Second edition first published 1980
Reissued as part of 1-volume *Christian Celebration* 1982
Third edition first published 1993

British Library Cataloguing-in-Publication Data
A catalogue record for this book is available from the British Library.

Library of Congress Cataloging-in-Publication Data
Available from the Library of Congress.

ISBN 0–225–66670–7

Typeset by Colset Pte Ltd, Singapore
Printed and bound in Great Britain by
Biddles Ltd, Guildford and King's Lynn

Contents

Preface

~~~~~

THE SUBJECT-MATTER of this volume of *Christian Celebration* is the revised liturgy of the sacraments of baptism, confirmation, matrimony, holy order and the Anointing of the Sick. To this has been added a consideration of the revised funeral rites.

After a prolonged study of these documents I have become conscious of the wide range and variety of knowledge that is necessary for an adequate treatment of them. What is to be found here is only an introduction. Even so, in covering so wide a range I cannot hope that the book is free of errors. For this I must beg the indulgence of the reader and express the hope that when he finds them he will let me know and I will correct them if a second edition should become possible.

There are other texts, notably the new breviary or 'Liturgy of the Hours' which I have not been able to deal with in this volume. Whether it will be possible to write yet another volume I do not know but for me the main work has been done and it is my hope that what I have written here will be of use to those who wish to celebrate the Roman liturgy in its present form.

I wish to record my sincere thanks to Mrs Olive Yeo who has typed the whole of this book.

Lent   J.D.C.
1973

PREFACE TO THE SECOND EDITION

WHEN I was writing the first edition of this book the Order of Penance had not appeared and in Chapter XI I speculated on what it might contain. The Constitution on the Liturgy (n. 72) had said that the rite and formulae of the sacrament were to be revised so that they might the more clearly express both its nature and

~

its effect. In addition there were the general injunctions of the Constitution concerning the requirements for any liturgical service: it is an act of the church, not a 'private function'; there must be a proclamation of God's word; the service must have a certain visibility and must be such that the people can take an active part in it. At the time it was not possible to see how the principles would be applied. With the promulgation of the *Ordo Paenitentiae* in 1973 all became clear. As expected, the rite of private penance was retained (though revised) and the corporate and ecclesial nature of the sacrament was expressed more fully in the second and third rites.

To provide some considerations on the new Order of Penance I wrote *The Ministry of Reconciliation* which first appeared in 1974. A second edition appeared with one or two corrections in 1976. This book is now out of print, though at the time of writing is still obtainable, and my publishers have thought that the usefulness of *Christian Celebration: The Sacraments* would be increased and its life extended if the chapter on Penance were re-written and, in view of all that has happened in the liturgical field since 1973, if some additions were made to the last chapter of the book, 'Pastoral Opportunities'. This I have done. Other changes are minor. One or two errors were corrected in the reprint of 1974 and misprints that escaped my notice have also been put right.

For the rest the book remains what it was. No doubt if I were writing it now some emphases would be different but I have seen no need to make any substantial changes. The book seems to have served its purpose as an introduction to the revised liturgy of the sacraments other than that of the eucharist which is dealt with in *Christian Celebration: The Mass*. Comments and correspondence from various parts of the world seem to support such a view and I wish to express my thanks to those who were sufficiently interested to send observations and corrections.

I did a good deal of the revision in France et ici je voudrais exprimer ma profonde reconnaissance aux membres de la Communauté de Notre Dame de la Pépiole qui m'ont toujours accueilli avec une grande bonté et gentillesse. Ils ont contribué plus qu'ils ne s'imaginent à cet ouvrage et à d'autres en me ménageant une locale et une ambiance où je pouvais étudier et écrire.

Notre Dame de la Pépiole   J.D.C.
1979

PREFACE TO THE THIRD EDITION

*T*HIS BOOK has been in use for nearly twenty years and still seems to be in demand. I've done my best to bring it up to date in the hope that its life will be prolonged a little further.

March   J.D.C.
1992

A List of Documents

SINCE THE number of new Orders is now considerable, I have thought it would be convenient to list in one place those used in this book. They have appeared at various times but the order given here is that in which they are considered in this volume.

Ordo Initiationis Christianae Adultorum, 1972; *Rite of Christian Initiation of Adults*, 1985.

Ordo Baptismi Parvulorum, 1969, 2nd ed. 1973; *The Rite of the Baptism of Children*, 1970.

Ordo Celebrandi Matrimonium, 1969, 2nd ed. 1990; various English editions of the 1969 rite.

Pontificale Romanum: De Ordinatione Diaconi, Presbyteri et Episcopi, 1968.

Pontificale Romanum: De Ordinatione Episcopi, Presbyteri, et Diaconi, 1990.

De Institutione Lectorum et Acolythorum; de Admissione inter candidatos ad Diaconatum. De Sacro Caelibatu amplectendo (Ministries of Reader and Acolyte with the Admission to the Clerical State and the Declaration on Celibacy).

Ordo Unctionis Infirmorum eorumque Pastoralis Curae, 1972; *Pastoral Care of the Sick*, 1982.

Ordo Exsequiarum, 1969; English edition, *Order of Christian Funerals*, 1990.

Ordo Benedicendi Oleum Catechumenorum et Infirmorum et Conficiendi Chrismae, 1971 (referred to in Chapters 2 and 9).

Ordo Paenitentiae, 1973; English edition with official ICEL translation, *The Rite of Penance*, 1976.

Their contents are as follows:

Decree of promulgation; *Praenotanda*, pastoral-theological notes, here called 'Introduction'; the rite; permitted variations; a collection of alternative texts (when not included in the rite); a collection of scripture readings which may be used in the celebration of the rites. With the exception of the Order of Adult Initiation and the Ordination rites, these orders are numbered throughout from the first paragraph of the introduction to the end of the book, including the rites themselves. Each part of the rite thus has its own number. Three, the Orders of Confirmation, Ordination and the Anointing of the Sick, where matters of importance for sacramental theology are concerned, were promulgated by an Apostolic Constitution of the Pope. Two, the lesser ministries and the admission to the clerical state etc., were promulgated by *Motu proprio* (*Ministeria quaedam* and *Ad Pascendum* respectively). The juridical status of these documents will be of interest primarily to canonists. The Apostolic Constitutions are the most important as they fully engage the papal authority.

The official texts, in Latin, of all these documents are published by the Vatican Press.

Abbreviations

~~~~~~

CL = Constitution on the Liturgy (1963), in the translation of Rev. Clifford Howell, SJ (Whitegate Publications, Cirencester, 1963).

Titles of other council documents are given in full.

CI = Christian Initiation to be found in *Ordo Baptismi Parvulorum*.

BP = *Ordo Baptismi Parvulorum* (infant baptism).

Occasional references to the General Instruction of the *Ordo Missae* (1969/1970) will be found under GI followed by the number of the paragraph.

LMD = *La Maison-Dieu*.

ST = *Summa Theologica* (St Thomas Aquinas).

AAS = *Acta Apostolicae Sedis* ('Acts of the Apostolic See').

Denz. = *Enchiridion Symbolorum, Definitionum et Declarationum de Rebus Fidei et Morum*, comp. H. Denzinger (1854) and others subsequently to the 31st edition (Barcelona, 1960) inclusive.

Denz.-Schön. = *Enchiridion* . . . (as above), 32nd edition with new numeration ed. A. Schönmetzer (Barcelona, 1963) and subsequent editions.

LXX = Septuagint (Greek).

Vulg. = Vulgate (Latin).

~

Translations

~~~~~~

For the Council documents (other than the Constitution on the Liturgy) I have used the translations in *The Documents of Vatican II*, ed. Walter Abbott, SJ (Geoffrey Chapman, 1966).

The Abbott translation has long been out of print. See now *Vatican II: The Conciliar and Post Conciliar Documents*, ed. Austin Flannery, OP (Costello Publishing Company, New York). Vol. I (2nd ed., 1988) gives all the documents of Vatican II and the documents concerning the liturgy that came shortly after the Council. Vol. II (1982) gives the Introductions (*Praenotanda*) in translation to all the Orders and certain other documents concerning the liturgy up to 1981. Two more volumes are in preparation.

Translations of the texts of the Orders are generally my own though I have made much use of the ICEL version for marriage. Thanks are due to the International Commission on English in the Liturgy for permission to use it here and in one or two other places. For scripture versions I have generally used the Jerusalem Bible (Darton, Longman and Todd, 1966) and occasionally the Revised Standard Version (Thomas Nelson and Sons, 1966).

Editions

~~~~~~

Editions of the Sacramentaries are as follows:

Verona (Leonine): ed. Mohlberg (Rome, 1956).

Gelasian: ed. Mohlberg (Rome, 1960).

Gregorian: ed. Lietzmann (Münster, 1921; reprint, 1967).

For patristic texts details of editions are given the text.

The most convenient edition of the *Apostolic Tradition* is *Hippolytus: A Text for Students. With Introduction, Translation, Commentary and Notes*, ed. Geoffrey J. Cuming (Grove Books, Nottingham, 1976).

~

To
Conrad Pepler, OP

πολλῶν ἕνεκα

The Sacraments and Life

~~~~~~~

T HE PLACE of the sacraments in the Christian life has varied a good deal in the history of the church. In the Middle Ages the sacraments were above all the sacred actions performed by the priest who alone had their secret. Including the eucharist, they were celebrated almost wholly without a ministry of the word which in any case was unintelligible to the people. They indeed brought a certain faith to the celebration and the sacraments existed in a society permeated by the Christian faith. This is some justification of the procedure. But the situation was not a happy one. It was all too easy to think that by going through certain ritual actions one was saved. With the Reformers' heavy emphasis on the word the sacraments ceased to play a dominant role in the Protestant world and came to be disregarded. On the Catholic side, the emphasis on the *ex opere operato* effect of the sacraments served to continue medieval tradition though, with the gradual renewal of the Christian life, they came to be celebrated in a new atmosphere of devotion. The realization grew that the reception of the sacraments required certain conditions and had consequences in Christian living though the notion that people should be prepared, 'evangelized', for them remained weak. The famous Mère Angélique Arnauld who, with papal permission, was made Abbess of Port-Royal in the first decade of the seventeenth century had no formal instruction for her confirmation and first communion and *she* was from an orthodox and devout family.[1] Detestable as Jansenist doctrines were and regrettable as were the unending controversies that ensued, the demand of Saint-Cyran, Mère Angélique herself and others of this period, some of whom were hardly formal Jansenists at all, that the sacraments, especially penance and the eucharist, required serious preparation and sincerity of heart, was right and reasonable.

In the eighteenth century, the age of the 'Enlightenment', sacramental practice waned. The *philosophes* and the Encyclopedists saw in sacramental worship hardly more than the relics of primitive religions which were now becoming known in an elementary way. Religion – if

there was to be religion–was to be based on a rather superficial rational-
ism. What could not be explained or justified on the shallow criteria of
the time must be rejected. Religion was the non-worship of an inopera-
tive Deity combined with a tedious moralism and an emphasis on duty.
In this atmosphere the sacraments had no place. Nor was all well
within the church. In France especially, in Germany, the home of the
Aufklärung, and even in Italy (e.g. the Synod of Pistoia), the clergy and
many of the laity were affected by the rationalist ideas of the time. The
sober, sacramental piety of a Challoner in the apparently dying Catholic
Church in England was not too common in Europe. The people, especially those of the rural parts of Europe, remained attached to the traditional rites, few infants remained unbaptized, but there was already a
suggestion of folklore about the whole business.[2]

As is well known, the Romantic Movement that began to affect ordinary life and thinking after the French Revolution created an atmosphere
that made possible the beginnings of the liturgical renewal. Not everything that was mysterious and inexplicable by the pedestrian principles
of a rationalist philosophy was to be rejected. The poets and writers
indeed exalted the irrational and there were a few theologians, the
fideists, who would cheerfully have fallen into the trap of irrationality
if they had not been called to order. There were those who would have
cried with Tertullian *Credo quia impossibile*. The early liturgical movement was not wholly free from such notions and when its leader,
Guéranger, decided to throw in his lot with the Ultramontanes, the
danger of a papalist fideism was real. At the same time the sacraments
were still seen as the religion of duty. Young ladies were prepared for
their 'duties' which did not mean the married state but confirmation,
confession and communion.

In the twentieth century, with the admission of young children to
communion, with its ever more frequent reception and with the gathering impetus of the liturgical movement, sacramental practice has steadily
improved. But until the Second Vatican Council we were still burdened
with fossilized medieval rites; even those sacraments which theologians
commonly called the 'sacraments of the living' (confirmation, the
eucharist, etc.) were administered in a dead language. In spite of and
no doubt because of this, efforts were made to secure a more lively
celebration of the sacraments. The clergy resorted to 'commentaries',
'catechesis', the value of the symbols (candle, white garment) was

enhanced and attempts were made to gather the local community for baptism. But the ritual remained unbendable,[3] as did the danger that sacraments would be seen to be divorced from ordinary living. The people were still almost wholly passive: a sacrament was valid provided the recipient put no *obex* in the way. They had little or no part to play except their physical presence and of course, in the case of baptism, to provide the baby!

Vatican II changed most of this but, what is more important, it consecrated a theology of the sacraments that had long been forgotten. This change can be summed up under three heads:

1. We are saved by faith and the sacraments of faith[4] which means that apart from the single exception of infant baptism, the participant must have a real, living faith in Christ before he can receive a sacrament;
2. As a result of this the sacrament is seen as the place of encounter with Christ in the fullness of his redeeming activity, called the paschal mystery;[5]
3. The people are not merely receivers of the sacraments, nor only participants. They are the celebrants (with the appointed minister) of the sacraments. This is marked by the constant appeal for their participation and by the emphasis laid in all the revised rites on the presence of the community.

If we are saved by faith, then we must have the faith preached to us (cf. Romans 10:14–17). Whether this 'preaching' is called 'evangelization', as seems to be the fashion now, or 'instruction' with all its daunting associations, does not for the moment matter. The axiom postulates and demands a living conscious faith which has often been *assumed* in the past but which cannot be assumed now. That is why the new rites require that there shall be no celebration of the sacraments without a proclamation of the word.[6] But faith is not to be regarded merely as a prerequisite of sacramental celebration. It needs to be expressed, and indeed is, in the celebration. Nor is this just a psychological device, though it has the immense value of enabling people to realize the truth of the axiom. The faith of the celebrants is manifested and concretized in the sacramental action itself. When a Christian engages in the celebration of a sacrament he is saying both by word and action that he believes in God and in his redeeming love made available to him in the sacrament. On the other hand, the rite of the sacrament expresses the faith of the whole church. *This* is what the church believes of, say, baptism or the eucharist and the new rites have this great virtue that they have spelt out more clearly than before what is the faith of the church as far as the sacraments are concerned. This is the meaning of St Thomas's phrase[7] that the celebration of a sacrament is a *protestatio fidei*, a profession of faith, first of the faith of the church and then of those who here and now are proclaiming it.

Further, it is because of the deep reverence for God and his saving purpose this faith witnesses to that the sacrament can be said 'to give worship to God'.[8] Through our 'faithful' approach to the sacraments we are showing our complete dependence on God, on God the Saviour, and when in the sacramental action this faith is manifested and externalized, then Christians at least can see that they are glorifying God. We are reminded once again of the phrase of Irenaeus: *Gloria Dei, vivens homo.* It is the man of faith who out of the depths of his being recognizes his need of God who gives him the glory.

But man approaches the Father only through the Son and he wishes to meet God, to enter into union with him so that he can live *in* God. In the sacraments, then, we approach Christ who has taught us that in these actions we call sacraments and which are the signs of his covenanted love, he is present. In them he takes up our faith, our love and whatever devotion we can bring to them and infuses into that faith and love and devotion his own divine life and love so that we can be united to the Father. The sacraments are not to be seen simply as adjuncts of the Christian life, sanctified lifts or elevators that transfer us to the supernatural order, nor merely as so many 'helps' (though they are that) to enable us to do those things we ought to do and avoid those things we ought not to do. They are the high moments of the Christian life when it achieves its most authentic expression. They are the most concrete signs of our faith, our love and our life, of what we really *are* – if of course we are at least trying to lead the Christian life.

Sacraments, then, are not isolated ecclesiastical rites but events in the flowing life of the church and in the life of man. It is the vocation of the church to go out to man, to preach the Gospel, to 'evangelize', to spread abroad a knowledge of Christ, to confront men with the life, passion, death and resurrection of Christ so that they may accept him by faith. But the faith they profess is not something extraneous to the sacraments.

~

These are, as we have said, concrete expressions of the faith that has come from hearing and the grace of God. There is a continuity between the faith in the heart and the faith expressed in the sacraments. When the convert is 'received', he is incorporated into a community of faith which by its very existence is the sign of faith in the world, the sacrament of Christ, as we have learnt to say, present in the world. Once incorporated, the convert then has to take up his task of proclaiming the faith to others and this, in the teaching of the new confirmation rite, he does by virtue of that sacrament. This too is the teaching of the Second Vatican Council: 'As members of the living Christ, all the faithful have been incorporated into him and made like him through baptism, confirmation and the eucharist. Hence all are duty-bound to co-operate in the expansion and growth of his Body, so that they can bring it to fulness as swiftly as possible (Ephesians 4:13).'[9]

Evangelization, then, liturgy and mission are all of a piece and the first and the third of these elements has for its purpose the drawing of men into an encounter with Christ in the liturgy. This is the perspective even of the Constitution on the Liturgy (9): the church has to proclaim the good news of salvation so that men may be converted and meet Christ. Even to believers the church must preach faith and repentance, must prepare them for the sacraments and 'invite them to all the works of charity, piety and the apostolate'. The sacramental community must be a missionary community, drawing its strength from Christ who makes himself present in the liturgy and leading men into it. Hence we get the saying 'The liturgy is the summit towards which the activity of the church is directed and at the same time the source from which all her power flows' (*ibid.*, 10).

So far then it is clear that the sacraments have been fully integrated into the Christian life, even if practice still limps behind theory, as it probably always will. There remains the question of the integration of the sacraments into life simply.

This is a more complex problem, the elements of which we have sketched out in a previous volume[10] and we do not intend to repeat what we said there. However, what we have to say about the sacraments should be regarded as particular examples of the view suggested there.

In the phrase 'the integration of the sacraments into life' life has a twofold connotation. It means first the life of the celebrants, necessarily therefore of Christians; secondly, it means the secular life of the world.

5

Not that these can be taken in fact as entirely separate, for Christians live in the world and secular, non-Christian people inevitably witness Christian celebrations. Witnessing them they pose certain questions or experience a certain bewilderment. *What* are these curious actions with their peculiar use of certain material objects? What do they mean? Are they just survival-taboos of the Christian tribe which derive from the pre-scientific culture? If inadvertently they are administered in a mechanical way, if the emphasis is on the sacraments as objects, as things, or on the quasi-automatic effect (You do this and that happens), then the modern secular man may be excused if he sees them as no more than sublimated magic. So, as far as the Christian celebrants are concerned, it is of primary importance that their faith, their acceptance of all that the sacraments imply (Christ and his redeeming work), should be made explicit even in the celebration. In a word, the sacraments must be seen as part of their life, as expressions of it, and secular man is perfectly justified in looking for the consequences of the celebration of the sacraments in the lives of Christians. This would seem to indicate that we should be much more demanding about who are fit candidates for the Christian sacraments.

But have the sacraments a deeper relationship to ordinary life? Or are they pieces of ritual imposed on life? An adequate answer to these questions would require what the theologians call a Christian anthropology, that is an examination of the nature of man as he exists in the concrete circumstances of his life.[11] Meanwhile it is possible to make some suggestions. Every human being is born and although in the eyes of modern human beings the wonder of a new birth is no longer the event it used to be — with the exception of the mother to whom it is always wonderful[12] — in the history of mankind it has usually been marked by some rite, such as circumcision. One of the most constant features of the life of man in the earlier stages of his development is the 'rites of passage'. People are born, are initiated, marry and die and all these events are marked by rites celebrated in common. The rites and the events of human living go together and the former are the expression and, I suppose it would be said, the sacralization of the latter. However that may be, these are all intensely human situations and even in these days, when so much of the natural rhythm of human life has been shattered, they remain to give pattern and direction to human living.

On even a superficial view the sacraments and other rites of the church, closely connected with them, correspond to these human situations. To birth corresponds baptism and there are those who would see confirmation as the counterpart of the rites of initiation in more primitive societies, though I do not think their point of view can be justified. To the 'natural' marriage of man and woman corresponds the sacrament that is simply called after it; to illness, the anointing of the sick, and to the final 'passage' of death, the rites that concern it. In this perspective the life-events and the rites are not mere juxtapositions. They witness to the need of man to refer the major events of life to a higher power, on whom he feels dependent, and implicitly he is asking that they should be taken up into the sphere of the divine, however he may conceive it.

It will be obvious that the Christian sacraments cover a wider field than that of the 'rites of passage'. Apart from the problematical sacrament of confirmation, there is the question of repentance as expressed in the sacrament of penance and there is that of holy order which, if it has parallels in primitive religions, is so far away from them in meaning as to make comparison misleading. Through these considerations we are brought to the question of the *seven* sacraments. It is well known that it was not until the twelfth century and largely under the influence of Canon Law that the present system of seven sacraments was established. For a St Augustine and a St Ambrose there were many more *sacramenta* (e.g. the foot-washing in the baptismal liturgy), as there are to this day in the Orthodox church. In Western Catholic terminology these are called 'sacramentals' and while this may be useful for theological categorization, there is a certain liturgical incongruity in the whole business. There are highly significant rites like that of the solemn profession of a monk (a second 'baptism'), the consecration of a virgin,[13] which have their interest precisely in as much as they are consecrations of particular ways of *life*. There is also the rite of the blessing of the holy oils[14] on Maundy Thursday. This is a specifically *paschal* rite looking forward as it does to the celebration of Easter which includes the administration of baptism and confirmation. That the primitive baptism/confirmation liturgy included a rite of anointing with oil is improbable but, against the biblical background, it was seen that oil was a significant symbol of the Holy Spirit and it was used as such. What is important is that the blessing of oil was not separated from the sacramental administration. In the *Apostolic Tradition* of Hippolytus the 'Oil of Thanksgiving' was blessed during the Easter liturgy and it was not until later (sixth century) that they were separated. The primitive arrangement, then, shows the close link between what later was called the 'matter' of the sacrament and the sacrament itself. Both the blessing and the sacrament were part of the one liturgical celebration. To put the matter in another way, the blessing and use of oil was a means by which the liturgical celebration could be made to meet the life-situation of the participants, for in the Mediterranean world olive oil was (and is) one of the staples of life.

The use of these *sacramenta* was then a way of reaching out into the life of the people and they should not be dismissed as mere ceremonial or a retrograde hanging-on to outmoded symbols. But on the assumption that the seven-sacrament scheme exists (which is accepted though with nuances of difference by the Orthodox) it will be useful to ask whether it has something useful to offer from our point of view in this chapter.

If you ask the question: why seven sacraments? you can, as a recent author has remarked, look at the question from two sides, from the point of view of revelation (what Christ willed) and from the point of view of man.[15] With the first we are not concerned for the moment, but the same author goes on to say that the material principle of the diversity of the sacraments (which convey the power of the paschal mystery in different ways) must appeal to the anthropological constituents of man:

The seven sacraments do not come from arbitrary decisions of Christ (and much less from a church which would dominate Christ). This diversity comes from the fact that the actions of Christ lay hold of or take up fundamental human situations to make them Christian situations.[16] The sacramental organism is an adapted organism. To be born, to pass to adult life, to review one's life with a view to a new start, to marry, to fall ill, are so many situations taken up by the sacraments and thus shown to be and established as divine–human situations. This constituent principle of the seven sacraments shows that the Christian life is the opposite of a life that is simply juxtaposed to human life. It is in fact the life of God penetrating to the anthropological roots of human existence. There are no sacraments that are not sacraments of Christ living his paschal mystery in man. But also, there are no sacraments that do not draw from the world and from

man the 'materiality' of their sign. The
thought of as the great and fundamental
or even the great axes by which the Lor
depths of our human nature and transfig

There are two points here worth ponderir
the sacraments Christ reaches down to the dee
not merely and superficially, as might be concluc
ment, to acquire the right kind of material sig⟩ ⸳⸳ wine, ⸣
etc.). That is not the whole meaning of the writ Christ who 'knows
what is in man' reaches down to human nature, to the very 'materiality'
of human nature (e.g. sexual love) because man is like this and because
it is only in this way that he can grasp existentially the divine reality
Christ wishes to convey. This is why 'the sacramental organism is an
adapted organism'. One could say that it is a conditioned organism, an
organism that is conditioned by the exigencies of human nature. Sacraments are, then, profoundly human and not just something 'stuck on'
to ordinary human living. They touch the deepest springs of human
existence and, to use the terminology of Karl Rahner,[17] they make it
possible for man in Christ to live out the human tragedy of birth and life
and death and suffering.[18]

But the sacraments do not just go down to the roots of the human
condition. They transform it. They are not to be thought of as actions,
even actions of Christ, that reach our human condition and leave it
where it is and as it is. The materiality of the human condition is the very
stuff of the Christian life. It is not merely a means, sanctified by grace,
by which we go to God. It is *in this* that we go to God. As we have said
elsewhere, it is in the wholeness of our human personality that we need
to go to God and in the sacraments Christ takes over these human situations and makes them specifically Christian 'grace-ful' situations, direc-
ting them and us to God. Here is an interpenetration of the divine and
the human that at least in principle makes it possible for us to live in God.
All is now taken up into him and through the enrichment he gives, we
are able to carry these riches, which are both his and ours, to the world.

If redemption is to be thought of as something more than an abstract
noun, as something deeper than a legalistic 'substitution' of Christ for
ourselves, it is here in the sacraments that we can see what it really is:
the penetration by Christ into human situations from which he removes,

~

...centredness and gives them a Godward direction. In this
...re able to establish or enter into the interpersonal relationship
...od in which salvation ultimately consists. Certain situations are
...-situations, such as that which involves the sacrament of penance, and
here the redemptive, reconciling aspect of the work of salvation is to the
fore. But in every human situation there is the danger of the movement
towards self, e.g. marriage and sickness, and here it is precisely the
re-direction the sacraments give that is important. Examples will make
clearer what we mean.

1. The sacrament of penance is the sign in the here and now of the
reconciliation we read of in 2 Corinthians 5:19: 'God was in Christ
reconciling the world to himself'. This he did in principle on the cross;
this he, with the Christian community, continues to do in the eucharist,
for all the power that was to be found in the cross is to be found in the
Mass. Indeed, the whole liturgy, including therefore the eucharist and
penance, is the sacrament-sign of the redeeming, reconciling work of
Christ in the world and for the world. The church as a community of
reconciliation and penance is in a special way the sacrament-sign of that
reconciliation by which it is conveyed to the world. Men and women
bring precisely their 'broken-ness' (contrition) to the sacrament and there
seek encounter with the reconciling Christ. They have experienced the
tragedy of (spiritual) death and alienation and now seek life and reconciliation. It is a normal human experience which in the sacramental
situation is 'redeemed' and one which enables them to insert their lives
into the reconciliation of Christ. There is more to be said and to it we
shall return later.

2. It may sound pompous and perhaps heartless to say that illness
and suffering, which are so personal, are part of the world's tragic experience, since suffering turns us in on ourselves so that at times, and even
against our will, our whole personality is shrunk to not much more than
a consciousness of pain. Yet it is so and when the pain has abated we
are aware that we are involved in something that exists outside us in all
the suffering of whatever kind that the human race experiences. We may
indeed think of illness and suffering as an assault on our personalities
that is quite unaccountable and if we do, we may find a clue to an understanding of it in the Old Testament view that illness, whether mental or
physical, is related to sin. Not in the crude sense that our suffering is
a punishment for our wrong-doing (though we can bring disease on

~

ourselves) but in the sense that just as sin, at least for the Christian, is a symptom of the disorientation of the world as we know it, so is illness. It throws our life out of gear and we sense a rift in the harmony of things. The good, health, is struggling with evil, disease, it is a conflict we now experience in our own personalities and not just something 'out there'. It is this maimed condition that Christ in his church invites us to bring to him and into this condition he inserts his healing, his comfort and his peace. Here you have an encounter between something that of itself is purely secular and the healing of Christ. And it is not unimportant to realize that healing means wholeness. The broken is repaired, the forces making for the disintegration of the human personality are turned towards integration. What has fallen into dis-ease and conflict is harmonized and the personality, now made whole, can once again turn itself out to Christ and to the world of men where its true vocation lies, even if the sick person is still confined to bed. Of all this restoration the sacraments of the sick are the sign, the sacrament-sign of Christ's healing, who is thus shown to be present in the world of suffering and pain.

3. Marriage may be regarded as the archetypal case of the co-inherence of the natural and the supernatural, the sacred and the profane, of the divine and the human. Here is a human love, earthy, warm and rich with every kind of fleshly association which yet reaches beyond itself to a total self-giving. It is this love that two people bring to God and in the encounter that ensues God's love meets theirs and transfuses it so that henceforth they are able to love each other with a love in which God is creatively present. None the less, their love remains fully human and yet at the same time is the sacrament-sign of their covenanted love as it is also the means by which they and their love are sanctified. Furthermore, this love is not restricted to murmured words or affectionate gestures. It is expressed in the very ordinary events of everyday life so that the very life-together-in-married-love also becomes the permanent sacrament-sign of the presence of God's love in their life. Here can be seen the involvement of God in the ordinary life of human beings, here we can see that God is not locked up in an ecclesiastical box but is to be found in human lives in all their ordinariness.

These situations are indications that the sacraments are not alien to human life. They celebrate it, they enhance it and are witnesses to the 'human-ness' of God who thus enters into it. It should not be supposed however that these situations (and others) are *proof* of the seven sacraments. First, not all the sacraments are so clearly connected with the human condition as those mentioned. If we give the impression that confirmation is the sacrament of adolescence *because* it corresponds to natural growth we are in danger of distorting its true nature. It is to be thought of as the perfecting of what is begun in baptism and this can be done at any age. We are so accustomed to think of baptism in the terms of infant baptism that it does not occur to us that a person baptized later in life has no possibility of 'growth' in the physical sense. Yet since confirmation has something to add to baptism it is perfectly right and proper that they should be confirmed. In other words, if we press the analogy between natural life and the Christian life too far we shall distort the sacramental organism. It is also difficult to find a credible analogy for the sacrament of holy order. We no longer live in a sacral order and the notion of the 'sacralization' of a human person is either unacceptable or meaningless. On the other hand, the dedication of a human being to a particular way of life, for instance monasticism, is covered by the rites of religious profession.[19]

All we can show, then, by this kind of investigation is that the sacraments are congruous with the human condition. We are thus brought to the consideration which is fundamental that the sacraments are 'given', they are part of Christ's revelation and in every sense of the word they are 'mysteries'. They are mysteries because they embody the mysterious presence of God active in human situations and are the signs of it. They are mysteries because they declare the faith of the church and that of the participants. They are mysteries because however well we think we understand them, their ultimate nature and effect lie beyond us. They are in fact part of the whole history of salvation which is a *datum*, something given, the pure gift of God, and we can only understand the sacraments as we understand the history of salvation. We look at it, we ponder on it, we 'see' that it is the divinely given way God willed to save us and that the sacraments are so many ways by which we are saved, justified and united through Christ in the Holy Spirit with the Father. Other ways would have been possible. A man could be saved by turning to God in wordless repentance or lifting up his heart in the wordless prayer of praise. But then we reflect, man himself is 'given', he is made by God, and the way of salvation is in accordance with the nature of the radical gift. In effect, so long as we do not see the sacraments as 'emerging' from the needs of human nature and thus finding their justification, it is safe to say that they meet the needs of human nature because God has arranged the matter that way.

There remains the question of the relationship of the sacraments with the world. It will be agreed that the celebration of the sacraments is not a missionary device but it does not follow that Christians can be indifferent to what the world thinks of them or indeed of the way we celebrate them. The sacraments are not only signs of a particular intervention of God in a particular situation, for instance baptism. As the Constitution on the Liturgy (2) made clear, they are signs of the church, revealing its nature, and when the Christian community celebrates the sacraments, it is constructing a sign of the church which may be read by others even if for lack of faith they cannot have a full understanding of it. What the church *is*, the sacraments declare; what the church believes, that the sacraments profess in word and action. It follows, then, as the same document teaches (34), that the liturgy of the sacraments, as the whole liturgy, must be simple and understandable to ordinary people. It is a matter of experience that the sacraments, when celebrated as they should be by a believing community, draw the non-believer towards the church and dispose him to listen or to come again. We also know that a bad celebration of the sacraments can repel people, sometimes for ever. We know too that in the new situation in which we are, the quality of the celebration depends on both clergy and people and sometimes, even when the former do all that is required of them, the people are reluctant to play the part that belongs to them. However, what is important is that it is the community that celebrates and it is the impression created by the whole community that will make an impact on others.

But the Constitution on the Liturgy[20] makes clear that the celebration of the sacraments is a beginning and not an end. Members of the church, by virtue of their status as Christians, have the obligation of carrying the Good News to the world. Nor is there any need to expound at length the truth that the mission of the church belongs to all the members of the church. It is however worth repeating that, according to the Constitution on the Church (31, 33), the mission of the people flows directly from their baptism and confirmation: 'These faithful are by baptism made one body with Christ and are established among the people of God. They are in their own way made sharers in the priestly, prophetic and kingly functions of Christ. They carry out their own part in the mission of the whole Christian people with respect to the Church and the world.' More concretely still: 'The lay apostolate is a participation in the saving mission of the Church itself. Through their baptism and confirmation, all are commissioned to that apostolate by the Lord himself' and since the heart of mission is love, a love that urges us on (2 Corinthians 5:14), it is in the sacraments but especially in the eucharist that they will find the source of that love.[21]

How all this is to be carried out is a large question but the Constitution on the Liturgy (2), which from this point of view might seem to be a less practical document, has an interesting emphasis. It sees the liturgy as the outstanding means by which the people may *express in their lives* and manifest to others the mystery of Christ and the nature of the church. It is the daily living of Christians that manifests the great mystery of Christ which is the mystery of salvation. It is in this daily living that the non-believer will (or will not) find, as it were incarnated, the love God has shown to men. Clearly this puts a very heavy responsibility on all of us who *dare* to celebrate the liturgy and perhaps we have not always thought of it this way. But at least we can say, however unsuccessful we may be, that the notion of the liturgy as simply a ritual operation is banished. As it must be approached with a living faith, involving the whole personality, so its consequence and, in a sense, its validity must be seen in the life of Christians. The liturgy lives and moves and has its being in the flowing life of Christian people who through it, through the mystery of Christ with which they come in contact, reach out to the world around them and strive by example and word to carry Christ to it.

Notes

[1] If a servant of the convent had not put a book of devotion into her hands, she would have had no instruction at all.

[2] For a not wholly satisfactory treatment of the period see Préclin and Jarry, *Histoire de l'Eglise*, 19/1, ed. Fliche and Martin (Paris, 1955).

[3] Even the placing of the Paschal Candle in the baptistery was regarded as 'odd' or even fanatical. It is now the rule!

[4] CL 59.

[5] CL 5.

[6] Infant baptism and the administration of certain sacraments to the dying or unconscious must be regarded as abnormal situations, however common the

former. As we shall see later, the principle is saved by the obligation parents have to educate their own children in the faith.

[7] ST III, 72, V, ad 2.

[8] CL 59 and ST III, 63, i.

[9] Decree on the Missionary Activity of the Church, 36 (**Documents**, ed. Abbott, p. 623) and cf. General Introduction to **The Rite of the Baptism for Children**, p. 7 (Geoffrey Chapman, 1970).

[10] **Christian Celebration: Understanding the Mass**, chapter 1.

[11] Not therefore the study of primitive man or even of the behaviour of modern man, though both can throw light on the subject.

[12] One mother, whose faith had been wavering, once said to me that after the carrying and birth of her child, not only did she herself believe more strongly in God but she found it difficult to understand others who did not.

[13] (Vatican Press, 1970).

[14] **Ordo Benedicendi** . . . (Vatican Press, 1971).

[15] Henri Denis, **Les Sacrements ont-ils un avenir?** (Paris, 1971), pp. 48–9.

[16] Literally, 'situations in Christ'.

[17] See **Christian Celebration: Understanding the Mass**, p. 208.

[18] They also make it possible for man to live out the joy of life because the sacraments are life-bearing and life-enhancing. The 'christened' man, while aware of death and suffering and indeed experiencing it himself, is also able to rejoice in the Lord and in his goodness to men.

[19] It is significant (to me at least) that the new rite of ordination no longer speaks of the consecration of a bishop but of his 'ordering': he is incorporated into the **ordo episcoporum**. In the rite, the word 'consecration' **is** used but the title is 'The Ordination of a Bishop'.

[20] CL 8, third paragraph.

[21] Constitution on the Church, 33. There is much more to the same effect in other conciliar documents, notably in that exclusively concerned with the laity.

The Symbolism of the
Sacraments

~~~~~~~

S INCE THE sacraments use a number of gestures and objects combined with gestures that are in fact constituent elements of the sacraments, it will be useful to say something about them at this point.
As we have attempted to show in a previous volume, the liturgy is
by nature symbolical.[1] It lives in the world of symbols through which it
manifests and conveys the mystery of Christ. Leaving out of account the
eucharist, which we have already considered, we can see that the liturgy
of the sacraments is particularly rich in symbolic objects and gestures.
Water is used in baptism, oil in baptism, confirmation, holy order and
the sacrament of the sick. Then there are certain gestures that are consti-
tutive of the sacramental action, such as pouring the water or immersion
in baptism, and others that are secondary, the signing with the cross, the
laying-on of hands (essential in confirmation and holy order), the wearing
of the white garment, the carrying of the candle in baptism, the assemblies that gather for the celebration of various sacraments, themselves
symbolic since they represent a greater and wider reality, the whole
church. Of these symbols it seems necessary to say something about
water, oil and the laying-on of hands for they are the most important
of all and their deeper significance is often unknown. The practice of
anointing with olive oil, for instance, instead of being a sign that conveys
a meaning, is in some parts of the world, including Northern Europe,
a barrier to understanding.

Symbolism of water

Until comparatively recently, water was an element whose significance
was understood by everyone. But since it has been tamed, tanked and
tapped and is available at will, people treat it as they do electric power.
It is always there: you just turn on the tap and it comes. Few have looked
down into the mysterious depths of a well, and those who have seen a
rushing torrent think of it as no more than a piece of scenery. A fountain

~

throwing up its water in all directions is just a show-p
some more imaginative town council or by a tycoon of yes
had nothing better to do with his money. In spite of the efforts
tists and lunarnauts to find water on the moon, we do not readily
water as the *source of life*. Yet this is how it was seen for untold thousands
of years and especially in the dry East where it became sacred because
men knew how they depended on it.[2] As is well enough known, in
Egypt the whole economy was dependent on the flooding of the Nile and
'in Egyptian belief . . . the *divine* waters could give life in every form in
which the mind could conceive it'.[3] The same was true of India: an old
text apostrophizes water, 'Water, you are the source of everything and
of all existence'.[4] Further, it was an ancient and widely prevalent belief
that water flowed from the womb of the earth or of paradise, a notion
that, transformed, found a place in the old text of the Blessing of the Font
at the Easter Vigil. There the font (spring, source) is the womb of the
church from which the waters flow 'for the renewal of the nations' and
new births come forth to the enrichment of the church:

> Look with kindness on the face of your church and increase in her
> the number of your children. She is that city of yours which you
> refresh with *flowing streams* of grace and there *you open up a spring
> to water the whole earth, her fountain of baptism for the renewal of
> the nations*. . . . May he (God) make this a life-giving water – this
> water prepared for man's new birth – secretly imbuing it with his
> own divine power, *that sons of heaven may be conceived and emerge
> from the spotless womb of this divine font reborn* . . .

Later, the ancient symbolism of water as flowing forth from the womb
of the world appears along with the theme of water as a necessity of life
for a desert people:

> In his (God's) name (I bless you) who bade you well forth from a
> *spring in Paradise* and branch into four streams and *water all the
> earth*. In the desert, when you were gall to taste, he gave you
> sweetness and made you fit to drink. When his people were
> parched with thirst he brought you from a rock . . .

According to some[5] – and it seems difficult to resist their view – the
symbolism is carried through to its logical conclusion. The water is
seen as being fecundated (*foecundet*) by the plunging in it of the phallic

een as a symbol of the Holy Spirit: 'May
ne down into this water . . . and charge
ough with power to give new life'.

ttle of this pregnant symbolism has been
f the blessing of baptismal water. Whether
archetypes or not, here is a symbolism that
k memory of people and yet is immeasurably
uted into a specifically Christian symbolism.
the early memories of mankind is lost, the
figure υ_   *mater ecclesia*, a mother of life and the bride of
Christ, is someth...ͷ   at would countervail the all too prevalent notion
of the church as an institution whose embraces have not always been as
tender as they might have been. It may be agreed that the prayer was too
long but either there was, somewhere along the line, a failure to see what
was symbolically important in the prayer or the symbolism was deliberately rejected. One wonders if it was thought to be too realistic: even the
word *foecundet* is removed from the text at the moment of plunging the
candle into the water, though the gesture is kept at least for the Easter
Vigil.

The new rite has however retained another aspect of water-
symbolism. In many different cultures the passage through water has
been seen as the symbol of regeneration and new life. The water could
be the sacred river, Lethe, or a spring or even the sacred bath (cf.
Ephesians 5:26, 27). By its cleansing and purifying power the candidate
entered into a new life. This is the symbolism of St Paul in Romans 6
which assumes baptism by immersion. In the prayer of the Blessing of
the Water, in both the old and the new editions, this symbolism is given
in the terms of the history of salvation. The Flood is a symbol of regeneration (*speciem regenerationis*[6]), marking as it did the end of sin and the
beginning of the virtuous life. The waters of the Red Sea, through which
the Israelites passed, is in the first place a figure of deliverance; they
moved from the slavery of Egypt into the freedom of the desert and there
through the covenant and its accompanying sacrifice they became the
people of God. This, says the prayer, is the symbol of the new people of
God who are delivered from sin by baptism. By its connection with
baptism the water thus becomes in the second place the symbol of
regeneration.

But the symbolism of water is ambivalent. If it is the source of life

~
18

and is necessary to sustain life, it can also stifle it. In the ancient world the sea at least was much feared on account of its mysterious, incontrollable strength and its power to kill. Water generally was seen as the abode of demons, of fearsome monsters like Leviathan (cf. Job 40:25) which God alone could master. When the baptismal liturgies were coming into existence from the second to the fourth centuries these memories were still vivid. The candidate had to be exorcized several times and the last time immediately before baptism. Turned towards the west, the abode of demons, he renounced the devil, even in some rites spitting at him, and then, turned towards the east, he professed his adherence to Christ. Then, before entering the water, he must strip, not wearing 'any alien object'[7] for fear, it would seem, that the devil should get a foothold. He was anointed all over with oil, prepared as it were for the *agon*, the struggle with the powers of evil. This notion is always implicit, as the symbolism itself shows, but occasionally it becomes explicit as in the Homilies of Narsai: 'The three Names (of the Trinity) he (the priest) recites, together with the rubbing of the oil upon the whole man: that hostile demons and vexing passions may not harm him'. It is not, the preacher goes on, that power resides in the oil itself but in God, the oil proclaiming [being a symbol] of the divine power: 'By his power body and soul acquire power; and they no more dread the injuries of death. As athletes they descend (and) stand in the arena, and they close in battle with the cowardly suggestions that are in them.'[8]

Not only, however, was the candidate exorcized, the water also had to be and the reason was precisely because it was regarded as the abode of demons. Once exorcized, the water could become the source of life and in it the candidate met not the devil but Christ. The first statement is amply illustrated by the (old) text for the Blessing of the Font, which, though edited, derives from the prayer in the Gelasian Sacramentary, dating, as far as this text goes, from the sixth century: 'Command, then, Lord, every evil spirit to be banished from this element, banished be the whole malice of diabolical deceit. No room here for this water to be imbued with an opposing power, flitting watchfully about it, insinuating itself by stealth and tainting it with poison.'[9] Nor is this exceptional. The Ambrosian prayer[10] is particularly vigorous: God is asked to exorcize the water so that it will have the power to put to flight every 'infestation' of the devil and 'to root out the devil himself' from those who are to be baptized. If these and other prayers[11] do not speak of the presence of demons in the water and indeed in some instances envisage the struggle as *beginning* with baptism, it is because the water has been exorcized and the demons have given place to the presence of Christ. For Narsai, the power of God dwells in the visible waters and destroys the might of the Evil One and of death.[12]

In most of the prayers this divine presence is given a more concrete expression. One of the constant features of these baptismal prayers, as of the patristic literature on the point, is the reference to the baptism of Christ. This is seen as the archetype of Christian baptism and also as its source. For Cyril of Jerusalem the water was 'consecrated' by contact with the divinity of Christ.[13] According to John Chrysostom, Christ 'cleansed' the waters and left them as a now 'sanctified' element for the sacrament of baptism.[14] Gregory Nazianzen brings a new richness and depth to the matter. He sees the baptism of Christ as a 'mystery', still effective: 'Christ is enlightened and at the same time, we are; Christ is baptized and we, at the same time, go down [into the water] and rise from it. John is baptizing, Jesus approaches, perhaps sanctifying the baptizer, but without any doubt burying the Old Adam in the waters, before us and on our account sanctifying them . . . Coming up out of the waters Jesus raises the whole world with him and cleaves open the heavens which Adam and his posterity and the fiery sword had closed.'[15] Christ is here very conspicuously the second Adam who is enacting in his own person the whole drama of salvation. Indeed the dimensions of Gregory's view are cosmic: the whole of creation is renewed and raised up by the baptism of Christ in the Jordan. The power of Christ in the baptismal water is very clear.

These ancient symbolisms perhaps make little appeal to modern man or to modern Christians though their transposition into the Christian register should make them meaningful to the latter. But can we be so sure? It was Jung's contention that modern man needs these symbols and periodical confrontation with them if he is to retain his psychological health. If this is so, it means that the way we use them becomes crucial. Baptism in the West (though not in the Eastern churches) has for centuries been by 'infusion', the pouring of water on the head of the candidate. Even the casuists said it must *flow* and it is a practice that retains one elementary symbolism, that of cleansing, though this was reduced to a 'washing away of original sin'. The difficulty is in presenting in celebration the deeper and more extensive symbolism of water, for if its effect is to be achieved on Jungian terms, it must make an impact of some force. Clearly, baptism by immersion does this and it is interesting to observe that in the baptismal Orders of 1969 and 1972 immersion is suggested, not merely because it is given as an alternative but because it is the method suggested in the first place.[16] The question is: how is it to be done? That baptism by immersion is not wholly impracticable can be seen from the practice of the Baptist Church though it is probable that in an individual Baptist church baptisms are not very numerous in the course of a year. This suggests the direction in which we should look. Baptism by immersion, quite apart from people's reluctance to undergo it, would have to be an occasional event, and in fact, if it were, it would make all the greater an impact. The plunging of the candidate into the water would recall not merely that it is the life-giving element in the natural order but the theology of St Paul in Romans 6:3, 4 that we are buried with Christ in the waters of baptism and raised from them by the power of his resurrection to a new kind of life, would be strongly suggested. This text, with its great depth of meaning, would thus come alive.

There are of course many difficulties, both psychological and physical, that stand in the way of restoring this practice and to these we shall return in our discussion of baptism.[17]

Symbolism of oil

While olive oil in the Mediterranean world is still a normal constituent of human living, in most parts of the world, including Northern Europe, it is not; and even in the Mediterranean world it is more likely to be thought of as the accompaniment of food than as anything else. In spite of its rich symbolism in the Old and the New Testaments, it remains difficult for us to use.[18] In industrial society it is thought of as a lubricant and those bold enough to examine the sumps of their cars know that it is a nasty, black mess. It does not help very much to be told that Greek athletes anointed themselves with olive oil to give strength and suppleness to their limbs. For as soon as you have to be told that this 'signifies' that, you are being told at the same time that the symbol is dead. Symbols are either significant or they do not exist. What then is to be done? Is the use of oil to be abolished altogether? There would seem to be no reason why it should not be for it is not necessary for the validity of any sacrament except that of the anointing of the sick.[19]

The question then resolves itself into this: is it desirable that we should try to keep alive a symbol that has lost almost all its significance? An answer in favour of its continued use can be given if we consider the biblical background and exploit its symbolism more adequately. If we look at the use of oil in the ancient world we find that it has certain parallels in our world. It is well known that the sun, especially in hot countries, dries up the skin and that over-exposure to it burns. In Egypt, it would seem, the high conical hair-styles, which are to be seen on bas-reliefs, were drenched with a perfumed oil which flowed down on the (bare) shoulders keeping the skin supple and giving off what was regarded as a pleasant odour.[20] Sunbathers of today do exactly the same with their various oils and lotions and for the same purpose. The perfume may be more delicate nowadays but the ancients had stronger stomachs. If this is true, we can the better understand the daunting picture of Aaron with his beard flowing with oil which runs down onto his vestments (Ps 133(132):2). For the psalmist it is a symbol of Yahweh's blessing, given copiously like the dew of Hermon, falling on the heights of Zion. Nor is it difficult to understand that oil has certain healing properties. It soothes pain, even if sometimes it will ultimately increase it if poured on a broken skin that then suppurates. But the ancients at any rate thought of it as healing and soothing. Hence its association with the sacrament of the sick (cf. Mark 6:13 and the parable of the Good Samaritan, Luke 10:29–37).

In the Bible, and in the ancient world from which in this matter it did not differ, oil has an even wider register of significance. It is used copiously, it is *poured*, it is mixed with perfume and on the human level it is the sign of love (Song of Songs 1:3), of honour (Luke 7:46 and Matthew 26:7) and of joy (Pss 104 (103):15; 45 (44):8) and it is clear that it received its significance from a generous use of it in a festive atmosphere. Water for the feet, oil for the head and wine that makes glad the face of man were ingredients of Eastern hospitality and feasting. But from another point of view it was a sign of election and consecration (1 Sam 10:1–6; 16:13), accompanied by the giving of the Spirit. It was this combination of unction and Spirit, we are told, that was the origin of the fundamental symbolism of oil.[21]

Although in the New Testament there is no reference to physical anointing (apart from Mark 6:13; Luke 10:34; James 5:14), the notion of a spiritual anointing is frequently found and it is possible to discern

~

in the early centuries of the church the combination of the physical gesture of the laying-on of hands with various anointings. These are always associated with the giving or outpouring of the Spirit in baptism, in what later was called confirmation, and in other rites too. These Christians seem to have felt a compelling need to externalize what they believed to be happening in the soul because for them unction did mean joy and richness and, in the end, the bounty of God. Nor was this— as happened later on in the Middle Ages—a mere copying of the Old Testament customs. The first Christians were filled with the sense of their union with Jesus, the Anointed of God, the Messiah, the Son of God.[22] He was supremely the Anointed and he was the source of the unction, the symbol of the manifold grace of the Holy Spirit, whom the sacraments communicated to them.[23]

The Church Fathers took over almost all this symbolism without difficulty. For those writing in Greek the relation of 'chrism' to 'Christ' was obvious, both coming from the same word, though it was more usually called *myron*. For Hippolytus the bishop anointed the baptized with the 'oil of thanksgiving'[24] and St Cyril of Jerusalem exploits almost every aspect of the symbolism, though he remains very close to the scriptures. Chrism is the exact image (*antitypon*) of that with which Christ was anointed who was filled with the Holy Spirit. The references to Luke 4:18 and Isaiah 61:1, 2 are given. Anointing with the *myron* is compared by way of Psalm 45(44):8 with the oil of joy with which Christ was chrismated in the incarnation because 'he is the author of spiritual joy'. Again, the oil is perfumed and the inevitable reference to 2 Corinthians 2:15 occurs, though Cyril is careful to point out that the perfume itself, no doubt on account of its richness, is a sign of the gift of Christ which has by the presence of the Holy Spirit become efficacious of his divine power: 'It is with this perfume that symbolically your forehead and other senses are chrismated; your body is chrismated with this perfume; your soul is sanctified by the holy and life-giving Spirit'.[25]

This is as far as we need go in the examination of the biblical and patristic literature. Subsequent writers will add little or nothing of importance. Abundance, joy, the self-giving of God in the 'anointing' of the Son, and healing properties seem to give the essential symbolism of unction. If its use is to be continued, this understanding of it is necessary, but how is it to be acquired? Since the Bible itself gives so rich a symbolism of unction, it is to this in the first place that we must go. Quite

~

apart from the liturgy, if people are to understand the Bible message, they will have to learn what the Bible is saying about it. We may well need to put off certain Western preconceptions, it may be a painful experience to enter into another culture for which oil was of considerable significance, but this is the cost we must pay if we are to understand it and incidentally to widen our understanding of how other people think and act. Once this is done and the symbolism of unction is firmly attached to Christ, the archetype of all anointing, the spiritual significance of the use of the oil in the sacraments should be apparent. This, as we have seen, is the approach that Cyril of Jerusalem made to the matter.

But present practice also needs to be improved. First of all, the quality of the chrism needs to be improved. For all the tradition, it was a perfumed oil and the perfume was supposed to be, on the human level, part of its charm and, on the religious–symbolic level, a sign of spiritual joy. In the patristic period it was thought of as perfuming not merely the candidate but the whole building where the sacramental rite was being celebrated. In the new rite (1970)[26] for the Blessing of Oils, the introduction (4) says that chrism is made of oil and aromatic or perfume-bearing substances (*ex aromatibus, seu materia oderifera*), leaving the rest to the imagination. How we are to get such a chrism is beyond the competence of the present writer to say and such is the corruption of one's taste in these matters that one can only think of brilliantine. But something obviously ought to be done to improve the present condition of a chrism that is called 'sacred'. If olive oil is difficult to obtain or if (as one may suppose) there is another oil that has significance for a certain region or culture, the chrism may now be made of it (3) and this may well facilitate a better understanding of the symbolism of oil.[27]

Secondly, the cautious dabbings of oil which are immediately rubbed off should give way to a more generous administration. In the early centuries the minister took it in his hand and rubbed it on or, in the case of confirmation, simply placed it on the head and one must suppose that sometimes it did run down on the neck. In the scriptural imagery the Holy Spirit is constantly said to be *poured out* on people and although the mixture of metaphors may not be to our taste, the sense of the gesture is clear: an abundant pouring is a symbol of the abundant giving of the Spirit. Where the head is anointed, as in baptism and confirmation, there would seem to be a case for the revival of the chrism cap which might be worn at least until the end of the service.

~

As for the continued use of the anointing before baptism, it is diffi-cult to see any justification for it. As we have seen, originally it meant an anointing for the struggle against Satan and the whole body was anointed. What significance can a dab of oil on the chest of a wriggling infant have? And has anyone with equanimity thought of the impression an anointing of this kind would have on an adult candidate and his friends? It might just as well be given up.

The laying-on of hands

The hand, along with the word, is one of the most expressive means of language that man has.[28] It has various significances but the gesture of the laying-on of hands is the most important. In the Old Testament it could mean consecration, the setting apart of certain men, e.g. the Levites, for the service of God (Numbers 8:10) and the giving of the Spirit of wisdom (Deuteronomy 34:9). In the gospels there are many examples of Jesus laying his hands on the sick to heal them but it is in the rest of the New Testament that the notion of the transmission of the Holy Spirit is principally found. Peter and John lay hands on the Samaritans and they receive the Holy Spirit, and Paul does likewise for the people of Ephesus (Acts 8:17; 19:6). Elsewhere, the laying-on of hands signifies the trans-mission of authority (Acts 6:6; 13:3) and in the Pastoral Epistles the giving of a *charisma* for a ministry or function in the church (1 Timothy 4:14; 2 Timothy 1:6, 7). In the liturgical tradition, the laying-on of hands is so constantly accompanied by the anointing with chrism that we must suppose that the former attracted the latter to itself because the anointing was seen as a more explicit symbol of the giving of the Spirit.

In the early church it was used far more frequently than now. During the course of the catechumenate hands were laid on the candidates; in the *Apostolic Tradition* the bishop laid hands on them after baptism and anointed them with 'the oil of thanksgiving'; and when people were reconciled to the church, either after apostasy or sin, hands were laid on them again. In all these situations the gesture signified the giving of the Spirit and perhaps it is worth reflecting on the implied doctrine that reconciliation after penitence is the work of the Spirit. A vestige of this once significant gesture remains even in the present ritual of penance where the confessor is instructed to raise his hand while pronouncing the words of absolution.

The gesture is seen at its most significant in the ordination of a bishop. The chief celebrant lays hands on the elect and the con-celebrants then do likewise, all in silence. The gesture itself is a pleading that the Holy Spirit may come upon the elect and incorporate him into the episcopal order. This is then made explicit in the ancien*r* prayer, that of Hippolytus (now happily restored to the rite), which asks that the *Spiritus principalis*, the sovereign Spirit, given first to Christ and then to the apostles, may fill his being so that he may rule the flock of Christ according to God's will.[29]

It needs perhaps to be emphasized that the laying-on of hands is a very ancient gesture, probably older than anointing, and evidently it is still significant. It needs little if any explanation. Hence, we can say that the antiquity of a symbol is no argument that it is no longer relevant. It may also however be significant that it is a human gesture, an action and not a thing, and it may be that this is the direction we shall have to move if we are to keep symbols alive. In the Middle Ages the anointings of the bishop and priest were regarded as all-important and it is interesting to note that they have become distinctly secondary rites in the revised liturgy of holy order.

Notes

[1] *Christian Celebration: Understanding the Mass*, chapter 2.

[2] See F. W. Dillistone, *Christianity and Symbolism* (London, 1955), pp. 185ff. The author points out that for Arabs water is so much the source of life that the same word is used for water and the male semen.

[3] Dillistone, *op. cit.*, citing the *Journal of the American Oriental Society*, 56, p. 158.

[4] L. Beirnaert, *ibid.*, p. 185.

[5] C. Jung, and Gerald Vann in *The Water and the Fire* (London, 1953), pp. 90-3. Gerald Vann also pointed out that the celebrant (in the then rite) breathed on the water making the form of *psi*, the first letter of the Greek word for life or life-principle (*psyche*)

[6] The ICEL translation virtually eliminates this phrase.

[7] *Ap. Trad.*, 21, p. 18.

[8] Narsai, *Hom.* 20. See E. C. Whitaker, *Documents of the Baptismal Liturgy*, 2nd ed. (London, 1970), p. 54. From this invaluable work other information about the baptismal liturgies is taken.

[9] Trans. *Layman's Missal* (London, 1962).

[10] *Missale Ambrosianum* (1949).

[11] See Whitaker, *op. cit., passim.*

[12] *Ibid.*, p. 55.

[13] Cyril of Jerusalem, **Cat. Myst.** III, i, ed. Piédagnel, p. 122.

[14] Both passages quoted in ST III, 39, i.

[15] Gregory Nazianzen, **Orat.** 39 in **Sancta Lumina**, 14–16, 20, the patristic lesson for the feast of the Baptism of the Lord in **Divine Office**, I (1974), p. 379.

[16] **Ordo Baptismi Parvulorum**, no. 60 (Vatican, 1969); **Ordo Initiationis Christianae Adultorum**, 220 (Vatican, 1972).

[17] As to practical difficulties, baptisteries and fonts would have to be constructed on quite different lines and would require piped warm water. Some new baptisteries in recent years have at least provided **flowing** water, which suggests life, and only a slight adaptation would be required to make immersion possible. See e.g. that at Our Lady of the Wayside, Shirley, Solihull, Warwickshire and St John's Abbey, Collegeville, USA, the best I have seen.

[18] Genesis 28:18; Exodus 30:25ff.; 1 Samuel 10:1ff.; James 5:14–15, etc.

[19] Not for baptism for both anointings may be omitted, not for ordination for the anointings in the orders of presbyter and bishop are now visibly secondary rites. Confirmation remains doubtful. It is still required (**Ordo Confirmationis**, 9, 27) though doing duty for the laying-on of hands. But in different times and places the laying-on of hands has been sufficient.

[20] See H. Lubienska de Lenval, **Liturgie du Geste** (Paris/Tournai, 1956), p. 47.

[21] The above is taken from X. Léon-Dufour, **Dictionary of Biblical Theology**, 2nd ed. (London, 1973), **s.v.** 'Oil' and 'Anointing'. The length of the latter article indicates the richness of the material on this subject in the Bible.

[22] Hebrews 1:9 and cf. Psalm 45(44):8.

[23] Cf. **Dictionary of Biblical Theology**, 'Oil'.

[24] **Ap. Trad.** 21, p. 20.

[25] Cyril of Jerusalem, **Cat. Myst.** III, 1, 2, 3, 4. The 'other senses' were the ears, the nostrils, the breast, for such was the Jerusalem custom.

[26] **Notitiae**, 62 (March 1971), pp. 89–91.

[27] The same is true of the oils of catechumens and of the sick, though the introduction does not say so. In neither of the prayers is the olive mentioned though it is in that for the Blessing of Chrism. It may be noted here too that the bishop may mix the chrism during the course of the service (5) and if this were done with really aromatic herbs the whole church would be scented with them.

[28] X. Léon-Dufour, **Dictionary of Biblical Theology**, s.v. 'Imposition of hands'.

[29] There is of course a laying-on of hands for the presbyter and the deacon and to this we shall return when dealing with holy order. Neither however is as impressive as that in the ordination of a bishop.

THREE

~

Baptism in the Context of
Christian Initiation

~~~~~~~

WHEN LITURGICAL rites are reformed people usually concentrate on matters of detail. This or that familiar feature has disappeared or has undergone a transformation and they feel upset or affronted. Until all the documents concerning Christian Initiation are translated and published in English and until they have entered into the ordinary practice of the church, it is possible that their broad significance will be overlooked. Infant baptism still remains the practical norm, the position of confirmation in the initiation process is still unclear and First Communion is hardly seen as part, the climax in fact, of Christian Initiation. The deeper significance of the promulgation of the Order of Baptism (1969) and the Order for the Christian Initiation of Adults (1972)[1] is that people be ome Christian by a whole process that involves their life as well as the community of the church. Christian Initiation is not (except very exceptionally) the pouring of a drop of water on the head of an infant but the total adherence of an adult person to Christ by faith and incorporation into him by baptism, confirmation and holy communion. It involves the Christian community which undertakes a certain responsibility for him, which must be present and which must receive him into itself.

Nor is initiation a purely mental (if engraced) operation. The candidate adheres to Christ with his whole personality. He is drawn into Christ by word, by rite and by symbol which 'speak' to his personality and enable him to engage both body and mind in the process of his becoming a Christian. In this sense the new order of initiation marks a return to a more fundamental and more organic view of both nature and grace. For as long as we have records of religion, man has approached God gradually through rite and symbol and his liturgy moved according to the rhythms of his natural life. His birth was marked by certain rites and at puberty he underwent (and in some places still undergoes) the ritual of initiation into the full life of the tribe and participation in the ancestral religion. These have proved to be the strongest bond binding him to

~

28

his people. In the Christian order there was the approach by faith in response to the proclamation of the word, the establishment of that faith and initiation into Christian living through the catechumenate, and finally climactic experience of sacramental incorporation into the community by baptism, confirmation and holy communion.

It is this vision that the new Orders have restored to the church and whatever the difficulties of adaptation, it is this that should be kept in mind. For far too long our sacramental practice has moved away from life. It has not even been parallel to it. The dislocation of the sacraments of initiation has been complete and, apart from baptism, the various sacramental acts bore no relation to the life-rhythm of the candidates. It may be thought that this is one reason why Christian practice has suffered such difficulties in recent years. A religion, a worship, that is not integrated with life can easily be shed and often is.

A further consequence of this restoration is that it provides the basis for a more coherent theology of the sacraments of initiation and it is to this that we must now turn.[2]

The organization of the material to be found in the Order of Baptism of 1969, which contains a general introduction to baptism, a special one on the baptism of infants and the rite for the baptism of infants and the Order of Adult Initiation, presents some difficulty. There is further the Order of Confirmation (1971) which is an integral part of initiation but which, owing to the complexities of the subject, must be dealt with separately. The order we follow here will then be: the general introduction to baptism, the Order of Adult Initiation, the baptism of infants and finally in a separate chapter, confirmation.

In view of what has already been said, it is not surprising that baptism is firmly set in the context of the sacraments of initiation but the matter is not left vague. Nor, on the other hand, does it unduly separate the different sacraments of initiation. All *three* sacraments of baptism, confirmation and holy communion combine to bring Christians to the full stature of Christ. This doctrine, which is wholly traditional, eliminates the need to examine too closely the respective effects of the different sacraments though, against this background, this may properly be done. As the Order says, baptism makes people members of the body of Christ and of the people of God. It takes away their sins, makes them a new creation and the adopted children of Christ, and it is important to notice that all this is effected 'by water and the Holy Spirit'. The Spirit is given in baptism too. But people are also sealed by the Spirit in confirmation, the more perfectly to conform them to Christ and to enable them to bear witness to him for the building up to its fullness of his body. In the eucharist, as well as receiving the bread of eternal life, they manifest, make the sign of, the unity of the people of God and 'by offering themselves with Christ, they share in his universal sacrifice: the entire community of the redeemed is offered by their high priest' (Christ).[3]

Such is the comprehensive vision of this document which it will be profitable to keep in mind when we have to examine the sacraments of initiation in greater detail. But at once two further elements may be noted. The first is that the newly baptized join with the Christian community to pray for the outpouring of the Holy Spirit 'so that the whole human race may be brought into the unity of God's family'. The vision is broad, as broad as the human race, and the church sees the eucharist as the dynamic centre of the redeeming love of Christ which goes out to the whole world, invisibly but surely gathering men and women everywhere into communion with Christ. The second thing is this: Christ is indeed working out his purpose for the salvation of mankind but through all three sacraments of initiation he calls his people to be his ambassadors, his fellow-workers to collaborate in that work (2 Corinthians 5:20; 6:1). By baptism, confirmation and the eucharist Christians are committed to mission in the church and for the world.

The nature of baptism

In recent years it has become ever clearer that baptism is the basic sacrament, with an importance that can hardly be measured. Ecumenically it is the sacrament of Christian unity. All who are baptized are members of Christ even if, as the *Decree on Ecumenism* says, those outside the visible unity of the Catholic Church have a less than full or perfect relation to it. But it is also basic in the life of the individual Christian who is called to live out throughout his days what he receives in baptism. In a phrase much used by the late Dom Gregory Dix, we have to become what we are and this is true whether we are baptized in infancy or later in life. It is not surprising, then, that the Order in the section called 'On the dignity of baptism' (CI 3–6) should offer a statement on the meaning of baptism, a statement that provides a very condensed theology of the whole sacrament. We can do no more than take up some of its points.

Faith

Throughout the whole series of documents on initiation and in the rites themselves the church shows a dominant concern for faith. This has always been explicit in the teaching and practice of the church but not since the early centuries have faith and sacraments been so closely integrated as they are now. Baptism, according to the Order (CI 2), is the sacrament of that faith by which, through the enlightenment of the Holy Spirit, we respond to the gospel of Christ; and the church believes it to be her fundamental duty to inspire all, catechumens, parents of children still to be baptized and godparents, to that true and living faith by which they adhere to Christ and enter into or confirm their commitment to the new covenant (CI 3). Even the language is remarkable, so different from the stale language of the catechism and the textbook. But if we turn to the New Testament we see that this teaching is no more than a re-statement of what is to be found there, though the evidence is so vast that one can do no more than cite one or two texts. Thus, in St Mark (16:16), a statement that seems to sum up so much of New Testament teaching on the point: 'He who believes and is baptized will be saved'. Of this Matthew 28:19 is no more than an elaborate echo: 'Go and make disciples of all nations, baptizing them in the name of the Father and of the Son and of the Holy Spirit'.[4]

When we come to the action of the apostles there is no doubt at all. First, there is the preaching, then there is the first conversion and in response to the question 'What shall we do?' Peter answers 'Be baptized in the name of Jesus Christ' (Acts 2:37–41). Faith comes from hearing, says St Paul, and for the hearing and the faith a preacher is necessary (Romans 10:14–17). The apostles first preached, men conceived faith in their hearts and then they proceeded to baptism. From Acts 2:42 we may conclude that the new converts then joined the eucharistic assembly. The pattern is constant and did not vary for the next five hundred years.[5]

Faith, then, is an indispensable necessity for baptism and it will be as well to see what kind of faith is in question. There has been a tendency to think of faith as static, as merely an assent, which could and should be protected by prayer but which once given remained much as it was. The Order speaks of a true and living faith by which people adhere to Christ and enter into a commitment to the new covenant which he

~

31

brought into existence. So the faith here spoken of is not merely an assent to the articles of the creed nor is it simply a minimal guarantee of orthodoxy. It is a faith that is the act of our whole personality going out to the person of Christ to whom we commit ourselves totally. At least, we do this in intention though we know that such a total giving is impossible in one act and that it takes years, perhaps a whole lifetime, to bring that commitment anywhere near perfection. The Christian life is a living out of this faith received in baptism, a faith that it enriches but always presupposes.

All this is to say no more than is said in the Constitution on the Liturgy (59): '(The sacraments) not only presuppose faith, but by words and objects they also nourish, strengthen and express it; that is why they are called "sacraments of faith". They have indeed the power to impart grace, but, in addition, the very act of celebrating them effectively disposes the faithful to receive this grace fruitfully . . .' Certainly in 'the very act of celebrating', according to the Orders of Initiation and Baptism, there is no doubt at all that faith is expressed and professed as well as witnessed to by the whole assembly. As the former shows very clearly, faith is presupposed, is deepened during the catechumenate, is professed in the 'giving back of the creed' and expounded in the several services of the word that make up so much of the catechumenate. In the latter, and just before the service reaches its climax in the act of baptism, the candidate is required to make a public profession of the faith in the presence of the assembly when he adheres to God, Father, Son and Holy Spirit. In the baptism of infants, there is understandably an even greater emphasis on the need for faith, a faith which the parents who are under-taking the Christian education of their children (BP 39) must profess. This faith is proclaimed in the word of God and the homily (44, 45), is prayed for in the intercessions and again is professed before the act of baptism and summed up by the celebrant in the words: 'This is our faith. This is the faith of the Church. We are proud to profess it, in Christ Jesus our Lord' (58, 60 and cf. 64).

Participation in the mystery of Christ

By faith and baptism, then, we come to Christ; but is he just a generalized figure, the *object* of faith, or even the teacher of faith? For the Order (CI 6), baptism 'recalls and effects the paschal mystery itself', it is a

~

celebration of the passion, death and resurrection of Christ and through it men and women are able to pass from death to life, are engrafted into his death and rise with him by the power of his resurrection.

This teaching raises the whole question of participation in the mystery of Christ which is central to Christian living. We are perhaps more accustomed to think of the matter in the context of the eucharist which in a unique way recalls and makes present the passion and resurrection of Christ. None the less baptism is a celebration of the paschal mystery and by it we are first made like Christ in his passion and resurrection. It is here, in Pauline language, that we first put on Christ, the Christ who suffered, died and rose again so that the barrier of sin might be destroyed and mankind could be reconciled to the Father. The similarity of the effects of baptism to those of the eucharist (or for that matter, to those of penance) has given theologians some little trouble. Perhaps it was precisely the separation and eventual categorization of the sacraments that produced the problem. In the sacraments, in the whole of the liturgy, we are celebrating the one mystery of Christ. It is contact with that mystery (a contact that may be and is initially made by faith also) that spells salvation, though we may approach it in several (God-given) ways and share in it in different ways. Baptism is the first way in which we are enabled to make our own and enter into the mystery, and the commitment spoken of earlier is necessarily a commitment to the suffering and glorified Christ. Our life as Christians is meant to bear the marks of both: 'If in union with Christ, we have imitated his death, we shall also imitate him in his resurrection',[6] not merely at the resurrection of the dead but here in our earthly life when, as we hope and pray, the power of the risen Christ is overcoming the deathward tendencies of the body.

Here again we are involved in a process. As St Paul says in the same place, we have to live a new kind of life that looks towards God through the risen Christ. Clearly this is a life-long process and it is at this point that we can see the connection between baptism and the eucharist. The latter, in all the early liturgies, is the culmination of the former; but at a level even deeper than that, we can see that if the Christian life is a dying and rising with Christ, then it is in the eucharist where we meet him week by week that we are able to appropriate the power of his death and resurrection. In the simplest language, by baptism we *begin* to be Christians; and to go on being Christians, to grow as Christians, to become the perfect man 'fully mature with the fullness of Christ himself' we need to be conformed again and again to the Christ of the passion and resurrection through celebration of the holy eucharist. At this deeper level, the Christian life is all of a piece and the truth under-lying the old system of the sacraments of initiation was a fundamental one. It may be thought that this is a sufficient reason to return to an ancient custom (retained by the Eastern churches) of communicating even infants after baptism. This would make sense especially when infants are baptized during the eucharist. In the Order of Infant Baptism the eventual communion of the infants is at least mentioned (67).

Incorporation into the community of the church

After all the writing and preaching in the 1930s and 1940s about the church as the mystical body of Christ as well as all the emphasis the Liturgical Movement laid on the people's share in Christ's priesthood, it was to have been expected that people generally would have come to realize that baptism effects the incorporation of the individual into the community of the church. But apparently the 'hang-over' from former times has not yet been dispelled. For many, baptism is still merely a rescue operation to save a child from the effects of original sin – which only shows that an inadequate and unintelligible rite helps to propagate false views. The thinking of the introduction and of the whole rite of baptism is quite different. The former says *tout court* 'Through baptism men and women are incorporated into Christ' (CI 2) and again they 'are incorporated into the church' (CI 4) which is the house of the Spirit and they become members of the holy nation and the royal priesthood.[7] In the rite this is symbolized by the anointing on the head after baptism and the words which accompany the action. The candidates have been freed from sin, regenerated by water and the Spirit, 'added' to the Lord's holy people and made members of Christ who is prophet, priest and king. Thus, they are incorporated into the people of whom Christ is the head and high priest. It is through baptism that they become sharers in the priesthood of Christ and therefore, in the words of St Peter (1 Peter 2:5), have for their task and vocation the offering of spiritual sacrifices which belong to the spiritual house of which they are living stones. As is now well known, in the liturgy and in the eucharist in a special way they exercise that priesthood by offering themselves in and through Christ.[8]

Here again the eucharist appears as the completion and culmination of baptism.

Two further points may be noted here, both of which are relevant to confirmation, which we treat below. The first is that the above prayer affirms that regeneration is effected by both water and the Holy Spirit, thus clearly indicating that the Spirit is given in baptism. Popular writing and preaching on confirmation has frequently overlooked this matter and the impression has been given that the Holy Spirit is given for the first time in that sacrament. It is an untenable point of view for how can regeneration, with all it implies, be effected without the intervention of the Holy Spirit? The second point is this: by the introduction into the same prayer of the teaching that the baptized Christian shares in the priestly, royal and prophetic qualities of Christ, thus implicitly quoting 1 Peter 2:5, 9 (not to mention other New Testament texts), the church is affirming that mission, the proclamation of the saving deeds of God, is part of the vocation of the Christian. The Christian is 'sent' by baptism and he does not have to wait until he is confirmed to exercise his ministry.

Fellowship with the Holy Trinity

The teaching on incorporation is carried through to its ultimate conclusion by another passage in the introduction. Incorporation into the church means entrance into fellowship with the Holy Trinity. Perhaps we do not even reflect on what the so frequently repeated teaching of the New Testament on the 'adoption of sons' means. It means adoption into the divine family: 'The blessed Trinity is invoked over those who are to be baptised. Signed in this name, they are consecrated to the Trinity and enter into fellowship with the Father, Son and Holy Spirit' (CI 5). This may be regarded as a most useful commentary on the significance of baptism in the name of the Trinity but it will be worth while to draw out its implications. The climax of the baptism rite, as the same text says, is the baptism in the Triune name, and we may add that it is also its final purpose. Incorporation into the church is but a step, normally a necessary step, to union with God. But he is Father, Son and Holy Spirit and it is into the life of the Trinity that we are introduced by baptism. We are initiated into the divine life and that life is essentially the lived relationship between Father, Son and Holy Spirit. Ceaselessly, without loss or diminution the Persons of the Trinity give themselves to each other and in the love they communicate to one another they enfold the baptized Christian who is thus able to participate in that creative love. As in the sacrament he receives the new life from Christ by the operation of the Holy Spirit, he is able to breathe out his love for the Father, a love that is transfused with the divine love and so acceptable to him. By baptism, then, the Christian begins to live the Christian life as from its centre and this, once again, is clearly a life-long task. Lastly, since the eucharist is pre-eminently the sacrament of love, it provides the principal means by which the Christian is able to live the divine life. This too makes it clear that the eucharist is the culmination of baptism.

Celebration

Liturgical documents are practical documents and if they are rightly concerned with theological ideas it is only so that they may be translated into action. It is not surprising, then, that the baptism Orders speak of celebration, though it is gratifying that they have chosen this word. It has been more common to speak of 'administering' or 'conferring' sacraments as if the laity were solely recipients. Celebration, which involves community and participation, is a much more significant word. If the sacraments are in the phrase of St Thomas Aquinas 'protestations of faith',[9] they are also the recognition of God's saving love which reached its culmination in the passion, resurrection and ascension of Christ, and the Order sees baptism as the celebration of the paschal mystery: 'Those who are baptised are engrafted into the likeness of Christ's death. They are buried with him, they are given life with him again and with him they rise again. For baptism recalls and effects the paschal mystery itself, because by means of it men and women pass from the death of sin into life' and the Order draws the practical consequences. The joy of the Christian community through its recognition of the paschal mystery should be reflected in the celebration itself (CI 6) and this is why the sacrament is to be celebrated during the Easter Vigil or on Sundays, and, as often as pastorally desirable, within the eucharist. All through the Orders we find this relationship between baptism and the paschal mystery being established, sometimes in quite small matters as when it urges that the Paschal Candle shall stand in the baptistery throughout the year.

How this sense of celebration is to be expressed is another matter. For adult baptism there is no difficulty. It is to be celebrated either during the Paschal Vigil or during a Sunday eucharist when the joy that belongs to celebration finds its natural expression.[10] With infant baptism there is a greater difficulty. Celebration at the Sunday eucharist is desirable but it is not always possible. However, what is probably necessary is that both clergy and laity should change their views about baptism and see it as a community action in which as many as possible should be involved. This is certainly the thinking of the Order for Infant Baptism (BP 4, 9) and some pattern needs to be established and become customary. In recent decades Catholics have been accustomed to going to only one service a Sunday, the Mass. Perhaps with the restoration of the Prayer of the Church to our Sunday worship, the baptism of infants could take place in conjunction with that service. If so, the texts provided by the Order, chants, hymns and acclamations could, on the assumption that they are set to music, be sung by all present and turn the service from being an 'administration' into a celebration. To achieve anything like this it must be admitted that we have a long way to go.

Community

As is immediately obvious, you cannot have celebration without community. It is *people* who celebrate, it is they who are the church, it is they who profess the faith of the church and it is they who sing God's praises. One of the more striking features of the Order of Christian Initiation for Adults is that it requires in no uncertain terms the help and presence of the Christian community not only at the liturgy but also throughout the whole process. In the case of infant baptism this is particularly important since the Order expressly teaches that infants are, in the traditional phrase, baptized 'in the faith of the church', the faith which is declared and professed throughout the rite. If it is *theologically* true that baptism incorporates into the Christian community, it must be made liturgically plain that this is what is happening. For this clearly some representation of the local community is necessary. Pastorally speaking, their presence is going to be of the greatest help to the candidates. They will realize that they are being incorporated into the great church of which the local community is an expression and they will be encouraged in their profession of faith by the faith of the surrounding community. Where infant

~

baptism is being celebrated, the weaker Catholic will feel strengthened and supported by the presence of the same community and will no doubt rid themselves of a certain feeling of isolation or even alienation that often overtakes them.

The above teaching is expressed in the liturgies of initiation, as we have attempted in part to indicate, but it seemed necessary to give it at this point. We are now in a position to consider the Order of Christian Initiation for Adults and the liturgy of adult baptism which is included in it.

Notes

[1] *Ordo Baptismi Parvulorum, Ordo Initiationis Christianae Adultorum* (Vatican Press). The numbers in the text refer to the Latin *Ordo Initiationis*. These numbers will be found in the right-hand margins of the *Rite of Christian Initiation of Adults* (1986).

[2] As already observed, the General Introduction falls into two parts, the first called 'Christian Initiation', with which we shall be dealing first. Its paragraphs or articles are numbered from 1 to 35 and will be referred to as CI 1, 2, 3 and so on.

[3] This last phrase from St Augustine, *De Civ. Dei*, X, 6.

[4] The first comes from the 'longer' ending of Mark and the scripture experts seem to think that Matthew 28:18-20 is a summary of a floating piece of catechesis. If so, it means that both passages became anchored at the end of the two gospels.

[5] The only exception is the baptism of infants who in the third, fourth and fifth centuries were baptized with their parents. It was not until later, as we shall see, that the pattern was broken.

[6] Romans 6:3-5.

[7] The texts referred to are Ephesians 2:22 ('the house where God dwells, in the Spirit') and 1 Peter 2:9.

[8] Cf. *Mediator Dei*, 92, CL 14, and *Christian Celebration: Understanding the Mass*, pp. 42-5.

[9] ST III, 72, 5, ad 2.

[10] It is to be supposed that adult baptism may be celebrated privately in very special circumstances though the Order does not envisage such a procedure.

~

The Christian Initiation
of Adults[1]

~~~~~~~

I T MAY be thought surprising that the church has found it necessary to restore the catechumenate. It may seem to deserve the charge of irrelevancy which has become almost a new mortal sin. If we think that way it means that we have become more conditioned by our situation than perhaps we like to think. Without reflection we have come to assume that infant baptism is the norm and that any other system of Christian Initiation is abnormal. For a very long time, perhaps for too long, we have assumed that we were living in a Christian society, however broad the connotation of 'Christian'. We readily deplore the unchristian spirit of our age but we do not realize that the arrangement we regard as traditional is breaking down. The baptism of infants of families of no apparent faith is already posing more or less acute problems and we must expect that the situation will get worse rather than better. Yet a mere refusal to baptize such children solves nothing and we are faced or soon will be with the prospect of pastoral action in their regard. If the requirements of the new Order for the Baptism of Infants are to be met, it seems inevitable that as the years go by there will be an increasing number of people who are not baptized. Instead of being brushed aside as an irredeemable residue, it will be necessary to think out pastoral approaches and techniques by which they can be drawn to the church and eventually incorporated into it. Adult baptism is not so much on the horizon as with us already.[2]

For some parts of the church this situation is not new and since the experience gathered there has led to the restoration of the catechumenate some account of its previous history will be in place here.

The 'homelands' of Europe, notably France, have been faced with a dechristianized society for some long time. Considerable numbers of children are not baptized and yet in adulthood, either through the pastoral action of Christians or on the occasion of marriage, they approach the church and often wish to be received into it. The existing structures proved inadequate to meet the situation and over thirty years

~

ago the French bishops set up an official catechumenate. In missionary areas adult baptisms of course remain common, but here again, and although there were elements of a catechumenate in existence, those engaged in the work felt it was inadequate. It was something outside the liturgy and running alongside it. It was thanks to the pressure from these two sources that in 1962 Rome issued a document restoring the catechumenate. It was not much more than a re-arrangement of the material to be found in the *Rituale Romanum*[3] of that time and with its rigidity and multiplicity of minor rites that could not be varied from one culture to another it proved to be unsatisfactory.

There was another factor of even greater importance. The bishops, whether in the homelands or in the missionary areas, asked that the catechetical formation of those approaching the church should be 'sanctified by the sacred rites of the catechumenate'. The word 'formation', which in the document is distinguished from 'instruction', points to a deeper understanding of initiation. The bishops were asking that potential converts should be not merely instructed but *initiated* into the Christian life and into the community of the church. Nowadays people who approach the church are usually not just 'changing churches', as was common in the nineteenth century. They are coming out of a world that is almost wholly pagan, a world that imposes considerable pressures on Christian and catechumen alike, a world that either does not know or rejects prayer, worship and all the moral effort that goes with the Christian life. Catechumens need to do a great deal more than to accept doctrines. They need to realize that they have to begin a new way of life that will involve a new outlook on life in general and probably a change of habits. And since Christianity is itself a life they need to be initiated into it. They need to learn how to live in the Christian community before ever they make a commitment that is definitive.

This is the background of the Second Vatican Council's decision that the rites of adult baptism should be revised and that the revision should take into account the (already) restored catechumenate (CL 66). This revision has now been completed with the promulgation of the *Ordo Initiationis Christianae Adultorum* which includes the rite of adult baptism. Since it is a very long document, the longest in fact to appear so far from the Congregation of Divine Worship,[4] it is necessary to give a summary of it.

At first sight the most surprising feature of the new Order is that it is a restoration, one might almost say, a resurrection of the Roman catechumenate of the last century of its existence, when in fact it was beginning to be obsolescent since by the end of the fifth century society had become largely Christian. The reasons for this choice seem to be fairly obvious. Instead of thinking up an entirely new system the revisers examined the tradition, as they have in all their work, and saw that it provided the necessary pattern even for today. It provided for the first approach to the church, it was progressive, it already contained the rites that were needed and it incorporated the whole process of initiation, baptism, confirmation and holy communion. Even so, a first reading of this document with its rites, so numerous and apparently complex, will tempt some to say that the whole thing is impracticable and irrelevant to the situation in which the church has to work today. This objection is foreseen and answered: pastors of the church will find here material from which they can construct a system suitable to their own circumstances (3) and in fact they are required to do so. But there is something more important still: the Order endorses the view set out briefly above that approach to the church and eventual incorporation into it is a gradual process that must be concretized in liturgical services and rites so that the candidate may grasp, with the whole of his personality, Christian faith and life and so be truly initiated into Christian living. In face of the complexity of the material and the evident difficulties of implementation these factors should always be kept in mind.

The first part of the Order (1–239) may be divided as follows:

1. Evangelization and pre-catechumenate.
2. The catechumenate.
3. The time of purification and enlightenment.
4. Sacramental initiation.
5. Mystagogy.

Evangelization and the pre-catechumenate

This is the stage with which most will be familiar. People approach the church out of interest, through contact with Catholics, out of a desire to make some sense of life and so on. After preliminary interviews they will ask for and be given some instruction, usually by a priest or some other person delegated for the purpose. Under the old system they were in due course received into the church either by baptism if they had not been baptized or by the rite devised for the purpose,[5] both being private ceremonies, and then admitted to holy communion. In this system evangelization, the pre-catechumenate stage and the catechumenate were so telescoped as to disappear from view.

The outlook of the Order is totally different. It assumes evangelization and in another context it would be relevant to ask what is meant by that and how we go about it. However, the Order requires that before admission to the catechumenate candidates should be in possession of the elements of Christian doctrine, that they should have formed their intention to change their life and conceived the beginnings of repentance (15). On the part of the 'applicant' this stage is meant to be a time of questioning (7, a) so that all major doubts are cleared up to make way for the proclamation on the part of the church of the Good News about the living God and his Son, Jesus Christ, whom his Father sent into the world to redeem it (9). The first conversion is to be the response to this proclamation of the gospel and at the same time help is to be given the applicants to purify their intentions and clarify their motives. Even at this stage the Order is concerned with Christian living and with what I suppose can be called an existential grasp of the faith (10, 11).

At this first stage too, the Order emphasizes the importance of community, as it does throughout. According to circumstances and individual dispositions, candidates should be enabled to experience the spirit of the Christian life as lived within the community or, if they are not in a position eventually to be incorporated into the catechumenate, to make at least external contacts with Christians (12 (2)). The Christian life is not communion of the alone with the Alone but a corporate life and of this life the church even as local community is the sacrament-sign. Therefore, the implication is, potential converts should experience this from the beginning.

All this may seem to be very foreign to the conventional notions of 'conversion' but the Order, which in any case is taking a world-view of things, is concerned to emphasize that there are people who are drawn to Christianity but who are as yet undecided or who on account of their situation, moral or otherwise, are unable and perhaps unwilling to take steps that will commit them to ultimate incorporation into the church. The Order calls them 'sympathizers' and no doubt in missionary areas they are numerous, but in the industrialized regions of the modern world they are to be found too. Among these people will be those who have been involved in divorce or other irregular situations and the question as to what can be done for them when they approach the church is becoming acute. It is something for the clergy or members of the parish to show sympathy for them but it is not enough. On the other hand, they cannot (at least for the time being) be incorporated even into a catechumenate. Hence the remarks of the Order, as given above, and its further recommendations that they and others whose situation is regular should be received at gatherings of the local community when there will be opportunity for conversation and the formation of friendships. Whether or not there is to be some external sign or rite marking their approach to the Christian community is left to local conferences of bishops to determine (12, 13).

In some ways, of course, there is nothing new here. In England, and no doubt elsewhere, what are called Enquiry Classes are held where potential converts hear about the elements of the Christian faith and are able to meet Christians and form friendships with them. But the *spirit* of the Order is rather different. It seems to suggest that the atmosphere should be really warm and one may doubt whether the authors of it envisage the somewhat bleak setting of a schoolroom. And they add one or two details that are important: the 'friend', who will become the sponsor accompanying the seeker throughout the period of initiation, introduces him and there will be some gesture, however informal, that the community is accepting him. He will thus not remain simply an 'outsider' who happens to be enquiring about the faith but will contract a relationship with the Christian community. He will feel that he 'belongs', however tenuous the relationship may have to be for some time to come. There is considerable pastoral wisdom behind this point of view. The process of converting a nation or an individual is a long one and often in the past it has been too hurried. It is a common complaint that the children of those who become converts lapse and in the history of the church the partial collapse of a recently converted community is a commonplace. It will be better to move slowly and build up an outer circle of 'sympathizers' who are won to the Christian faith and life by their experience of the Christian living of a community (cf. 12 (2)).

The catechumenate

It is during this stage and the next ('purification') that the whole richness of the church's mind on the formation of a Christian is revealed. By word and human contact, by symbol, rite and gesture which correspond with deep human needs, the catechumen is led from an incipient faith into the fullness of the Christian life. It is important to realize this since the organization of these two stages of Christian Initiation will be difficult and in the text it looks over-complicated, even ritualistic, although offsetting this is the considerable faculty of adaptation that is assumed and enjoined by the Order. At any rate it would be a gross misunderstanding of the restored catechumenate to see it as no more than the ritualization of what might, mistakenly, be thought a very simple matter. Conviction about the Christian faith is one thing, practice is another and since Christianity is rather a life to be lived than a doctrine to be believed, it is absolutely necessary that people, especially modern people, should be initiated into Christian living during the time of their preparation.

For this stage the Order assumes that the candidates have an initial faith, have undergone the first (moral) conversion, have been familiarized with prayer and have made contact with the Christian community. That granted, the catechumenate is 'of the highest importance' for it is at this point that the candidates *publicly* declare their desire to be incorporated into the church and the church, performing her apostolic function, publicly admits them as potential members (14). In addition, there are certain social consequences. Now they belong 'to the household of Christ', they are fed by God's word in the Christian assembly, they are strengthened by liturgical rites and they may receive certain liturgical blessings. There is a special marriage rite for them[6] and if they die during their catechumenate they are buried with the Christian funeral rite (18).

The content and style of the catechumenate are indicated (19 (1), (2), (3), (4)). They consist of a suitable catechesis integrated with the liturgical year and supported by Bible Services. Teaching on the church's doctrines and the Christian precepts is to be given but above all the candidates are to be led to a deeper understanding of the mystery of salvation. They are to be assisted to live the Christian life and, even while catechumens, they are to learn to bear witness to Christ. Finally, there are the liturgical rites which we describe below. However, it is necessary to say a word about a suggestion that is contained in 19 (3).

It raises a quite big question whether catechumens are to be admitted to the eucharistic assembly proper. The Order urges that catechumens should take part in the ministry of the word along with the faithful, and therefore at public Masses, but it also says that they are to be 'kindly dismissed' unless there are difficulties 'for they should await baptism, by which they are incorporated into the priestly people when they will acquire their right to celebrate the new worship of Christ'. An unpopular suggestion, one imagines, for it has been the custom to 'get them to Mass' for fear they will not acquire the habit. This fear is dispelled by the Order which provides the means to teach people how to worship and the question remains: how far is it right to allow and even invite people to the eucharist when they cannot communicate and must in the nature of the case appear to be 'outsiders'? It is a large question, as yet without an answer.[7]

The liturgy of the catechumenate (106–131)

The first rite is naturally that which admits people to the catechumenate. Candidates with their friends and members of the local community meet in the place designated, preferably the narthex of the church which will thus return to its ancient function. The celebrant greets them, expresses the joy of the church at their coming, reminds them of the significance of the event and invites the whole company to take up the places allocated to them. During this Psalm 62:1–8 may be sung. There follow the questions ('What do you ask of the church of God? Faith . . .') and the first commitment.[8] This is preceded by a brief address of the celebrant who reminds them that since they have followed the light 'the way of the gospel is now open' to them. He concludes by asking the candidates if they are willing to take the way of Christ in faith and each replies 'I am ready'. The sponsor and the others present are asked for their support which they promise in the same terms.

According to different situations and needs (e.g. where certain kinds of 'magical' religions are prevalent), there may follow a brief exorcism and renunciation of evil. Otherwise the celebrant concludes this part of the rite with a collect and an expression of thanksgiving.

There follows the signing with the cross which signifies the new status of the candidates and the protection of Christ: 'Receive the cross on your forehead. Christ himself protects you with the sign of his love. Learn to know and follow him.' There is a second signing on all the senses which however may be wholly or partially omitted. The celebrant recites the formulas while others sign the candidates: 'Receive the sign of the cross on your ears that you may hear the voice of God . . . on your eyes that you may see the glory of God . . . on your lips that you may respond to the word of God . . .'.[9] This signing is an example of a symbolic Christian gesture that may in certain circumstances be very appropriate and its use could well be extended to other situations: e.g. the appointment of a lay reader.

This part concludes with a collect which is the old prayer of the catechumenate, now slightly re-edited: the church prays that now the candidates have been signed with the cross, they may be protected by its power and that, keeping the commandments, they may come to the glory of the new life.[10] The catechumens are now led into church with the old formula revised and enriched: 'Come into the church that you may have part with us at the table of God's word'. There follows a Bible Service during which there may be a giving of the gospel text and general intercessions for the catechumens. Finally, there is the dismissal with a reminder to the candidates to be assiduous in coming to church to hear the word of God. If Mass follows, they may stay but clearly the Order thinks it is better they should not.

During the period of the catechumenate, which may last for several years, giving time for the candidates' faith and conversion to 'mature' (98), the Order provides for a series of Bible Services, exorcisms and blessings. It is here perhaps more than anywhere else in the restored catechumenate that the nature of the process by which people become Christians is made clear. Yes, there is instruction in the doctrines of the Catholic faith; yes, they are to be encouraged to practise the precepts of the Christian life and to join in worship so far as that is possible for them; but all this is taken out of the realm of the merely intellectual or exhortatory. These things are inculcated in the context of liturgical rites which are intended to be *formative*. In the Bible Services, for instance, the catechumens will not merely hear the word of God, they will pray about it and in their endeavours to live the Christian life they will be supported by the exorcisms and blessings provided for them.

As to the exorcisms, the Order (101) says they are intended to be positive and deprecatory and the six prayers for this purpose amply prove that this is so (113–118). The emphasis on the devil is very light (113: *spiritum malignum* without a capital 'S') and they are much more requests that the catechumens will grow in virtue and will resist the evil that comes from their own nature or from the surrounding world.

The blessings are prayers, which may be used at the dismissal of the catechumens, even more positive, intended to encourage the catechumens on their way to the church, to show the care of the church for them and, as the texts of the prayer show, direct their minds and hearts to the rebirth that is to be the conclusion of the whole process.[11]

The time of enrolment, purification and enlightenment (152–207)

The Order sees this as the really decisive stage. The catechumens make a deliberate and final decision to proceed to the reception of the sacraments of initiation and, for its part, the Christian community, after consultation between the clergy, sponsors and catechists determines to admit them to full membership (135). The part to be played by the community is striking and very demanding and one wonders how far it will be practicable in the circumstances of the modern urban parish. In urban parishes people hardly know each other sufficiently to be able to offer opinions about the fitness of candidates for baptism and there is of course in any case all the danger of petty dislikes playing their part. Unless and until urban parishes can be organized on rather different lines it will be for those who have been responsible for the formation of the catechumens to make the necessary decisions and the local community will at the liturgical service endorse them. This is in fact provided for in the Order (144).[12]

The nature and purpose of this stage of purification and enlightenment (wholly traditional terms though others may be used) can be gathered from the following. It coincides with Lent when, with the Christian community, who recall and renew the grace of baptism at this time, the catechumens will be helped to ponder on the meaning of the paschal mystery which the sacraments of initiation communicate to each of them (21). This in fact explains the nature of the liturgical arrangements for this stage. At this time it is conceived that there will be a period of more intense spiritual recollection and formation. The hearts and minds of the candidates are to be purified by an education of the conscience and by penitence and it is these elements that are insisted on rather than further instruction. It is to this end that 'scrutinies', which form part of this stage, are enjoined. Their purpose is first to reveal what is still weak or perverse in the candidates' conduct so that this may be put right (ut sanetur) but secondly to show what is good, strong and holy that it may be established in them. The enlightenment comes with the exposition and 'giving' (traditio) of the creed and the Lord's Prayer. The first is seen as a summary of the Good News of salvation, which they will accept with joy, and by the latter they will learn to recognize the deeper

~

significance of their being children of God, an acknowledgement they will make when (eventually) they recite it 'in the midst of the eucharistic assembly' (25 (1), (2)).

At this stage, too, they become the 'elect' (another traditional term)[13] not simply because they are enrolled and their names entered in a register but because, says the Order (23), the church's act of calling and choosing them is founded on the choice God has made of them (22). This statement, based no doubt on texts like Ephesians 1:4, restores to currency a certain theology of vocation in the sense of calling and of the conversion, which is its consequence not merely for those usually called converts but for all Christians. It is evidence of how serious the church considers this matter of becoming a Christian. Conversion is not a sociological or psychological accident; it is evidence of God's call, indicated perhaps by the conditions of one's life, but manifested in the call and election of the church and sealed by the sacraments of baptism, confirmation and the holy eucharist.

The liturgy of this stage

First, it is to be noted that this liturgy is firmly integrated into that of Lent, the rite of admission taking place on the First Sunday of Lent (140). This links it with the preparation of the whole Christian community for the celebration of the paschal mystery at Easter.

The liturgy consists of the following: the rite of admission, the scrutinies with exorcisms and the giving ('tradition') and the rendering of the creed and the Lord's Prayer.

First, the catechumens are presented and then in terms that remind one of the ordination service, they are invited to come forward and their sponsors are questioned about their fitness. In their turn, the catechumens are asked about their intentions: do they wish to be initiated into the sacraments of Christ, baptism, confirmation and the eucharist? and they answer that they do. They are then formally elected: 'You are now chosen that you may be initiated into the sacred mysteries at the coming celebration of Easter'. There follow intercessions for them, concluded with a collect and the dismissal.

There are three scrutinies which are to take place on the Third, Fourth and Fifth Sundays of Lent after the homily. These are not 'examinations' nor are they enquiries into the moral fitness of the candidates. They are prayers for their spiritual strengthening and they take the place of the General Intercession of the Mass (154). After the prayers there is what is called an exorcism for which three collects are provided, each of which echoes the theme of the respective Sunday gospel, thus restoring the sense of these gospel passages for Lent.[14]

On appointed weekdays during Lent there is the 'tradition' of the creed and the Lord's Prayer. The celebrant addresses the candidates, and leads them in the recitation of either the Apostles' Creed (which thus returns to our liturgy!) or, at choice, the Niceno-Constantinopolitan Creed which we use at Mass. There follow a prayer for the elect and a laying-on of hands with a prayer. The service of the 'tradition' of the Lord's Prayer follows the same pattern and naturally includes the gospel passage (Matthew 6:9–13) in which the Lord taught it to his disciples.

At an appointed hour on Holy Saturday the elect are assembled, if possible, and then 'give back' the creed and the Lord's Prayer. The rite of the *Ephphetha* (the opening of the ears and mouths of the candidates to hear and speak the word of God) may be performed as may the anointing with the oil of catechumens. The candidates are to be anointed on the breast and the hands and other parts of the body, if desired. Presumably there are parts of the world where these rites are still acceptable but they present considerable difficulties for modern Western man. Local conferences of bishops may allow their omission and it is to be hoped that they will.

The Order gives the impression that these weekday rites are not so important as the others and there will be practical difficulties in finding suitable times for them. *Ephphetha* and anointings apart, there is however a case for them. The Order, with sound psychological insight, sees the value of active participation here as elsewhere in the liturgy and the ritualization of the giving back of the creed and the Lord's Prayer should help the candidates to feel more personally committed to what they are undertaking. Simple gestures involving personal choice should not be undervalued.

*The initiation: baptism, confirmation and the holy eucharist
(208–234)*

Since confirmation demands separate treatment and since there are few special features of the eucharist on this occasion, this section will deal principally with what is now in effect the rite of adult baptism.

Three aspects of the new liturgy of Christian Initiation stand out and deserve attention.

1. These sacraments are now normally to be celebrated within the Easter Vigil. This is not to be regarded as merely a good liturgical arrangement. It indicates that baptism, confirmation and the eucharist are all means by which the Christian participates in the paschal mystery, the passion, death and resurrection of Christ. This more than preaching or lectures will teach the Christian people that these sacraments are so related.[15]

2. The ancient relationship between baptism, confirmation and the eucharist is visibly restored. The candidates proceed from one sacrament to another in an ordered sequence for, even if a bishop is not present, they may be confirmed.[16] This will do more than anything to inculcate in the Christian people (including the clergy) that this is the right order of events and pastoral practice will, presumably, eventually be affected by it.

3. Adult baptism appears in its 'pure' state, totally different from the complex and obscure rite of the now-obsolete *Rituale Romanum*. The reason for this is that the old rite had telescoped the whole of the catechumenate into a series of prayers and gestures which in that context were meaningless.[17] Since the catechumenate has been restored and everything belonging to it has already been done, there is nothing left but to baptize the candidate. This means that it is a very simple rite, simpler now than that of infant baptism which has retained certain features of the catechumenate, and its description can be brief.

The liturgy of adult baptism

The service of baptism begins after the homily of the Mass. Either before or during the singing of the Litany of Saints, the candidates are gathered in the baptistery. Before the Litany begins the celebrant addresses them: 'Let us beseech our God and Father for these his servants who ask for baptism. He has called them and led them to this moment to give them light and strength so that courageously they may adhere to Christ and profess the faith of the church. May he renew them through the Holy Spirit whom in a few moments we are going to call down on this water.'

Although this is not a fixed text (213) it is very important. It is at baptism that the Christian commits himself to Christ and undertakes to profess the faith and is regenerated by water and the Holy Spirit. This text has, as we shall see, interesting implications for confirmation.

The Litany, during which there is a special petition for the catechumens, is sung and is immediately followed by the Blessing of the Font. The three prayers to be found in the Order of Infant Baptism may be used at choice, the first being a shortened and unfortunately emasculated version of that in the old Roman Missal.

The renunciation of evil and the profession of faith follow.[18]

It may be thought that since the catechumen during the time of preparation has renounced evil, has been exorcized and professed the faith in one way or another, a repetition here is superfluous. The Order takes up this point explicitly (211). The renunciation of evil and the profession of faith, it says, here have their full force: 'Since baptism is a sacrament of faith by which catechumens adhere to God and at the same time are reborn, these acts by which they now renounce sin and Satan fittingly precede the act of baptism itself. By these acts, which were prefigured in the covenant with the patriarchs of the Old Testament,[19] the candidates adhere for ever to the promise of the Saviour and the mystery of the Trinity. By their profession, which they make before the celebrant and in presence of the community, they signify their will, matured in the time of the catechumenate, to enter into the new covenant with Christ. In this faith, handed on to them by the church, a faith they have already embraced, they are (now) baptised.' It is to be seen, then, as a summing up and declaration in the presence of the community, of all they have already undertaken. The text invites commentary, which however would take us too far. It may be said *en passant* that the covenant-language, thus brought back into currency in an official document, throws light on the whole of Christian living. We are a covenanted people, enjoying, if we will, the benefits of God's fidelity to his promises but we in turn are required to be faithful to God who has shown us his mercy in Christ. We note too that the existing faith of the candidates is an active element in their baptism and we recall the 'form' of baptism in the *Apostolic Tradition* of Hippolytus.[20] The minister asked if the candidate believed and it was the candidate who professed the faith, upon which and without further ado he was plunged into the water. It is difficult to think of a more striking example of active participation than this and it is a pity that the church has not restored this mode of baptism at least for adults.[21]

After this, there remains only the act of baptism, which may be by immersion (which is put first in the text) or by affusion. In the first case the celebrant immerses either the head or the whole body under the water; in the second he pours the water on the head in the way with which we are familiar. Acclamations or other chants to accompany the acts of baptism are recommended.

The post-baptismal rites remain, the clothing in the white robe and the lighting of a candle (done by the sponsor from the Paschal Candle). There is also the question of the post-baptismal anointing about which we say a word below. There is a minor difficulty about the white robe. What sort should it be? Presumably the modern sort of alb, shaped and held together with a linen girdle, would be suitable to both men and women but some experimentation is needed. Sponsors could perhaps provide it and it could be worn throughout the following Mass. The formula for the handing of the candle to the newly baptized is eloquent:

You have been made light in Christ.
Ever walk as children of light.
So persevering in faith,
may you meet Christ when he comes again
with all the saints in the court of heaven.

The omission of the post-baptismal anointing if, as will usually be the case, confirmation immediately follows, is puzzling. The introduction offers no commentary and yet if the chrismation is to take place it is grouped with the *ritus explanativi* (white garment and candle) which surely means rites that unfold the meaning of baptism. The text of the prayer accompanying the chrismation teaches that the neophyte is 'joined' to the people of God and made a member of Christ who is priest, prophet and king. Neither the rite of baptism nor that of confirmation has this teaching elsewhere and the implication seems to be that all that is conveyed by chrismation is conveyed by confirmation. Could the alternative also be true, as it was assumed to be true in pre-Carolingian Gaul when presbyters chrismated and this was regarded as confirmation? It would seem more probable that chrismation is regarded as an expendable extra (in spite of Hippolytus who has both chrismation and confirmation) especially as, according to the Order of Infant Baptism (24 (4)), if the number of candidates is very great, it may be omitted. The conclusion must be that in spite of the long (Western) tradition, chrismation is not to be regarded as important.

Of confirmation itself all we need say at this point is that it is to be regarded as normal, almost *de rigueur*, even though no bishop is present. It is only *peculiari de causa* (and one wonders what *that* could be) that it is to be omitted (244).

There are few special features of the Mass. The creed is naturally omitted; the neophytes are to take their part in the General Intercession; there are special inserts into the eucharistic prayers, not merely for I but also for II, III and IV; communion, it is recommended, should be given in both kinds to the neophytes, their sponsors, relations and any concerned in their instruction. Before the *Ecce, Agnus Dei* the celebrant may speak briefly of the greatness of the eucharistic mystery which is the culmination of initiation and the centre of the Christian life (234).

The conclusion or mystagogy [22]

A word must be said about this phase with its ill-sounding name, 'mystagogy'. It is well known that in the classical period of the catechumenate there was a final stage in Easter week when the neophytes were initiated into an understanding of the mysteries of baptism and the eucharist which they had received at the Vigil. The catechetical instructions of a Cyril of Jerusalem and an Ambrose of Milan, to mention no others, remain to show what was done at this time. The candidates met daily in church and the bishop led them into a deeper understanding of what they had done and received. During this week they wore the white garments with which they had been clothed after baptism. The Order has kept the general sense of this phase but has not thought good to ritualize it.

Its purpose is to deepen the neophytes' understanding and appreciation of the paschal mystery and to help them to harmonize their daily living with it (37). This is to be achieved by hearing the word of God, by a particularly frequent celebration of the sacraments[23] and by an ever closer association with the Christian community (38, 39). The Order urges that the neophytes should be particularly careful to gather with their friends for the celebration of the Sunday Masses of Eastertide of which the readings of Year A are especially appropriate to their condition (39, 40).

This time could well be marked by some weekday meetings when questions about doctrine or practice arising out of the catechumenate experience could be discussed. It has been found that this is sometimes necessary.

What it all comes to is that the newly baptized should, with their sponsors, friends and the local community, celebrate the Sunday eucharist at this time with a special joy and appreciation.

Simpler and abbreviated forms of initiation

The first (240–277) is intended for 'extraordinary circumstances' when the candidate cannot undertake all the stages of the catechumenate or when the Ordinary is satisfied with his sincerity and maturity (240). Three things are assumed: (a) sufficient knowledge of the faith; (b) the assistance of a sponsor; (c) familiarity with the local Christian community. The last two emphasize, as the Order does throughout, the need for the support of the community in the person of the sponsor and the presence of the community into which the candidate is to be incorporated. The rite itself is again intended to emphasize that conversion and incorporation into the church are public acts, manifesting the assent of the candidate, his desire for initiation and the acceptance of him by the local community (241–244).

The rite, which is to be celebrated at Mass, may be done as one action and consists of the questions (to both candidate and sponsor), a collect and the ceremony of introduction to the community. The ministry of the word follows with intercessions, exorcism and the first anointing. The act of baptism follows with confirmation and holy communion and their attendant rites as in the longer form.

However, directives are given (274–277) for the incorporation of certain rites from the longer form and for their distribution over an appointed period of time. Unless circumstances (envisaged by the Order (274)) make it necessary to abbreviate the whole rite, this will surely be the better way. Further, if the intentions of the church are not to be frustrated in this matter, this catechumenate is a quasi-necessity. In fact, this shorter form, properly used, will be the one that most practical in the circumstances of the large urban parish.

The Abbreviated Order (278–294) is intended for those in danger of death whether a catechumen or not. In the latter case, he must give certain signs that he wishes to turn to Christ and that he is willing to take up the full catechumenate on recovery. The rite is simple and impressive. There are the questions ('This is eternal life; that we may know the true God and Jesus Christ whom he sent. This is the faith of Christians. Do

~

you know this? I do'), there is the support of a sponsor or witness who promises to help him; there are intercessions, renunciation of evil and profession of faith, the baptism, confirmation and the administering of holy communion.

On those baptized in infancy but not instructed (295–305)

If the elaborate catechumenate seems impracticable, it cannot be said that the revisers lack pastoral sense. They have provided for almost every pastoral situation that is likely to be met with in normal parish work and in this section (chapter IV) they give certain 'pastoral persuasions' as to how to deal with those who were baptized Catholics in infancy and have never been confirmed or received holy communion. Their remarks are deliberately called 'persuasions' (suasiones) and might be translated as 'suggestions'. What they come to is an adapted catechumenate, though the Order insists that such people are in an entirely different situation from that of catechumens (295). Sponsors and the local community are again in the picture and the text suggests that incorporation into the Christian community through liturgical rites such as those of the 'giving' of the creed, the Lord's Prayer and the gospels is the method by which they should be initiated into the sacraments they have not yet received. No Order, however, is given and the pastoral clergy are thus left with wide possibilities of adaptation. It is however insisted that these people should be adequately prepared by instruction and attendance at liturgical services.

The injunction (296), however, that the instruction should be protracted may or may not be practicable. Sometimes it is true that people approach the church and it is only after many conversations that it is revealed that they were baptized Catholics in infancy. The more usual case is of those who wish to get married and now that most people plan their weddings far ahead there is time to initiate them into the faith by instruction and by the sacraments of penance, confirmation and the eucharist. If the minister in charge of all this presides at liturgical rites he has the power to confirm also (cf. canons 882, 883 and RCIA 339). However, even in these cases the general outlook of the Order should be regarded as helpful. The 'giving' of the creed, the Lord's Prayer and the gospels suggest where the emphasis should lie in whatever instruction can be given and if these 'traditions' are done as simple rites in

~

church, the instructions are more likely to be effective. In addition, preparation for the sacraments through the use of the liturgical texts will make the whole process concrete and meaningful to them.

The initiation of unbaptized children

A quite common situation in parish life is the need to receive into the church children who were not baptized in infancy. Their parents may wish to become Catholics or have already done so, or the parents, though Catholics, were for one reason or another unable to have their children baptized when they were born. There is also the phenomenon of families who through pastoral effort have been 'reclaimed' for the church. Whatever the situation, the question of initiating such children has posed certain problems. Often enough, for want of documents, they have been baptized conditionally in a miserable little ceremony, that made little or no impact. This Order caters for this situation and offers a most attractive way of initiating such children.

The Order is based on the lines of the classical catechumenate, set out above, but there is an important observation on the need for a very considerable adaptation (312). The local bishops' conferences are to see to this adaptation not merely of the rites but, and this is of immense importance, of the *language* of the texts: 'When this Order is turned into vernacular languages, care must be taken to accommodate the addresses, the intercessions and the prayers to the capacity of the children'. For this work the bishops will obviously have to invoke the aid of skilled catechists and it is clear that this process of adaptation could lead to a harmonization of the instruction given in the classroom and the liturgy performed in the church. It is also clear that at least one or two versions will have to be made to adapt the Order to different age-ranges. What is suitable to a child of eleven will not be suitable to a child of seven.[24]

Quite properly the Order sees the initiation of such children against the background of the family, who have a decisive part to play, and in the context of what it calls 'the catechetical community' of which the child is a member. These two groups are the immediate community in the presence of which all the acts of initiation are to be performed though the larger, parish, community is also to play its part at certain moments of the initiation.

The Order begins with a rite of entry consisting of a few simple questions (e.g. 'Why do you wish to be a Christian?'), and a dialogue between the celebrant and the parents and/or sponsors during which the children go to their parents and ask their consent to be made Christians, a consent which the parents are required to give *viva voce* to the celebrant. He then signs the children with the cross, enrolling them among the members of the church, and invites their parents to do likewise. The children are then led into the church where a simple Bible Service is celebrated[25] during which a copy of the gospels may be handed to the child. The service ends with intercessions and a collect. After this, the children, now called catechumens, are dismissed. It is taken for granted that if the eucharist is to be celebrated they will not be present for it.

In the event of this catechumenate being prolonged some of the rites of the adult catechumenate may be used, scrutinies, exorcisms and the pre-baptismal anointing. All are to be adapted to the situation.

The last stage is the sacramental initiation, baptism, confirmation and the celebration of the eucharist. It does not appear from the Order (349) that the prayer of blessing of the baptismal water may be adapted and no doubt it is supposed that one or other of the alternative blessings in the Order of Baptism, which are rather simpler, will be used. However, just as in the case of eucharistic prayers there is need for texts written for young children, so is there here. The best people to *initiate* the composition of such prayers would be the bishops' conferences themselves.

The admission of the validly baptized into full communion

This Order, tucked away in an Appendix at the end of the book, has an importance much greater than the simple little rite it encloses would seem to indicate. The thirteen articles of its introduction set out a whole ecumenical theology on the admission of members of other churches to full communion with the Roman Catholic Church. The desire not to give offence whether by language or practice is very evident. Such converts are to be sharply distinguished from catechumens (5), no abjuration of heresy is required and the rite is drawn up so that the candidate may enter into the unity and (full) communion of the church (1). For this reason nothing other than what is necessary is to be imposed (*ibid.*, with a reference to Acts 15:28).

The rite of reception, which normally is to take place within the Mass, again strikes the same ecumenical note. It is an action that should be seen as a celebration of the church which finds its culmination in communion in the eucharist (3, a). Thus are brought together communion with the church in the sense of membership and communion in the sacrament which is both creative of union and its chief expression. But the Mass is to be celebrated simply and without any suggestion of 'triumphalism' (*magnificentiae*) and the Order enjoins that two factors shall decide the style of celebration: ecumenical propriety (*boni*) and the bond with the parish community. According to the Order, then, most often a Mass with a small community will be best though the circumstances of each case are to be taken into account (3, b).

The preparation, which includes instruction of the candidate, is apparently to be private, i.e. without any liturgical acts. He is to have a full knowledge of the faith but his spiritual formation is also to be attended to. He is to see that his adherence to the church is the fulfilment of all he has received in baptism (5).[26]

The conditions for reception no longer include, as we have seen, the abjuration of heresy and the Order repeats the instructions to be found in the Ecumenical Directory (14, 15) on the subject of conditional baptism which is *never* to be given as a matter of course but only after the necessary investigation if there is any reason to doubt the validity or existence of the first baptism (7). In any case, it is to be given privately. The local Ordinary is to decide exactly what is to be done (*ibid.*). Confession of sin is to be made beforehand to a confessor who is to be warned that the candidate is to be admitted into full communion with the church (10).

The rite is very simple. It takes place after the homily in which the celebrant gives thanks for the event, points out that baptism, which the candidate originally received, is the foundation and ultimate justification of what is happening. He continues with references to the sacraments of confirmation and communion which the candidate is to receive. The celebrant then invites him to make his act of faith either in the terms of the Apostles' Creed or of the Niceno-Constantinopolitan Creed. At the end and at the prompting of the celebrant the candidate then says: 'I believe and profess all that the holy Catholic Church believes, teaches and proclaims as revealed by God'. The celebrant then pronounces the formula of admission ('You have full communion with us in the faith which you have professed') and confirms the candidate. He with his sponsor(s), friends and others will go to holy communion and all may receive it in both kinds (11).

Finally, it remains for local conferences of bishops to adapt the rite according to circumstances, if they think fit, and to add to or

58

subtract from it (12). It is difficult to suppose that anyone will want to abbreviate it.

After the liturgically jejune rite of former times with its heavy legalistic flavour this new rite must be welcomed on every ground.

Pastoral reflections

When the Order of the Christian Initiation of Adults (RCIA for short) appeared in 1985 in its English edition (the excellent work of the ICEL) it was taken up in English-speaking countries with some enthusiasm. This was both gratifying and important. Gratifying, because it indicated that what on paper seems a complicated series of liturgies could be and was taken up by the pastoral clergy in their parishes. Important, because it introduced a new element into the pastoral life, a liturgy that involves many members of the parish community and eventually the whole of it. Here the Christian community visibly, through word, rite and sacrament, is doing the work for which it was intended. It is reaching out to the world around it, it is proclaiming the faith of Christ and gradually incorporates into the church by baptism, confirmation and the eucharist those who have been willing to listen and make the necessary commitment. It has already had a beneficial effect on those parish communities which have celebrated the rite since it has involved people of various gifts from catechesis to hospitality and when generalized could have a profound influence on the life of the church in any given diocese or region.

There are however one or two matters of concern. In England and Wales the RCIA was made 'official' and in several dioceses bishops have marked their responsibility for it by presiding in their cathedrals at the enrolment ceremony. Others have presided at the baptism, confirmation and the eucharist at the Easter Vigil either in their cathedrals or, if they are auxiliary bishops, in selected parish churches. In this way the role of the bishop as the chief minister of these sacraments has been made plain. There seems however to be a discrepancy between what is done on these occasions and episcopal practice in the matter of confirmation generally. It is still customary for children to receive first communion about the age of seven and then, two, three, four years later, to be confirmed. The discrepancy is all the more glaring in those parishes where parish-centred sacramental programmes are in use (usually known as the Brusselmans Scheme). Here children with the constant participation of their parents are gradually initiated into their first eucharist. No account is taken of this in the bishops' planning of confirmations and the scheme itself cries out for confirmation to be inserted into it. More will be said about this in connection with confirmation.

Another concern is that adequate distinction does not always seem to be made between catechumens as such (i.e. the non-baptized) and those who have been baptized in other Christian churches. Yet the RCIA and other documents are emphatic that this distinction must be respected. It is wrong to treat a baptized person as if he or she were not baptized. Yet, it seems, both are included in the same programme.

This points up another difficulty. When the implementation of the RCIA was made official it was not made clear that in the circumstances of England and Wales at least it is highly improbable that there will be catechumens every year. You cannot manufacture them! No harm will be done if the organization of a catechumenate is an occasional affair. People will be all the more willing to help for neither they nor the clergy can or should be kept on the go all the time. The catechumenate is very demanding of time and energy.

In this Decade of Evangelization however the church as a whole in this country and parishes in particular should see it as their duty to exercise the mission that is theirs by reaching out in ways best known to them not only to the unchurched but to those who have never had a connection with any church at all. If this is done there will be non-baptized potential catechumens and if they can make the first commitment then a true catechumenate can be organized. It would seem a good thing if several parishes in a given area jointly organized a catechumenate, thus sharing resources and the work-load.

There is however a larger question looming here. Is the dechristianization that is proceeding in this country and in the West generally to continue? If it does, it is likely that by the end of the decade there will be a very large number of the non-baptized and if they are to be incorporated into the church the catechumenate and all that goes before it and with it will become a necessity. It will not be just 'official', it will be a necessary part of normal pastoral life.

The RCIA involves a series of rites, or, better, liturgies, word–prayer services, the laying-on of hands, anointings, assemblies with the local parish community and finally the celebration of the sacraments during the Easter Vigil. There may be a temptation to 'cut corners', to omit or downgrade matters that are judged to be of lesser importance. To do so would be to misunderstand the nature and purpose of the catechumenate and the doctrine that it implies. In the past we have thought of entrance into the faith as a matter of catechetics whether to the baptized or the unbaptized. 'Instruction' was all important and the more, it was thought, the better. The catechumenate has a higher importance and a deeper impact. The whole of it from the first introduction to the climax in the Easter eucharist is a process of formation. It is not easy to become a Christian. Mentality, habits, attitudes and sometimes morals have to be changed and the rites of the catechumenate are all directed to the *formation* of a Christian man or woman. Becoming a Christian means to enter into a new life, life in Christ and life as a member of the Christian Church, and the catechumenate is the means whereby people are initiated into Christian living.

If however 'instruction' is not normally the way to Christian living, some is necessary and the question is, of what sort should it be? The RCIA document is emphatic that instruction must be directed to Christian living: 'The living God is proclaimed and Jesus Christ whom he has sent for the salvation of all; *the hearts of the seekers are opened to the Holy Spirit so that they may believe and be freely converted to the Lord and commit themselves sincerely to him*'. This process is continued through much of the catechumenate and the word–prayer meetings are a model of how it should be done. There is the reading of the scriptures, there is prayer and there is the exposition of what has been read or what the scripture has suggested. This will ensure that the language of the catechesis will remain concrete, full of images, as is acceptable to people now. In discussion (in small groups if necessary) after the talk, questions can be raised, difficulties sorted out and more extended explanations of doctrines or morals given as may be necessary. Finally, the catechumens are exhorted to live the Christian life or to begin to do so by showing concern for others, perhaps visiting the sick and so on. To help them to do so each catechumen has a friend, a 'sponsor', who will encourage and support him or her in this and other matters.

There has now been sufficient experience to show that those parishes that have organized the catechumenate have undergone a considerable renewal. Catechists, friends, sponsors, the givers of hospitality, the clergy have all been working together for the same end. In a sense the catechumenate is a model of what a parish should be. It is far-reaching in its consequences and coupled with evangelization (without which it cannot exist) it could revitalize the church in our time.

To unfold all the riches of the catechumenate cannot be done here and I would refer readers to a full commentary, available in two editions.[27]

Notes
~

[1] For the purposes of this chapter this term covers all that is to be found in the *Order of Christian Initiation for Adults* (1972) from the first approach of a seeker to the church to mystagogy which is the final stage. In the Order the various items, including the *praenotanda* or introductions, are numbered from 1 to 239. Whether they refer to these or parts of the rites it is these numbers that will be given in what follows. In this chapter it will also be necessary to include sundry variations of the Order and the rite of admission of a baptized Christian into the Catholic Church. This rite is to be found in an Appendix and is separately numbered.

[2] In one parish known to the present writer at least three people received adult baptism during the Easter Vigil in 1971.

[3] Text in **AAS**, 54/6 (May 1962), pp. 310ff. Cf. also for French translation *Documentation Catholique*, 59/1, p. 380.

[4] Longer by thirteen pages than the *Ordo Missae*.

[5] Involving abjuration of and absolution from heresies they were totally innocent of!

[6] *Ordo Matrimonii*, 55–56.

[7] J. Gelineau, in *Nelle Vostre Assemblee* (Brescia, 1970), pp. 72–3, raises the question not only in connection with catechumens but with those public ceremonies and certain marriages and funerals where most of the congregation are not Christians in any real sense. What right have we to expose the holy mysteries to them? Are we not laying ourselves open to radical misunderstanding? And here and elsewhere he suggests that catechumens should be dismissed before the eucharist proper: 'The restoration of the catechumenate invites us to ensure a certain pedagogy to assist the approach to the sign of the Christian mystery . . . *It is not normal* that a catechumen should be present at the eucharist in which he is not permitted to receive holy communion.'

[8] No. 76; in the Latin, *Prima adhaesio*.

[9] I am unable to find the source of this manifold signing. The rite may be omitted either in whole or in part (85). There is a similar rite, though *after* baptism, in Cyril of Jerusalem, cited above, p. 27.

[10] There is an alternative.

[11] Certain features of the next stage may be anticipated in this (119).

[12] The decision-making does not of course exclude the bishop. There will be previous consultation with him and at the service either he or his delegate will announce the decision (23).

[13] In different parts of the church and at different times various terms were used for catechumens: 'elect' was a Roman term; *photismenoi*, 'those to be enlightened', a Greek term.

~

[14] In the early Middle Ages they were in fact the 'scrutiny' gospels and when the catechumenate fell into disuse they were moved to certain weekdays. They have now been restored to their original places.

[15] For sound pastoral reasons this liturgy may be celebrated at Whitsuntide or on Sundays.

[16] *Ord. Confirm.* 7b.

[17] And even then managed to make no reference to confirmation and the eucharist!

[18] If the pre-baptismal anointing has taken place earlier on Holy Saturday morning, it will of course be omitted here.

[19] Entry into the covenant involved the repudiation of idolatry, with all its attendant immorality, and adherence to God. It was the constant cry of the prophets.

[20] *Ap. Trad.* 21, p. 19.

[21] It would not necessarily involve baptism by immersion.

[22] 'Mystagogy' simply means 'an introduction to the mysteries'.

[23] *Sacramentorum* is the word used but since the eucharist can be the only one in view, it must be that the word is used in the sense of 'mysteries', the 'sacred mysteries' of the new Order of the Mass.

[24] It is difficult to discern from the Order what age the compilers had in mind. They speak of 'several years' in one place (307). For young children this is far too long. Experience shows that it is a matter of months rather than years, and even months seem an eternity to an eight-year-old. We may suppose that this question of age is one that the bishops should consider.

[25] Scripture passages are suggested (326), some of which do not seem very appropriate.

[26] We also read that during the time of preparation he may communicate in certain sacred acts and a reference is given to the Directory of Ecumenism, 19, 20. These will include blessings, 'sacramentals' and presumably attendance, though obviously not communion, at the eucharist. He is **not** a catechumen, so may attend 'the sacred mysteries'. Here again however circumstances will alter cases and it will often be necessary to initiate a candidate gradually into a kind of worship with which he may be quite unfamiliar.

[27] *Rite of Christian Initiation of Adults: The Final Texts with Commentaries* (Dublin, Columba Press, 1986); *The Rite of Christian Initiation of Adults: A Study Book. Approved Text and Commentaries* (London, St Thomas More Centre, 1988). The commentaries by Patrick A. Purnell, SJ, and J. D. Crichton are the same in both volumes; in the English edition, one by Ann Tomalak replaces one by Briege O'Hare.

~

Infant Baptism

~~~~~~~~

*T*HIS IS not the place to go into the vexed question of infant baptism. Even the recent bibliography on the subject is enormous, for theologians of almost every denomination have been discussing it very vigorously for some years. The Catholic Church (Roman and Orthodox) has accepted the practice from a very early age (though the New Testament evidence is indecisive) and still accepts it. It will be as well, however, to spell out what the church means by it. As the whole of the new Order of Baptism makes clear, it means *the baptism of the infants of believing and practising parents* (even if the question of belief is sometimes a matter of discussion) *who intend to bring up their children in the faith of Christ*. This is fundamental to an understanding of the new Order and it is regrettable that while the rite has proved to be very acceptable to both clergy and people, its implications and the plain teaching of the introduction have not been so welcome. If that teaching is not accepted, it is very difficult, if not impossible, to find any justification for infant baptism. In recent years the church has reiterated again and again that we are saved by faith and the sacraments of faith. Both are necessary and yet there seems to be an ineradicable tendency in certain quarters to act as if the former were unnecessary. The indiscriminate baptism of infants (because otherwise they cannot be saved?) leads only to the multiplication of nominal Christians who have no real attachment to the church and yet who are held by certain juridical requirements of the church.[1] If the new rite of infant baptism is approved of, it is equally important that its implications should be accepted and put into practice. Anything less is sheer ritualism.

Faith

The first of these implications is in fact faith and since, in the view of the Order, faith on the part of the parents is an indispensable necessity for the admission of a child to baptism, it is necessary to say something

~

further about it here. It is to be noted that throughout the introduction
and the rite, it is the faith of the *parents* that is in question and, to
anticipate for a moment, it would be quite intolerable to use this service
unless the parents can give evidence of a credible faith. It would be to
perpetuate precisely that insincerity and inauthenticity with which our
liturgy has been afflicted for so long. It is not surprising, then, that no
less than seven times during the service, the faith of the parents is called
into play or mentioned (39, 44 (45), 47, 56, 58, 60, 64). Particularly
important are the following: the parents undertaking to bring their child
up in the faith (39), the scripture readings and homily (44, 45) whose purpose is to evoke and renew their faith, the address before the profession
of faith when they are reminded that it is by faith they are led to undertake the Christian upbringing of their children (56), the profession of
faith itself (58) and perhaps most important of all, the assent they make
just before the act of baptism (60): 'Do you wish your child to receive
baptism in the faith of the church which we have just professed together?'
This faith has been made sufficiently explicit and indeed inclusive in the
ancient formula of profession which, with slight alteration, goes back to
the time of Hippolytus in the early third century.

This teaching, which has always been implicit in the rite of infant baptism and explicit in the documents of the church, is further unfolded in
the introduction. Since infants have not a personal faith (*fidem propriam*)
they are baptized in the faith of the church (*in fide ipsius Ecclesiae*, a phrase
found at least as early as St Augustine) and 'church' here is not left as
an abstraction. It is represented by the parents, godparents and members
of the local community who during the course of baptism profess it
(BP 1, 2). It is obvious that the parents too must have a 'personal faith'
and the profession in the rite is not to be regarded as a mere form of
words that may be uttered without conviction.

Nor of course does the Order leave the matter there. Both before and
after the celebration there is something to be done. Beforehand the
parents are to be prepared and if necessary instructed in the faith (5 (1),
8) and afterwards means are to be found to help parents to fulfil the
obligations they have undertaken (BP 7 (1)). But the over-riding importance of faith for both the parents and the child is underlined. The Order
uses a remarkable phrase to introduce the subject: 'To fulfil the true
meaning of the sacrament'[2] the children are later to be formed in the
faith in which they have been baptized. As the Latin has it, *Ad veritatem*

sacramenti complendam (3), which might be translated 'to achieve the authenticity of the sign' (which of course is the sacrament), as if to suggest that without this subsequent formation the sign is not authentic.[3] Baptism is one of the sacraments which, in the ancient phrase,[4] *significando causant* and in the case of baptism if the subsequent formation is not given, the significance of the sacrament is prevented from having its full effect. Furthermore, the introduction goes on to state that baptism is the basis of Christian education in the course of which the child will gradually be led to understand God's plan of salvation effected in Christ so that ultimately he will affirm and ratify the faith in which he has been baptized.

Infant baptism is theologically not without its difficulties. As is clear from the general teaching of the New Testament, normally faith comes before sacrament. But against the background as given in the new Order it is justifiable. An analogy may help to show this. The child lives in its mother's womb for nine months and is totally dependent on her for life and nourishment. After birth it remains dependent on her and on the family group, a dependence that becomes increasingly important as it grows. It is from the family it receives the stimuli to discern the outline of its world, to speak and to become conscious of belonging to a community. Psychologically, the child lives in the womb of the family until about the age of twelve and only then begins to become independent, a person. What is true in the natural order is largely true in the supernatural order. During childhood parents have the responsibility (now made very clear in the Order) of seeing that the child does grow in faith and, if all is well, he does so grow, making ever more explicit and personal assents to the faith given in baptism. During this time Christ will become a person to him. In short, the parents and the family group communicate the faith to the child or perhaps actualize the faith given as a potentiality in baptism. In any case, baptism is to lead on to confirmation and the eucharist (in that order), as the introduction (BP 5 (5)) and the final address of the rite make clear (BP 68).

In all this teaching there is clearly a whole programme of Christian education suggested and the presupposition is that it is the parents who will do it though with the assistance of bishops, clergy and (unspecified) lay people (BP 7 (1)). There is much to be done on this field and, as we suggest elsewhere, one of the most fruitful developments in the contemporary church would be the training of lay-catechists among whom it is to be wished that large numbers of parents would be included. Not only are there great numbers of children who cannot get to Catholic schools but it is a fact of experience that schools in this all-important matter of Christian education are well-nigh powerless to bring up children as Christians without the active co-operation of their parents.

Community

In infant baptism the community has a role of peculiar importance. As we have observed, by baptism people are incorporated into Christ and made living members of his body the church. As the Constitution on the Liturgy (41, 42) and the new Order of the Mass (GI 7) have it, the local community, normally the parish, is in its liturgical celebrations the sign or 'sacrament' of the whole church throughout the world and although it is into the one, holy, Catholic and apostolic church that we are admitted by baptism, it is through the local church that this is achieved. Further, it is in the faith of the church that children are baptized and therefore, says the Order of Infant Baptism, the local community should be represented when the sacrament is celebrated. 'The people of God, represented by the local church', it says, 'have a large part to play in the baptism of both adults and children' (BP 4) and as far as the children are concerned, 'they have a right to the love of the community both before and after baptism'. This love will be shown by their presence, by the prayers, in which they join, for the child and the family and above all by giving their assent of faith with the celebrant after the parents have made their profession of it (*ibid.*). Parents, community and celebrant all join in making the profession of a faith that is common to all, and thus is made very concrete the saying that the child is baptized 'in the faith of the church'.

This of course represents a change of emphasis in the practice of baptism that has been typical in recent centuries. It was for the most part a *private* celebration, and there are those who would still have it so. But just as the full significance of the eucharist cannot be seen unless it is a community celebration, so with baptism. Psychologically the family group will feel strengthened in its faith by the presence of the community and where weaker parents are concerned, they will be encouraged by the presence of a believing community ready to support them in their undertakings.

~

Celebration

There is little to add to what we have said about this matter in connection with adult baptism. Here the presence of the community will make
it possible, however improbable it may seem at the present time, that
'sung baptisms' will become the custom. The Order lays down (BP 9) that
baptisms are to be celebrated on Sundays (and only once a day) or at the
Easter Vigil and that they may take place within the Sunday eucharist,
though this should not be done too frequently. Experience however is
showing that, in modern pastoral conditions, celebration within the Sunday eucharist is the only way in which the community dimension and a
note of joy can be obtained. Since there are in most churches several
Masses on a Sunday any one of these can be chosen and thus it would
not be more or less the same people who every time witness the baptism.
On the assumption that some form of afternoon or evening service can
be maintained (and it is more and more difficult to do so) baptism should
be celebrated then.

Pastoral preparation

The introduction to the Order of Infant Baptism is a strongly pastoral
document showing an awareness of the importance of the matter and
also of the difficulties encountered in its practice. It can no longer be
said, if it ever could, that the church takes infant baptism as a matter of
routine. As we have seen, baptism requires a follow-up, the further Christian education of the child. But it also requires preparation which conditions the time when baptism is to take place.

When should baptism be celebrated?

To the question when a child should be baptized, the Code of Canon Law
(867) says within the first weeks after birth. The new Order of Baptism
has a quite elaborate answer which is based on the great principles that
run throughout it: namely, faith, the role of the parents, community and
celebration. All these factors are to be taken into account in fixing the
time when a child should be baptized and the conclusion must be that
baptisms may be less frequent than they used to be but that more children will be baptized on a single occasion. But here again, it will be *local*

conditions that dictate the best course of action. In a very populous parish, there may already be many baptisms every Sunday and to group them, say, once a month would impose a burden on both parents and priests. What is desired is that baptism shall be a celebration and not just an administrative act.

In detail, then, the Order says that the following factors should be taken into account in arranging the baptism of a child. (1) The health of the child: if there is any danger then baptism must be given as soon as possible; (2) the health of the mother, that is, it will be necessary to wait until she has got up or returned from hospital, for the Order is emphatic that the parents of the child should be present (BP 4 (2)); (3) sufficient time to make the necessary preparation of the parents and (4) to organize the celebration, not merely in church, one would say, but also in the home. Relatives, friends and others will want to come and time should be given to invite them. These indeed are envisaged as taking some part, if necessary, in the preparation of the parents before baptism (BP 5 (1)). This is but another illustration of the importance of community in the whole celebration of the sacrament.

The preparation of the parents

Normally, then, the child is to be baptized in the first weeks after birth (BP 8 (3)) but the parents are asked to let the parish clergy know, either before birth or immediately after it, that they wish their child to be baptized. Granted this and the circumstances being normal, the parish priest or one of his assistants will visit the family and give them such instruction as may be necessary. No doubt this will not be necessary for every child of the same family nor need the instruction be lengthy or heavy-handed. The text of the rite is the best basis for such instruction for it expresses in concrete form the content of the introduction and at the same time covers matters of ceremonial which concern the parents. It is not possible to celebrate this rite without some preparation and where parents of weak faith are concerned, it would be intolerable that they should be required to undertake serious obligations both on their own behalf and on that of the child without being given time to reflect on them.

Even if a house-visit should prove impossible (and in the circumstances of the large urban parish this may well be so), an interview with one or both of the parents before baptism is indispensable. There are several matters (e.g. the insertion of the child's name(s) in the litany) that need discussion before the baptism and make contact with the parents necessary if the rite is to be celebrated with conviction and in the spirit the church now demands. As far as the minister of the sacrament is concerned, this is a matter of obligation but one which he cannot carry out properly without the collaboration of the parents: 'Every celebration of baptism should be done with dignity and accommodated so far as may be necessary to the conditions and desires of the family' (BP 6 (2)).

The question of delay

If all were for the best in the best possible of worlds, the above arrangements would provide no difficulty. But we know this is not so and the Order envisages the situation where parents have insufficient faith to make the promises or have shown by past experience that they do not in fact bring up their children as Christians (BP 25). Here the Order sees that some delay is necessary and requires local conferences of bishops to lay down guidelines for their clergy in the matter. They, in the light of such instructions, are to make a judgement *when* a child of such parents should be baptized (BP 8 (4)). The Order does not in fact contemplate the possibility of *refusal*. Such refusal may well come from the parents when they have been confronted with their obligations. But, as everyone knows, the whole situation is a very delicate one, calling for considerable tact and prudence. On the one hand, it is intolerable that a sacrament of faith should be administered without faith and that its normal effects should be frustrated by a lack of Christian education and, on the other, it is extremely hard even to *seem* to refuse a sacrament which normally is necessary for salvation. Rigid rules however in one direction or another are not likely to solve the problem, which is an essentially human one and therefore untidy.

First, then, since the Order does not speak of refusal it would be a mistake, perhaps because one has *a priori* notions about the problem of those who have been baptized though lapsed, to indulge in talk about refusing baptism. The Order speaks of *delay* and even a suggestion of this may cause trouble.[5] If a parish has been able to establish the custom that baptisms are only administered after interview (and this seems to be the situation in most places), it is highly likely that the difficulties of a case can be solved, one way or the other, at this point. It is the priest's duty to help the parents to understand what they are undertaking and if at this point they feel they cannot undertake their obligations, it is they who will withdraw perhaps for further reflection. On the other hand, it is not for the priest to be too demanding. Some may have difficulties about this or that point of Christian teaching. This does not mean they have no faith[6] or even an insufficient faith. This, we have indicated above, is to be thought of as a global faith which can be expressed in the terms of the creed professed in baptism. Again, an insistence on regular Sunday worship or even 'Easter duties' as a condition of the admission of the child to baptism would be too rigid a rule. If, however, parents of a weak or wavering faith (and there seem to be quite a number of the latter nowadays) make the first approach, this should be regarded as a positive sign that they have some desire to do what the church wants them to do. They may of course have all sorts of folk-lore notions in their heads (and it may be as well to discover what part the grandmother is playing behind the scenes) but their very approach offers something on which to build. Once baptism and the other sacraments are seen as something more than pieces of isolated ritual, their celebration is seen to offer pastoral opportunities. Finally, there will always be a greater or smaller residue of cases where it will be impossible to admit a child to baptism at once but the Order does not see this as the end of the affair. It is but a beginning of a new pastoral effort which will seek to bring back the parents to a true faith when they will be able to have their children baptized. If this new Order of Infant Baptism suggests a whole programme of Christian education it also suggests a whole programme of pastoral care to which a good deal of thought needs to be given.

In the event of one parent not being able to make the profession of faith, the Order shows a wide comprehension and a great respect for the human conscience. This will often be the case where there is a mixed marriage. In interview one finds often enough that though the non-Catholic partner is not a practising Christian he or she is able and willing to make the profession of faith with the Catholic. Where this is so, they should be invited to do so and to take as full a part in the rite as possible. Where however one or other of them cannot do this but is willing to allow the child to be brought up a Christian, he (or she) may remain silent (5 (4)).

Godparents

The most significant change in the new Order is that the parents occupy the central place in its celebration. They ask publicly for the baptism of their child, they sign him on the forehead at the rite of admission, they renounce evil and profess the faith, the mother holds the child at the font, the father holds the lighted candle and at the end there is a blessing for each of them (BP 5 (3)). They are active participants in bringing their child to the new birth by water and the Holy Spirit. Nevertheless they can and should be supported by godparents who represent both the extended family, which can be of such support to parents and children in a world that is increasingly impersonal, and the Christian community which should be the first to show their care for them. The primary role of the godparents is to assist the parents to fulfil their obligations and they seem to have no direct relationship with the child. This is what they undertake to do in the rite (BP 40). In practice of course the two go together. The minimum requirements for godparents are that they should be 'sufficiently mature' (not children therefore), and must have been baptized, confirmed and have received holy communion. They must be Catholics. But it is possible to admit members of the Orthodox Church as godparents and members of other churches as witnesses to Christian baptism (CI 10).[7]

The ministers of baptism

According to Canon Law (861) the ordinary minister is either the bishop, a priest (usually the parish priest) or a deacon. Bishops, says the Order (CI 11), are no longer to be seen as 'extraordinary' ministers intervening only on very important occasions. Nor yet are deacons though they must receive the necessary delegation. But it is not just a matter of rights and duties. Bishops, says the Order, are the dispensers of the mysteries of God and presidents of the whole liturgical life of the diocese (12) and, in accordance with the principles of the Constitution on the Liturgy, their role has to be made visible. There would seem to be a strong case therefore for bishops to celebrate baptism when for instance they come for confirmation. If in addition certain children could be admitted to first communion on the same occasion, the bishop would visibly appear as the president of the whole process of Christian Initiation. The objection that this would mean a very long service can be answered by providing that there are only small numbers of children involved.[8] As for deacons, they are now able to administer baptism as a matter of course but in a large parish they will also usefully concelebrate the sacrament with the other clergy (BP 61). In this way the presbyteral community will match the community of the people.

The place of baptism

For centuries the place of baptism has been the parish church and many were the bitter battles fought over this issue in the Middle Ages. Battles apart, this is still the situation with the Order (BP 10, 11), though the bishop may permit other places if there is real need. Again, the reason for this is not just the protection of the rights of parish priests but that the parish church is the normal place of assembly for the Christian people and since they have a role of considerable importance to play in the celebration of the sacrament, it should be the normal place of baptism. Modern conditions may however modify this and a *real* community may well be able to meet in some other place than the church. A link with the wider parish could be established by prayer at the eucharist both before and after the event for the candidates and their parents.

The baptistery and the font (CI 18–28)

The new Order of Baptism changes many things and makes almost superfluous some of its own injunctions. It says for instance that the water must be clean, a very difficult matter under the old regime where the water was changed only once or twice a year and was infused with holy oil into the bargain. With the strong recommendation (*optandum est*) that the water should be blessed every time (which implies that it must be fresh for every baptism), even in Paschaltide if it seems opportune, there is little danger that it will be anything but clean. In the light of the remarks of the Order itself (CI 21) and of the structure of the service the recommendation could have been much stronger. It is in the prayer(s) of blessing that the symbolism of the water is expounded and much of its precise sacramental significance is made plain. It is an integral part of the rite and its omission would be regrettable.

As has already been provided for in many new churches, the water

~

may be flowing and in this case it is the flowing water that is blessed and not a certain quantity of it. Finally, an echo of the *Didache*, it may, when necessary, be warmed – a humane provision in winter.

It was hardly to have been expected that baptism by immersion would be recommended but so it is (CI 22) and both here and in the rite (60) it is put first, even if in the former place it would seem to be restricted to places where it is customary. Whether or not this is so (and the two ways are distinguished by the lightest Latin disjunctive, *vel*), it is hardly a live issue in most Western countries as yet.[9] Mothers will be understandably reluctant to allow it though if the font looked more like a 'bath of regeneration' and was filled with warm water, some of their reluctance would no doubt disappear. It is the view of the introduction, at any rate, that immersion better expresses the meaning of baptism in which we die with Christ in the waters and rise from them with him to the new life of the resurrection.

The font should not only be kept clean (and not used as the repository for miscellaneous and forgotten objects) but is also to be beautiful, worthy of its purpose. Which is but another way of saying that just as the altar is a symbol of the eucharist, expressing something of its nature, so the font and the baptistery should express by their form something of the meaning of baptism. However, it is not just a question of having a beautiful font and baptistery. Both are the focus of a community action and their arrangement is conditioned by that fact. The thinking of the Order marks a considerable break with more recent tradition. The baptistery has too often been an obscure and undistinguished part of the church which gave the impression that infant baptism was a private action in which the smallest number of people possible would be involved. The first principle, then, that now comes into play is that baptism, like the eucharist, is an action of the Christian community and the baptistery must be such that the people can gather there and take part in the celebration of the sacrament. Even the pattern of the rite is to be taken into account: it requires a ministry of the word and that too must be provided for. Given current conditions, then, it is not surprising that a considerable freedom is left to the local clergy in arranging the place of baptism. Where the baptistery is small and possibly dark, cut off from the body of the church, a font may be set up wherever it is found most convenient and that means a place where a community celebration can take place. As in all the recent liturgical reform, the role of the people is paramount. Generally speaking, where it is not possible to devise a large compartment of the church for baptism, a place with seats and big enough to hold twenty, thirty or even more people, it would seem best not to have a fixed font at all. A large bowl of silver or copper will meet the requirement of the Order that the font should be beautiful.[10]

In fact, four places can be envisaged for the celebration of the sacrament: (1) somewhere near the main entrance where the minister will welcome the baptismal party and ask the first questions; (2) a place for the ministry of the word during which the people will no doubt like to sit down; (3) the place for 'the celebration of the sacrament' which could be the conventional baptistery or some other place in the church, e.g. near the sanctuary; (4) before the sanctuary for the conclusion of the rite.

The liturgy of infant baptism

This already lengthy account of baptism is significant of the great change in the church's thinking on the subject. Compared with the baptism of infants, that for adults is quite simple if only because the issues are so much clearer. Since however we are in a situation that is still new and indeed since for the first time in the history of the church we have a rite for infants that is truly adapted to their condition, some examination of the rite is necessary.

A summary of the rite

1. The reception of the baptismal party whom the minister welcomes. The first questions establishing that the parents undertake to bring up their children in the Catholic faith. The signing of the child by the minister, parents and godparents.

2. The celebration of God's word. One or two scripture readings, the homily, the intercessions.

3. The prayer of exorcism (two texts provided) and the anointing with the oil of catechumens.

4. The celebration of the sacrament: the blessing of the water, the parents' renunciation of evil and profession of faith, the baptism, the anointing with chrism, the clothing with the white garment, the giving of the candle (the *Ephphetha*, if retained).

5. The conclusion: the procession to the sanctuary, the final address with the Lord's Prayer and the blessings.

Commentary

It may be said at once that though the rite is new, it discreetly incorporates (and adapts) much that was to be found in the old liturgy of initiation. The first questions include the old 'naming' rite (which has persisted through the centuries in almost every baptismal rite) and the signing with the cross represents the former rite of the enrolment of catechumens. The ministry of the word corresponds to the former and lengthy instruction given during the catechumenate and the intercessions and brief litany take the place of the great prayer sung by the assembled community while the baptisms were taking place. The exorcism and the anointing with the oil of catechumens were also part of the catechumenate and the renunciation of evil was associated with the latter. The profession of faith has its parallel in the candidates' profession of faith both before and during the act of baptism. The post-baptismal chrismation is at least as old as Hippolytus (died *c.* 235) and the clothing with the white robe is of equally ancient date. The giving of the candle is a medieval rite and appears for the first time in the eleventh century.[11] The conclusion of the rite is new.

The first thing to be said about this liturgy is that it is so much more than a piece of ritual. It is addressed to people, it constantly engages their attention and requires their very active collaboration. The celebrant too is required to act in a human and welcoming fashion (BP 36, 41) and throughout the rite he delivers various (brief) addresses to the people to arouse their faith and to lead them to a fuller understanding of the paschal mystery of which baptism is a celebration. At the same time, the rite leads them into the praise of God whom, through chants and hymns, they thank for the continuing work of salvation made present by the celebration of the sacrament. In short, it is an act of worship and not merely an 'administration'. All this is expressed in detail and in various ways throughout the rite.

Thus *the first questions* emphasize the importance of the parents' faith and inculcate the commitment they are required to make on behalf of their child.

The signing with the cross is to be regarded (BP 41) as the sign that the child is admitted to the Christian community.

The celebration of God's word, which is the newest feature of the rite, has a peculiar importance. It is a practical application of the axiom which underlies the whole of the revised liturgy: no sacramental celebration without a proclamation of the word. In infant baptism it is intended to renew and deepen the faith of the parents and godparents and of all who are assembled for the celebration and it is the function of the homily in particular to draw out the meaning of whatever readings are chosen and to lead the people on to an understanding of the baptismal mystery. It is not desirable that the homily should be lengthy but it should aim at achieving at least this. In the event of infants being over-vocal the Order recommends that they should be taken to another place, though this should be done by someone other than the parents or godparents to whom in a special way the word is proclaimed (BP 43).

As for the readings, the Lectionary offers a rich anthology which it would be difficult to improve on. The following, all from the New Testament, carry a fundamental message: Romans 6:3–4 (we die with Christ in baptism and by him are raised to a new life); 1 Corinthians 12:13, 12 (we are all baptized in one spirit and form one body); Ephesians 4:1–4 (one Lord, one faith, one baptism); 1 Peter 2:4–5, 9–10 (a royal priesthood); Matthew 22:35–40 (the law of love); Matthew 28:18–20 (go and make disciples of all nations); Mark 1:9–11 (the baptism of Jesus); Mark 10:13–16 (let the little children come to me, a text used in the Sarum Manual and retained by the Book of Common Prayer); John 3:1–6 (unless a man is born again . . .). This is but a selection and leaves out the Old Testament readings provided, since they offer special difficulties and will be used only for groups whose knowledge of the Bible is rather deeper than is usual. The celebrant is left a wide choice though it would seem that he should use at least one gospel passage; the baptism of Jesus provides most valuable material for the homily. It should be noted too that between the readings, psalms or hymns may be sung and though the latter are very scarce, this will be the right place to introduce some singing.[12]

The intercessions speak for themselves but it should be noted that in the short litany the patron(s) and other saints may be invoked.

The sense of the exorcism is not, as in the former rite, that devils should be cast out of the candidate but that when we are born and whether we like it or not we enter upon the struggle between good and

~

evil which is part of the human condition and which will go on to the
end of time. The prayer is for the protection of the child in that struggle.
The second (alternative) makes this clearer than the first: May these
children who are going to experience the wickedness of the world and
the power of Satan be protected by the power and grace of the passion
and resurrection of Christ. Incidentally, the first of these prayers is the
only text in the whole rite that mentions original sin.

With the exorcism is combined *the anointing with the oil of catechumens* which in the earlier rites of baptism was called the oil of exorcism.
Its sense is the same as that of the prayer. This is one of the rites that
local conferences of bishops may 'for grave reasons' allow to be omitted,
and the reason is pretty obvious. If everything else in the rite is perspi-
cuous in meaning this is not, and for an explanation of it one has to go
back to a much earlier age of the church's history. This rite seems to
derive from the anointing that took place just before the baptism.[13]
The candidate was stripped, anointed all over with oil and invited to
renounce Satan and all his works. Even if one could find a suitable opportunity to give this explanation, it is hardly likely to seem relevant to the
modern parent. A prayer for the protection of the child against evil is
comprehensible and welcome but a dab of oil on the breast seems to
mean precisely nothing, especially since, as we have observed above, the
use of oil is one of the most opaque symbols for modern people of
industrial society. By the decision of the bishops it has to be retained in
England and no doubt some other places. It would have been better to
leave its use to the discretion of the parish clergy. However, for them
there seems to be an escape route in CI 35 which says that in preparing
and celebrating the rite the minister of the sacrament is to take account
of 'the desires of the faithful'.

The first element of the celebration of the sacrament is *the blessing*
of the water for which three prayers (to be used at choice) are provided.
The first of these includes all the great types of baptism of the Old
Testament (the creation of water, the rescuing of Noah and his family
from the destruction of the flood, the passage of the Red Sea 'a figure
of the baptized') and much of the doctrine of the New (the baptism of
Christ, the piercing of his side on the cross and, right at the end, the
Pauline teaching on burial and resurrection in Christ). Perhaps too much
is packed in here though something can be done to interpret the text by
using as readings Romans 6 and the incident of Christ's baptism. The

prayer is based on the ancient text found in the Gelasian Sacramentary and, as we have observed above, it is a pity that in the revision the vivid symbolism speaking of the font as the womb of life fecundated by the Holy Spirit has been eliminated. The two other prayers given are much simpler and will often if not usually be more appropriate. The first of these has, in its first part, the literary form of a Jewish prayer of blessing (*berakah*): 'Blessed be God, the only Son, Jesus Christ. From your side flowed blood and water that by your death and resurrection your church might be born'; and the people's acclamation may be in similarly Jewish form: 'Blessed be God'. The second half of the prayer consists of petitions responded to by the people asking for the blessing of the water. Among other things, these two texts suggest interesting possibilities for new eucharistic prayers.

The renunciation of evil and *the profession of faith* come *after* the prayer of blessing and this is a little odd. The renunciation was traditionally associated with exorcism. The candidate was anointed with the oil of exorcism, turned to the west (the supposed abode of evil spirits) and then turned to profess his faith in baptism. In this rite a much more appropriate place for the renunciation would be before the prayer of exorcism. Presumably the revisers had before their minds the ancient pattern where the renunciation was immediately followed by baptism.

There are two formulas for renunciation, the second of which may in many circumstances be more appropriate: it begins with a general renunciation of evil and Satan appears lower down the list. It is foolish not to recognize that some people, while they are fully conscious that there is much evil in our world, have difficulties about Satan and a baptismal service does not seem to be the occasion to rub their noses in a difficult doctrine. In any case, local conferences of bishops may vary these formulas (BP 24 (3)) and the criterion will be the different levels of culture and knowledge of the Christian message. There is however a good case for making them more concrete and to specify what people are being required to renounce. No doubt there is no need to go as far as mentioning pornography though the fourth-century Christians knew that when they rejected the devil's *pompa*, they were rejecting the sadistic–sexual excitements of the arena.[14] This was not a vague expression.

Of the profession of faith there is little need to say more than a word. It is the old Roman baptismal creed almost exactly in the form of

Hippolytus's *Apostolic Tradition* used in the act of baptism itself. To the profession of faith are attached two formulas which are worth noting. The first (BP 59) said by the celebrant and community together runs: 'This is our faith, this is the faith of the church which we are proud to profess in Christ Jesus our Lord'; and the second (60) is this: 'Do you wish *N* to receive baptism in the faith of the church which together we have all professed?' Thus written into the rite is the doctrine that has been laid out in the introduction.

The chrismation, one of the oldest baptismal rites of the Western church, has always signified the incorporation of the baptized into the church which is the body of Christ who is priest, prophet and king. This is now spelt out clearly in the text of the prayer that precedes the anointing. The best commentary on it is 1 Peter 2:2–10. The Christian people by baptism are made priests who through Christ can offer 'spiritual sacrifices' to the Father. They are 'prophets' sharing in the church's mission to bear witness to Christ in the world and they are 'kings' in that they collaborate with him in making the world a better place until it reaches that fulfilment appointed by God and can be offered by Christ to his Father (1 Corinthians 15:25–28). All this, and it is important to note that it includes mission and witness, is effected by baptism and the Christian does not have to wait for confirmation to be 'sent'.

In view of the former undesirable practice of putting a square of linen on the head of the child, it is necessary to emphasize that *the white robe* is meant to be a real garment, in fact the traditional christening robe which for long enough it has been the custom to clothe the child with before baptism. It is the desire of the church that it should be put on after the chrismation (though immediately after the baptism would be the more logical and traditional place). Mothers need to be told of this and experience shows that when they understand the purpose and significance of the gesture they readily accept the new way of doing it. Unless local custom indicates otherwise, its colour must be white. This no doubt is for traditional reasons (in the early church the candidates were clothed in white) but, although the formula accompanying the gesture does not say so, it is as well to reflect that white is the messianic colour in both the Old and the New Testaments.[15] As the formula does say, the candidates by baptism have been clothed in Christ and the colour of the robe indicates that they share in the 'lordship' of the Messiah who will come at the end 'with great power and majesty' to 'gather his chosen ones from the four winds, from one end of heaven to the other' (Matthew 24:30, 31).

In practice, the church desires the family to give the robe and this is usually done, but there is a good case for the parish, or a society in the parish, to give it. If this were generally done, it would be possible to design a garment rather more convenient than the Victorian-style things with narrow sleeves which are so difficult to put on.

The father (or a godparent) is to light *the candle* from the Paschal Candle, the purpose of the rite being to indicate the connection between the celebration of baptism and the paschal mystery.

The conclusion of the whole service takes place before the altar. The parents are reminded that baptism leads to confirmation and holy communion and that the children, as are all Christians, are children of one common Father, and to express their sonship all join in the recitation of the Lord's Prayer. Then come the blessings, one for the mother, one for the father and one for the whole assembly. The first of these replaces the old churching ceremony and is readily acceptable to the young mothers of today.[16]

Some critical observations

If the supreme test of a rite is that it 'works', then the new Order must be said to be good. Again and again parents have expressed their satisfaction, even their delight, with it and if it is celebrated in a relaxed and friendly fashion, it becomes the occasion of a real meeting with people. There are however one or two points that could be improved.

The formula which the celebrant addresses to the parents at the beginning asking if they are ready to bring up their children as Christians is complicated and unwieldy: 'You have come to ask that your children should be baptized. Are you aware of your duty to bring them up in the faith so that, as Christ taught, they may keep the commandments of God, that is love the Lord and their neighbour?' The ICEL translation does nothing to improve the Latin. At first, they had 'raising' children but evidently the English-speakers of Great Britain objected. We speak of 'raising' crops, not children. But ICEL then opted for 'training them in the practice of the faith'. Then they go on: 'It will be your duty to bring them up to keep God's commandments as Christ taught us *by* loving God . . .'. The awkwardness of the translation indicates the awkwardness of the Latin. It is merely an inexpert re-writing of the old formula. Is the 'faith' here spoken of identical with keeping the commandments? In fact, the phrase is far too condensed. *Two* questions are needed: (1) are you willing to bring the children up in the (Christian) faith? (2) are you willing to bring them up to *live* as Christians keeping God's commandments . . .? It may be objected that this is to perpetuate the old notion that you can be brought up 'in the faith' and remain uncommitted to Christian living. There may be some truth in this but you can distinguish the two and parents ought not to have to do a vast amount of ratiocination before making this answer.

As we have observed above, the anointing with the oil of catechumens provides difficulties to some parents and it is difficult to understand why it was retained.[17] The prayer of exorcism and the brief formula to be used *without* anointing sufficiently make the point of the whole rite.

As we have also indicated above, it would have been better to attach the renunciation of evil to this rite for whatever historical precedent the revisers had in mind (whether they deliberately conflated the renunciation that occurred in the catechumenate with the profession of faith or were thinking of the renunciation that occurred almost immediately before the act of baptism), in this rite the position of the renunciation next to the prayer of exorcism would have been much more comprehensible to modern people. It is the *parents* who will have the primary task of shielding their children from evil.

A small practical improvement in the second and third prayers of the blessing of the water would make it easier to use them. The people do not readily respond 'Blessed be God' after each paragraph. They need a phrase to 'lead them in'.

In spite of the revision of the prayer, chrismation remains ambiguous. If the number of children to be baptized is exceptionally large it may be omitted (BP 61) though one has to suppose the Order has something like dozens of children in mind. And in the adult form when confirmation follows, it may be omitted altogether. This does not seem very satisfactory. Chrismation either has some meaning or it has not. If the latter, it should be omitted altogether. If the former, why omit it on any occasion? On the principle written into the official documents themselves, which place this among the *ritus explanativi*, its purpose is to unfold or explicitate certain aspects of baptism. The prayer now says explicitly that it signifies the candidates' incorporation into the people of God. It seems to be worth saying since this meaning is given nowhere else.

One notes that the new Order continues the old and undesirable custom of addressing the unwitting child in at least one place, i.e. for the giving of the white garment. It would have been better to devise another form of words addressed to the parents and the assembly.

The *Ephphetha* rite has been retained for optional use and in England it is not normally to be used. If it is, it is to be explained. It once formed part of the last exorcism done shortly before the baptism and in imitation of what Christ did (Mark 7:32–5). It was itself regarded as an exorcism. The old gesture, involving the touching of the ears and nose of the candidate, was a deviation from the gospel incident it was supposed to repeat. This at least has now been put right and the formula interprets it as meaning that the ears are to hear the word of God and the mouth is to proclaim the faith. Understandable enough, but the rite is in a very curious place (it would have come better in connection with the ministry of the word) just before the blessings and it is difficult to understand why it was retained at all. It is no more than an archaeological remain.

The problem of infant baptism

It is undeniable that the question of infant baptism is a matter of concern for both Catholics and those of the reformed tradition. The New Testament has been scrutinized anew to see whether the practice is justifiable or whether some firmer authority can be found for a practice that is very ancient. This is not the place nor is it within the writer's power to add anything to theological discussion. But one or two things may be said to help a pastoral orientation on the subject. First, the New Testament certainly makes it clear that *normally* people approach Christ by faith and then by the sacraments, even if in the New Testament there were one or two occasions (e.g. Acts 16:30–33[18]) when children may have been baptized. Secondly, neither the introduction to the Order of Baptism nor the service itself gives any emphasis to original sin. What conclusions, if any, are to be drawn from this it is impossible to say but it is worth noting that, as we have shown above, the positive side of the sacrament receives very great emphasis. Again, the possibility of delaying infant baptism is written into the introduction with the obvious implication that some infants will not in fact be baptized. It is not for a document like this to say how such children may be saved but at the practical level

~

it does mean that a whole new policy of pastoral practice in their regard needs to be worked out.

It can, I think, be said that this document represents a change of emphasis in the church's teaching and this reflects a change of mentality among the people too. Even good Christians no longer feel the urge to rush the child to the font at the earliest possible moment and some are seriously questioning the advisability of baptizing infants at all. Since they are being brought up in a Christian community, first the family and then the parish, would it not be better to wait until they can give their assent to this all-important event in their lives with the enormous consequences that follow from it? If, on the other hand, infant baptism continues to be the custom, as seems most likely, what view does the church take of the baptized at a later age refusing to endorse what has been done in infancy on his behalf or being unable, through loss of faith, to ratify what has been done? Does the subject remain free to choose or not to choose? How is such a person to be regarded in his relationship to the official church? Is he an apostate or just 'lapsed'? Does he remain bound by the church's laws? These questions are already being asked and it is well enough known that a considerable number of young adults are rejecting (not merely slipping away from) the faith of their baptism.

If these questions were satisfactorily answered, we could continue the practice of infant baptism with greater tranquillity. It must be said too that the consequences of *not* baptizing infants would be incalculable. Not only would the whole system of sacramental initiation (first communion and the rest) be overturned but the very pattern of Christian education would be wrecked. Even more important, the child would not be living in Christ in the way it does from baptism onwards. The best way to meet this problem of infant baptism would seem to be to insist on its positive side, on what is *given*. This, regeneration, life in Christ and in the Trinity, may only be germinal and the seeds have to grow to become the full flower of the Christian life. But there is a *datum* and if we think there is not, we are in danger of thinking that God can only do what man permits.[19] It can be said, that if we take in the *whole* teaching of the new baptismal Order and *if it is put into practice*, infant baptism remains theologically credible and practically of the greatest importance. Perhaps we have got too individualistic and tend to forget the organic relationships that are the stuff of family, with the consequence that we do not see as clearly as we ought that it is perfectly natural that Christian parents should want their children, who by blood belong to the Christian community of the family, to be incorporated i**ñ**to the greater family of the church by which they themselves live. After that, all will depend on the love, intelligence and skill of the family to bring up children as lovers of God.

This in turn suggests or reminds us of what the Order (BP 4, 5 (5)) has to say about the help to be given by the Christian community in the upbringing of children. For this a vast programme of adult Christian education, directed to parents as well as to others, should be initiated if we are to have the sort of Christians that the church so badly needs and that the sacrament of baptism envisages.

Since the promulgation of the Order of Infant Baptism there has been a good deal of discussion in some places of the possibility of an enrolment service for those children whose parents are unable to undertake the obligations required by baptism. Such a practice would certainly mitigate the difficulties involved in the delay of baptism, would ensure that the children were registered and provide a tangible link between the family and the church. A service, perhaps adapted from the enrolment rite of the Order of the Christian Initiation of Adults (75–87) including some expression on the part of the parents to receive further instruction, would seem to be appropriate.

Notes
~

[1] In marriage, for instance. A Roman Catholic baptized in infancy and with no knowledge of the church cannot contract a valid marriage outside the church, unless, improbably, he or she is granted a dispensation from the 'form'.

[2] Thus far ICEL translation.

[3] Though of course valid!

[4] Cf. ST III, 62, i, ad 1. St Thomas's phrase is **efficiunt quod figurant**.

[5] There are those who like to insist on their 'rights' and who never perform their duties.

[6] Whatever may be the truth of the old tag 'if you doubt in one matter of faith, you doubt the lot', it is of no use in pastoral work and any insistence on it can only do harm.

[7] In an earlier booklet **Companion to the New Order of Baptism** (1970), p. 16, basing myself on the text of the Order, I gave it as my opinion that Christians of other denominations, as well as the Orthodox, could be admitted as godparents. It seemed to be a modification of the instructions of the Ecumenical Directory (ET, 1967, no. 57, p. 23). Such an interpretation is however ruled out by a reply from

the Secretariat for Christian Unity which states that the directive in BP is not to be regarded as an extension of the Directory. Cf. *Notitiae*, 62 (March 1971), pp. 92–3. One can only comment that the Latin of the Order should have been more precise.

8 This too of course raises the vexed question of the size of dioceses but does not the bishop's liturgical (and pastoral) role provide one criterion, and a fundamental one, for the division of dioceses?

9 It is of course the normal way of baptism in the Orthodox Church.

10 In some modern churches the font is placed on the sanctuary balancing, as it is said, the lectern. Perhaps too formal an arrangement and there is the danger that having cleared our sanctuaries of a lot of unnecessary furniture we are now replacing it with 'liturgical' objects which lead to a new kind of clutter. However a baptistery that is off-sanctuary but at the sanctuary end has much to be said for it. It would also be the most convenient place for the Paschal Candle, even in Paschaltide. The transporting of the Candle from one place to another is far from convenient.

11 See **The Church at Prayer**, III: **The Sacraments**, ed. A. G. Martimort (ET, Collegeville, MN/London, 1988), p. 69, n. 27.

12 See **Praise the Lord**, ed. John Ainslie, Stephen Dean and Paul Inwood, rev. ed. (London, 1972), nos. 1–5 (and cf. also certain Easter hymns).

13 I say 'seems' because there were exorcisms and anointings during the catechumenate, but in the Order this anointing is put in the traditional place immediately before the blessing of the water.

14 See for example St Augustine, **Confess.**, L.6, 13, the incident of Alypius at the games drunk *cruenta voluptate*.

15 The texts are well known and too numerous to cite.

16 But this too needs explaining to them in the instruction given before the baptism.

17 It has been said that it was retained because the Orthodox still have it and there was a desire to keep a link with their practice.

18 The gaoler 'and all those belonging to him' (**kai hoi autou apantes**) were baptized after his 'household' (**oikos**) had believed.

19 See L. Brockett, **The Theology of Baptism** (Cork, 1971), pp. 78–9.

See now for this chapter **Rite of Baptism for Children** (Veritas, Dublin/Geoffrey Chapman, London, 1992).

The Sacrament of Confirmation

~~~~~~~

THE RESTORATION of the liturgy of Christian Initiation has now firmly established that confirmation is part of that process and already the separate celebration of confirmation has a certain air of anomaly. Given current practice, the Order[1] had perforce to appear as a separate rite though there are signs that the practice of a thousand years is coming to an end. All the new documents on Christian Initiation constantly speak of baptism, confirmation and the eucharist as being the sacraments by which people are made Christians and assume that this is the order in which they are going to be received. Further, the permissions given in certain circumstances to presbyters to confirm (e.g. the initiation of adults, the confirmation and first communion of children baptized but not instructed) mean that more often than for centuries confirmation can precede communion, as of course it ought. Whatever questions may be raised about the age of confirmation the repeated statements of the RCIA and even the rite of Infant Baptism must be taken into account. If these statements are to be regarded as the 'mind of the church' then confirmation must always precede communion. That is the norm and if other practices are followed, they need special justification.

Since almost all the problems concerning confirmation have come from its peculiar history, it is necessary to give some account, necessarily summary, of its practice through the ages. History may not be determinative of truth but in liturgical practice it plays a role of peculiar importance.

Confirmation does not appear as an identifiable rite until the beginning of the third century and whatever may be the meaning of Acts 8:15–17 and 19:5 ff., these texts seem to have played no part in establishing confirmation in the first three centuries. The first text in which confirmation (though not under that name) can be identified is the *Apostolic Tradition* of Hippolytus.[2] Before baptism the bishop blesses the 'Oil of Thanksgiving', the baptism and profession of faith follow and then

~

a presbyter anoints the candidate with that same oil. After putting on his clothes, he goes to the bishop in church ('in the assembly') who lays his hand on him while saying a prayer. The bishop then pours out the 'Oil of Thanksgiving' on his hand and lays the latter on the head of the candidate saying 'I anoint thee with holy oil in God the Father Almighty, and Christ Jesus and the Holy Ghost'. After this, he 'seals' or signs the candidate on the forehead and gives him the kiss of peace. He then joins the assembly for the prayers after which the members of the assembly exchange with him the kiss of peace. The eucharist follows.

For so early a document this is an elaborate ritual and is carefully described by the writer. The second anointing by the bishop seems to be clearly identifiable as 'confirmation' though it receives no great emphasis. The prayer asks that the candidates may be filled with the Holy Spirit that they may serve God. There is no question of the candidate being sent on 'mission' and, what is more important, the action of the bishop is part of a continuing process that begins with the rites before baptism and ends with the eucharist. It was in fact a true concelebration of the local church, presided over by the bishop and performed by him, the presbyters and deacons with the participation of the assembly.

A similar picture is given in a well-known passage of Tertullian, of perhaps a slightly earlier date, quoted in the Apostolic Constitution placed at the beginning of the Order (p. 7).

> The flesh is washed (he wrote) so that the soul may be made spotless:
> the flesh is anointed so that the soul may be consecrated:
> the flesh is signed so that the soul may be protected:
> the flesh is overshadowed (*adumbratur*) by the laying-on of the hand
> so that the soul may be enlightened by the Spirit:
> the flesh feeds on the body and blood of Christ so that the soul may be filled with God.[3]

If we compare this with a longer but less precise description in the same author's *De Baptismo*, viii, we find that in both there is an anointing immediately after the candidate emerges from the water and that there is a laying-on of the hand by which the Holy Spirit is given. Both texts are close to the *Apostolic Tradition* of Hippolytus, particularly the first. There we note a signing but unfortunately Tertullian does not say this was a sign with oil. What is clear from both texts is that the laying-on of the hand is already the traditional gesture for the giving of the Spirit. The anointing seems to refer back to baptism, as does the first anointing in the *Apostolic Tradition*. In all three texts this Roman and Western rite has been taken as the paradigm of the sacraments of initiation but in the face of history this can hardly be maintained. In the fourth century St Cyril of Jerusalem knows a post-baptismal anointing but only one. In the area of the Syrian church (*Didascalia*, Narsai, St John Chrysostom) there is no post-baptismal anointing of any kind and these writers show that they believed that initiation, including the giving of the Spirit, was achieved by baptism and the eucharist. A curious passage from the compiler of the *Apostolic Constitutions* (also most probably Syrian), who knew the *Apostolic Tradition* very well, is worth repeating. After giving a conventional description of the post-baptismal anointing he writes 'But if there be neither oil nor chrism, *the water is sufficient for both the anointing and the seal*'.[4] The compiler certainly believed the Spirit was given but evidently he did not see either hand-laying or anointing as essential. For him, both 'anointing' and 'seal', which he regarded as important, did not need physical gestures for them to take place.

All this may be thought to be a 'primitive' theology and liturgy which would have to be 'developed', or merely the aberration of a local church, though the practice was widespread and lasted for some long time. In any case, it is very close to what we can discern in the New Testament on the subject of baptism. Again and again we find there that in baptism the Spirit is given in contexts where there is no mention of 'confirmation'. The *whole* effect of initiation was achieved by baptism and the eucharist.

In addition to all this, the Eastern church took a different way from the Roman. To preserve the integrity and order of the sacraments of initiation the Eastern church preferred to allow the presbyter to confirm candidates immediately after baptism and even in the case of infants to communicate them. This is still the custom and the link between the bishop and the celebration of the sacrament is maintained by the require-ment that the chrism or *myron* must always be consecrated by the bishop.

To return to the West, the witness of St Ambrose is particularly important. He was in the Roman tradition but, as we know, he could be independent of it[5] and he witnessed to a post-baptismal signing, the washing of the feet (in which consciously he differed from Rome), the clothing with the white garment and the signing of the forehead which was the gesture for the giving of the seal of the Spirit which he calls *signaculum spiritale*. After the font, he wrote, 'it remains for the "perfecting" to take place, when at the invocation of the priest (*sacerdos* = bishop) the Holy Spirit is bestowed, the spirit of wisdom and understanding, the spirit of counsel and strength, the spirit of knowledge of godliness, the spirit of holy fear, as it were the seven virtues of the Spirit'.[6] Whether this text from Isaiah 11:2 ff. was already part of a prayer of invocation or whether it suggested to the compilers of the Roman Sacramentaries the theme of a prayer, it was destined to have a long history before it. Coming as this rite does at the end of the elaborate rite of baptism, it witnesses to a quite developed notion of confirmation.

Rome, too, always remained faithful to its own tradition, even when adult baptism with its catechumenate had disappeared.[7] The pope presided at the Easter Vigil at the Lateran, a liturgy which included the sacraments of initiation, and in the stational or regional churches of Rome the same liturgy took place, assistant bishops in Rome conferring confirmation.[8] In the Gelasian Sacramentary the prayer accompanying the bishop's hand-laying and consignation takes up the text of Isaiah mentioned by St Ambrose and is practically identical with the prayer now said towards the beginning of the confirmation rite when the bishop extends his hands over all the candidates. It is certainly an ancient prayer and may be older than the sacramentary itself.[9] Its sense is made clear not only by the content of the prayer but by the rubric which says that 'the sevenfold Spirit' is given to the candidates by the bishop.

However, in other parts of the West, confirmation by a bishop was by no means the invariable practice. In Rome and no doubt in big city centres like Milan it was possible to conform to the Hippolytan model but even in rural Italy (until Innocent I put a stop to it) and certainly in Gaul and Spain, presbyters were authorized by synods and bishops to confer confirmation. The reason was that by the fifth century, especially in the two latter countries, the structure of the church was beginning to change. As the church moved into the great rural areas of Europe (and we recall the continual journeyings of St Martin in Gaul before the end of the fourth century), it became increasingly difficult to maintain the pattern of the city church organization with the clergy of various degrees gathered round the bishop. Priests, with perhaps the assistance of a deacon and a reader, were taking charge of groups of Christians, later called parishes, geographically distant from the episcopal see, and it became difficult if not impossible for parents to approach the bishop for the confirmation of their children. Yet Christians were so convinced that the integrity of the sacraments of initiation should be preserved that the Gallic and Spanish churches authorized priests to administer these sacraments. Infants were baptized, confirmed and communicated in one service, though the rite that did duty for confirmation was the *first* post-baptismal anointing, a fact which caused some confusion when later on the Roman system was introduced into the Carolingian church. But efforts were made at this time and throughout the ensuing centuries to secure that people should present their children to bishops for confirmation; and bishops and synods, mostly in vain it would seem, constantly enjoined on the faithful the duty of presenting their children either within a week of baptism or at the Easter celebration or during Easter week.

In this same region, about the middle of the fifth century, appeared a document that would have an extraordinary influence on the theology of confirmation, and a word must be said about it here. It was a sermon preached by Faustus, first a monk of Lérins then bishop of Riez. In it he tries to tackle the problem raised by the apparently growing custom of priestly confirmation and to answer the question: what does the bishop's hand-laying effect? In the course of his answer he says that it gives an *augmentum gratiae* and strengthens the Christian for the struggle of the Christian life. In one place he even uses the military metaphor though not quite in the sense that it has been used more recently. This teaching that was eventually condensed in the Scholastic *augmentum gratiae ad pugnam* had its extraordinary influence because it was incorporated into the False Decretals (which were concerned to exalt episcopal power) and from them passed into the *Decretum* of Gratian and finally into the Scholastics of the twelfth century whence St Thomas took it. On the way it acquired a bogus authority through its attribution to a non-existent pope (Melchiades – there was one called Miltiades). Medieval theologians were in no position to check the matter.

The text, which, I think, is unique, is so out of line with the Western tradition of the time that one is prompted to ask if there were special reasons for its peculiar character. Faustus had been an earnest monk of Lérins, he was a zealous bishop, but he also moved in the semi-Pelagian circles of southern Gaul. He was suspected and eventually accused of heresy in this respect.[10] Given this background, it is not surprising that he put what was regarded as undue emphasis on the role of the human will in salvation and the spiritual life. It was with this last that he was most concerned, he was thinking of the combat of the spiritual life and to do him justice his teaching went a good deal deeper than the soldier-of-Christ view that was later based on it. It cannot, I think, be regarded as an authentic addition to the theology of confirmation.

When in the ninth century the liturgy of the Roman books was being imposed by Charlemagne we note a further step in the disintegration of the pattern. Chrismation by the presbyter was regarded as the sign of the giving of the Spirit. What then was to be made of the episcopal hand-laying and anointing? Alcuin and later Rabanus Maurus introduced a new notion. For both of these writers the laying-on of the bishop's hand meant that the candidate receives the Spirit 'to preach to others'. A somewhat *ad hoc* interpretation it must be admitted because both Alcuin and Rabanus Maurus were convinced that the Spirit had already been given, though the latter made no difficulty about that. From a liturgical point of view, what is even more curious is that candidates were baptized, chrismated by the presbyter and communicated and only after that was confirmation given by the bishop, usually at a separate service, a favourite time being seven days after Easter.[11]

By the tenth century the ancient order of Christian Initiation had broken down. Baptism, which was given almost immediately after birth, was no longer celebrated within the Easter Vigil. If the bishop was not available, as was usually the case, confirmation was delayed indefinitely and the whole complex of notions and phobias that militated at this time against frequent communion militated also against the communication of infants at baptism. So you have three separate celebrations: baptism given within a day or two of birth, confirmation at some unpredictable moment and communion.

This separation of the sacraments of initiation received a certain, if unwitting, sanction when the Fourth Lateran Council (1215) decreed that those who had reached 'the age of discretion' must receive holy communion at least once a year. This suggested that communion now had to be received separately from baptism and, given the circumstances of the medieval church, it meant in practice that most would receive communion before confirmation. It is true that synods and individual bishops made strenuous efforts to see that children were confirmed even as early as the age of one and in synodal law at least the age was usually not more than seven. This witnesses to a realization that confirmation should both be near in time to baptism and come before communion, but the facts were against the legislation and that it had to be repeated again and again shows that it was not effective.[12]

By the end of the Middle Ages the age of confirmation seems to have risen to ten or twelve or even fourteen and it is this situation the Church of England seems to have inherited. The continental Reformers retained what is best described as a para-liturgy, a profession of faith and commitment to Christ, which was performed (of course by a non-episcopal minister) at about the age of fourteen.[13] Rome held to the tradition from which it has never wavered: confirmation must precede communion and it is worth noting that the 1595 edition of the *Pontificale Romanum* still envisages infants being presented for confirmation.[14] It may be remarked too that Rome never endorsed the practices of the churches beyond the Alps.

The last stages of the history are familiar. As long as the age of first communion remained at ten or twelve confirmation beforehand was a possibility and in certain countries, like Spain and South America, confirmation has always been given before communion. But when Pius X decreed that children of seven years or less could be admitted to communion that possibility became remote. Hence what seems to be the prevalent custom: communion at seven or so and confirmation at any age thereafter until about twelve. This system seems to make the worst of all possible worlds. It should be noted however that the Canon Law (788) still speaks of 'seven years', a requirement that is modified by the new Order (11).[15]

It will have been seen that the factors making for the present position were almost wholly non-theological and confirmation after communion or even a late age for confirmation were not endorsed by the Roman tradition.[16]

In recent years there has been a vast debate about confirmation in its every aspect, all sorts of questions have been asked, some of which still lack a definitive answer. The tradition has been re-scrutinized and the history revealed. It is this untidy situation with which the revisers were faced when they came to re-write the confirmation rite and it is both practice and theology they have had to take into account.

93

As a preliminary to a further consideration of the Order, we may note the following:

1. It is a separate service though in the liturgy of Christian Initiation it appears as part of it.

2. There is an insistence on the *order* of the sacraments of initiation: 'The faithful who have been re-born in baptism are strengthened by the sacrament of confirmation and finally fed by the bread of life in the eucharist, that by these sacraments of Christian Initiation they may receive more of the treasures of the divine life and be brought to perfect charity'.[17] The Introduction (1) sees confirmation as a stage through which baptized Christians must pass though here it does not mention the eucharist, as the Order of Baptism does (1) and of course the Order of Adult Initiation.[18] However, the point is made in another way: normally confirmation is to be conferred during the eucharist (13).

3. Although the Order refers to adult catechumens and children who have not been baptized in infancy as receiving baptism, confirmation and the eucharist at one service, it goes on to say that 'in the Latin Church confirmation is generally *delayed* until the age of seven'. This clearly echoes the Code of Canon Law (1917) and expresses the Roman tradition. Like the Code, it seems to leave the way open for infant confirmation.

4. Local conferences of bishops however may, for pastoral reasons, decide on a later age (*aetate maturiore*).[19] These reasons are indicated: the purpose of the delay should be (a) to form people in a more perfect obedience to Christ so that (b) they may bear more effective witness to him. Dom Bernard Botte, however, who was a member of the original commission on confirmation, points out that the papal constitution 'which engages the pope's doctrinal authority' has nothing to say about this and, as we have seen, affirms that it is the second stage of Christian Initiation. The matter of age was deliberately left to the local conferences of bishops, a decision that Dom Botte thinks wise, given the practical difficulties of the administration of the sacrament. While expressing his trust in the bishops' wisdom, he ends with a *mot* from an experienced bishop which Dom Botte begs the bishops to reflect on: 'You cannot build a sound pastoral action on bad theology'.[20] With which sentiment one cannot but agree. The above 'pastoral reasons' are an aspect of the theology adopted by the Order of which we will now give some account.

The theology of confirmation

This is to be found in three places: the Apostolic Constitution that prefaces the Order, in the rite itself and, to a lesser extent, in the Introduction (1, 2).

The main feature of the teaching of the Constitution is the wide scriptural context in which it places the sacrament. Christ was baptized and the Spirit came upon him (Mark 1:10 and par.) and he began his mission under the impulse of the same Spirit (Luke 4:17–21). He promised the Spirit to his apostles that they might bear witness to the faith before persecutors (Luke 12:12) and before he suffered he announced that they were to receive the Spirit of truth who would remain with them for ever (John 15:26, 14:16). Then at Pentecost they and Mary and the company of the disciples received the Spirit. The proclamation of the new messianic age followed and those who believed were baptized and received the gift of the Spirit (Acts 2:38).[21]

Christians, continues the text, are incorporated into Christ and conformed to him, made his living members, by baptism, confirmation and the eucharist. In baptism they receive the remission of sin, the adoption of sons and the 'character' by which they share in the priesthood of Christ.[22] In confirmation they receive the Holy Spirit himself 'by whom they are endowed with a special strength',[23] signed with the 'character', are bound more perfectly to the church and contract a stricter obligation to be witnesses to Christ and to propagate and defend the faith. Finally, confirmation is so bound to the eucharist that confirmed Christians are fully (*plene*) inserted into Christ by the eucharist.[24]

It is remarkable that in the above account no reference is made to the action of the Holy Spirit in baptism, though the baptismal texts always do so, as indeed does this Order (24, 25). The theology of the Constitution is in some ways more conventional than that of the Order. Secondly, though 1 Peter 2:5 and 9 are used to show that Christians receive a share in the priesthood of Christ at baptism no reference is made to the fact that the same text says that Christians have a vocation to proclaim the saving works of God (verse 9 precisely[25]). In fact, the exegesis of the scriptural texts is a great deal less simple than the Constitution indicates.[26]

There follows a treatment of the 'matter' and 'form' of the sacrament which recognizes a pluralism of practice in the past but opts for

~

chrismation as the 'matter'. The 'form', which has been changed, is (literally) 'Receive the seal of the gift of the Holy Spirit', a text borrowed from the East where it has been used since the fourth or fifth century. This, we are told,[27] is a decision that engages the Pope's teaching authority and so is of great consequence. The extension of the hands over all the candidates together is not essential to the rite but is an integral part of it and retained as explicitating its meaning. The gesture, combined with its accompanying prayer, clearly expresses the giving of the fullness of the Spirit.

When we turn to the rite itself and, to some extent, to the Introduction we find this doctrine expressed rather more subtly and there is other teaching that does not appear in the Constitution. The latter says that in confirmation the baptized receive the Spirit poured out on the apostles at Pentecost and by this gift they are (a) more perfectly conformed to Christ and are (b) strengthened (here the medieval teaching appears) so that they may bear witness to Christ for the building-up of the church in faith and love.

The homily suggested for the use of the celebrant, while setting confirmation in the context of the Pentecost event, deepens the notion of both conformity and witness. The gift of the Spirit the baptized receive in confirmation is a spiritual seal (an expression used by St Ambrose)[28] which will conform them more perfectly to Christ and make them more perfectly members of his church.[29] Conformity to Christ as the effect of the post-baptismal anointing is much emphasized by Cyril of Jerusalem whom the homily seems to be following here. For him candidates are conformed to Christ (*summorphoi*) and by the symbolic act of anointing (*eikonikos*) they are made images (*eikones*) of Christ.[30] But the context of Cyril and of the homily is first the baptism of Christ, when he received the Spirit, and secondly the beginning of his preaching (Luke 4:17–21). The Holy Spirit is operative on *both* occasions and the second is seen as the fulfilment or working out of the first. The candidates have a mission because they are conformed to Christ who was 'sent', who had a mission. How far Cyril thought of this as a separate 'effect' from those of baptism is very doubtful. For him the supreme model was the *baptism* of Christ in which he saw concentrated all that was unfolded in the liturgical rite. Conformity to Christ is mentioned again (24) and this, with the emphasis on incorporation and service of the mystical church, provides a theological basis for confirmation as understood by the Order. It must be admitted that it is very much more satisfactory than the teaching current since the thirteenth century and then later hardened and narrowed to a defence of the institution.

Conformity to Christ or imitation of Christ, always according to the homily, is to be found in two ways. The sign of the cross with chrism signifies the power of the Spirit enabling the candidates to bear witness by their lives to the passion and resurrection of Christ, that is to the paschal mystery and, it is hinted, the living out of the paschal mystery is the consequence of confirmation. This is a deeply traditional teaching though it must be confessed that in the earliest centuries it was associated with baptism and the eucharist. Secondly, Christ is the head of the body, the church of which Christians are living members, and like him who came to serve and not to be served, the confirmed are to be the servants of all. But this service is raised above the level of mere moral exhortation. It is a service that springs from a *datum* which is nothing other than the *donum Spiritus Sancti*, the Spirit who gives himself and who at the same time gives to each, again according to the homily, the charismatic graces meant for the building-up of the Body in unity and love. Here too the teaching of Vatican II is discernible.[31] All receive the gifts for service inside and outside the church, revealing it as the Spirit-filled body of Christ. Given this teaching and the fact that confirmation is set in the context of the Pentecost event, we can see emerging in this rite a pneumatology which has long been wanting in the Western church. For a very long time the church was seen as institution and even when new emphasis came to be made, as in the theology of the mystical body, the church was attached to Christology. It was the body of *Christ* and by the use of terms like 'the extension or prolongation of the incarnation' it was seen almost wholly in relation to the latter. As some Eastern Catholics said even as late as Vatican II, Western ecclesiology was wanting in emphasis on the Spirit in the church in general and in the liturgy in particular.

This teaching is carried forward and given, as I think, a different *nuance*, first in the rite of the laying-on of the hands and then in the new 'form'. In the invitatory to the prayer for the Holy Spirit the celebrant asks that the Spirit may come to 'confirm' the candidates (who have already been born by water and the Holy Spirit) with the abundance of his gifts and by the anointing to conform them to Christ. Perhaps the Greek Fathers would have put the matter a little differently though the use of 'confirm' here in conjunction with the giving of the gifts suggests the view held earlier in both East and West that the second giving of the Spirit was to *establish* his indwelling in the candidate (unless of course rejected by sin). As we shall see, the earlier notion in the West is that 'confirmation' has the sense of 'establishing' and completing what is done in baptism. The 'sealing' is a sort of guarantee that the Spirit will always be present. If this is so, then it is merely the echo of a text which though not about 'confirmation' understood in the modern sense is often in the background of patristic teaching.[32] 'But it is God who *establishes* us with you in Christ and has commissioned us; *he has put his seal upon us* and *given us his Spirit* in our hearts as a *guarantee*' (2 Corinthians 1:21, 22).

More significant still is the new 'form' which marks a conscious change from the past. But to be understood it needs to be put back in its context. St Ambrose, an assiduous student of the Greek writers of his time, speaks of the *signaculum spiritale* which takes place after baptism and, interpreting the gesture, he writes 'After the font, it remains for the "perfecting" to take place'.[33] The word *perfectio* (and its cognate forms) corresponds to the Greek word *teleiosis*, so much used by the Greek Fathers, and it too means 'perfecting', 'accomplishing', 'achieving' something that has been begun. Confirmation is a perfecting or completing of the work of God begun in baptism. It is not primarily a perfecting or strengthening of the candidates in the moral or psychological order though, as in baptism and the eucharist, that is on the horizon. This, I believe, is the sense of the words 'Receive the seal of the gift of the Holy Spirit'. The anointing with chrism or *myron* seals, makes safe, establishes the candidate in the Spirit who gives himself to him and who, as the prayer for the Spirit over the candidates indicates, 'completes' the process of initiation in which the Spirit has been active from the first conception of faith until now.[34] As all the texts of the New Testament and of the liturgies show, we are regenerated 'by water and the Holy Spirit'. The Greek Fathers and St Ambrose, whose *signaculum spiritale* could be translated 'the seal of the Spirit', say that the gift of the Spirit is now 'sealed' by the post-baptismal rite whether it is the laying-on of the hand or anointing or both.

This too seems to have been the teaching in earlier times in the West. To leave Hippolytus aside for the moment, we find that the earliest form of the sacrament, as given in the Gelasian Sacramentary, is *Signum Christi in vitam aeternam* (the sign of Christ for eternal life). This is laconic enough and its interpretation must remain doubtful but it says nothing about being 'confirmed' (as the twelfth-century form does), and it seems to hark back to the *signaculum spiritale* of St Ambrose. When in fifth-century Gaul the word *confirmare* began to come into use, it did not mean 'confirm' in the modern sense. An examination of the semantics of the word shows that it meant 'to establish', 'to complete' or 'to perfect'.[35] And this sealing, ratifying or completing referred directly not to the candidate but to the gift. In the same context it is also interesting to learn that the eucharist is spoken of occasionally as the *confirmatio* of the whole process of initiation. This witnesses to a profound insight into the nature of the eucharist in which the Spirit is present and gives himself so that the church may be built up ('it is the eucharist that makes the church') and become *koinonia*, communion, indwelt by the Holy Spirit. What is begun in the first conception of faith and is carried forward by the catechumenate, baptism and confirmation reaches its climax, its *confirmatio* in the holy eucharist.

All this teaching should have important pastoral consequences. In this perspective, confirmation *after* first communion does not make much sense. Confirmation is related both to baptism which it completes or perfects and to holy communion in which the whole of Christian initiation reaches its achievement. One of the enormous disadvantages of the separation of these three sacraments is that the organic relationship between them is almost totally obscured. We may rightly try to distinguish 'moments' in the whole process of initiation when this or that effect is achieved but we are not going to make much sense of them if they occur in the wrong order. In this matter the paradigm case of Hippolytus still seems to have validity, especially if we understand his liturgy as *a continuing action* in which the effect or effects are to be attributed to the *whole* action, including the eucharist which immediately followed the liturgy of baptism and 'confirmation'.

Whether and how far this teaching can be harmonized with the missionary–witness theme, so strongly emphasized in the Order, is another matter.[36] It is worth noting that in the renewal of baptismal promises there is no reference to witness or mission and it cannot therefore be regarded as a commitment of the candidate to witness or mission.[37] An attentive study of the texts however shows that they do not directly relate the missionary element in the Pentecost event to the candidates. As we have seen above, the giving of the Spirit is directly related to the imitation of Christ in his passion and resurrection and to service. But since it is into the church, the body of Christ, that they are incorporated and since the church has from Christ the mission to preach the gospel to every creature, confirmation can be seen as the sacrament-sign of that mission. Further, if we can see the setting of confirmation in the context of the Pentecost event as evidence of a certain pneumatology, we can also see that confirmation represents a deepened relationship to the church as the Spirit-filled body of Christ in which the Christian lives and moves and has his being. It is through the Christian that the Spirit, working through faith and the sacraments, and especially those of initiation, shows the church to be the 'pneumatic' body, a body permeated by him.

As for the act of confirmation proper, the controversy whether it is effected by the laying-on of the hand[38] or by anointing no longer seems to be an urgent one. The new Order sees the signing of the forehead with chrism *as* the imposition of the hand and commentators make it clear that the celebrant is no longer required to perform the awkward gesture of laying-on the hand (which in practice meant four fingers) and at the same time anointing the forehead with the thumb:[39] 'The sacrament of confirmation is conferred by the anointing with chrism on the forehead *which is done by the imposition of the hand* and the words . . .'.[40] This really marks a return to early medieval custom, witnessed to by Innocent III, the second Council of Lyons and the Decree for the Armenians that was drawn up after the Council of Florence. The hand-laying rubric was absent from the revised Roman Pontifical of 1595 and was inserted into the rite as late as the time of Benedict XIV (died 1758). In practice it will mean that the gesture is much easier to make.[41] The laying-on of hands (no longer called 'the extension of the hands') at the beginning of the rite is regarded in its proper role as a liturgical gesture explicitating the meaning of chrismation.[42]

There remains the question of the translation of the formula. 'Receive the seal of the gift of the Holy Spirit', which is its literal translation, by its complete lack of emphasis and, as one may think, a failure to ask what it means, conveys almost nothing. The French have adopted the translation 'Receive the mark (seal?) of the Holy Spirit who is given to you',[43] which is very close to the version first suggested in the commission by Dom Bernard Botte,[44] *Accipe signaculum Spiritus sancti qui tibi datur—* and it is a pity it was not adopted. He insists that the central truth of the formula is that it is the Holy Spirit who is given and that it is this

~

that must be emphasized in vernacular versions. With this we can agree though one asks: but what then is the force of 'seal'? The translators of the ICEL text have investigated the scriptural background of the text and point to 'seal' (cf. Ephesians 1:13), 'gift' (Acts 2:38 'you shall receive the gift of the Holy Spirit') and 'Gift' in the sense of the Holy Spirit himself (cf. Luke 11:13; Acts 1:4; John 14:26, etc.) which must all be taken into account. Their version is 'Receive the seal of the Holy Spirit, the Gift of the Father' which seems to do justice to the scriptural contexts.[45] It makes clear 'the personal nature of the Gift', suggests its origin (the Father) and since the action of the Son is evident throughout the rite there was no need to attempt to bring in this element explicitly. This version has now been confirmed by the Roman Congregation for Worship.

Some critical observations

The theology of the Order offers a grand vision and is an infinite improvement on the etiolated theology so long associated with confirmation. But should all this richness be associated with it? Are not the effects of confirmation also those of baptism? According to the New Testament it is by baptism that we are made members of Christ (1 Corinthians 12:12, 13 etc.), are conformed to Christ in his passion and resurrection (Romans 6:3, 4), and receive the Spirit, for we cannot be regenerated without the Spirit (Galatians 3:26, 27; 4:6, 7; cf. Romans 8:14–16; Titus 3:5). By baptism too we are called to service (1 Corinthians 12:12ff.) and receive a mission to proclaim the saving deeds of God (1 Peter 2:4–9). The Order seems to leave us with the dilemma: if these functions are given in baptism, what is confirmation for? And if it is said that it is *for* all these functions, what becomes of New Testament teaching?

My own view, for what it is worth, is that in the New Testament all the effects of baptism and confirmation were concentrated in the former sacrament, and confirmation, as subsequent centuries have come to know it, is an unfolding of the content of baptism. This view would seem to be supported by the witness of the Syrian church whose theology may be said to be undeveloped but where we find the deep conviction that the Spirit is given in a rite which had no elements of confirmation. Such a view would also help towards an explanation of the situation in Europe where for centuries millions of Christians must have died without confirmation as we have come to know it. Confirmation by the presbyter with the *first* post-baptismal anointing is a solution that had something to be said for it. There is however another way of looking at the matter. It would appear that there is more than one theology of Christian initiation in the New Testament, the Pauline one which saw 'baptism' with the giving of the Spirit as complete in itself, and the Lucan one which saw the church as 'endowed with a special outpouring of the Spirit for the promulgation of the gospel'.[46] This is to be distinguished from the gift of the Spirit at baptism for regeneration and cannot be 'harmonized' with it in the context of the New Testament. It was the Jerusalem church, presided over by the apostles, which had so conspicuously received the gift of the Spirit. The consequence of this was the spread of the gospel. When we come to texts like Acts 8:14–17 and 19:5, 6 which have been used as 'proof-texts' of confirmation, they are to be seen as acts of the Jerusalem church to establish the unity of the church. For this purpose the emergent local churches like that of Samaria, Antioch and others must receive the Spirit both to show their unity with the mother-church and to guarantee that they would play their part in the spreading of the gospel. Since it was on the apostles that the Spirit had come at Pentecost, it was their function to communicate the Spirit to these churches. But the main point was to maintain the unity of the church. Perhaps we could add that in one sense it was an act of 'authority' but it is significant that authority meant the communication of the Spirit. The whole church had to become visibly the living, breathing, Spirit-filled body of Christ.

The two texts from Acts are cited in the papal constitution and the second (only) in the homily and it is a question whether in the former document they are to be seen rather as an argument *ex traditione* than as one *ex sacra scriptura*. Such is often the style of papal documents. It does however seem possible to discern the above Lucan theology in the homily where it is said that the Spirit is given for the building-up of the church and for its unity in love.[47]

The rite (20–32)

Like all the other sacramental actions of the reformed liturgy, confirmation is normally to be celebrated within the Mass after the ministry of the word. The bishop sits and the candidates are presented to him by the parish priest or others concerned in their instruction. If they are children, they are to be presented by their parents or sponsors. Unless they are very numerous they are to be called by name.

The homily follows, in which the celebrant takes up the themes of the readings and uses them to lead the candidates to a deeper understanding of 'the mystery of confirmation'.

The homily ends with the invitation to renounce evil and profess the faith: 'Before you receive the Spirit, be mindful of the faith which you or your parents or godparents professed with the church'. The renunciation consists of but one sentence and the profession of faith makes special mention of the Holy Spirit: 'Do you believe in the Holy Spirit, Lord and giver of life, who today in a special way is given to you by the sacrament of confirmation as he was to the apostles on the day of Pentecost?'

After concluding the profession of faith the celebrant, standing, pronounces an invitatory, there is silence and then the prayer for the coming of the Spirit with the sevenfold gifts on the candidates.

For the chrismation either the candidates approach the celebrant or he them while the sponsor places his right hand on the shoulder of the candidate. The celebrant anoints the forehead with his thumb (nothing is said about his laying the hand on the top of the head) while he pronounces the formula. To this the candidate replies *Amen*.

The Order then says that the sign of peace is to be given. The General Intercession (replacing that of the Mass) follows. The formula is given as a model only but it is good and might well be used regularly. It prays for the candidates, for the parents and sponsors, for the whole church and for the world.

The rest of the Mass follows (there is a special *Hanc igitur* for use in the Roman Canon) and candidates may receive communion in both kinds. The Mass concludes either with the solemn form of blessing or with the special 'prayer over the people' which incorporates the old phrase (originally an introit) 'Confirm, Lord, what you have effected in us . . .'.

Commentary

While the organization of the presentation of the candidates may present some practical difficulties, it is evidently intended to express the desire of the parents to have their children confirmed or, in the case of adults, to express the intention of the local community to do likewise. It is a significant gesture and should be kept wherever possible. It is another reason for keeping the number of candidates small.

At first sight, there is an anomaly in asking the candidates to renew their baptismal promises. In the new baptismal Order children do not make any and the situation is only saved by the clause 'which you or your parents . . . have professed'. We may suppose that there was some compromise at this point. The revisers did not want to give way to the pressure of certain powerful groups to turn confirmation into a 'sacrament of Catholic Action' or of commitment.[48] Confirmation is not the sacrament either of childhood or of adulthood and where grown-ups who have just been baptized are concerned further acts of commitment are out of the question. It is because some have thought confirmation had something to do with adolescence that this notion has been prevalent.

We have already spoken of the invitatory. Its underlying theology is very balanced. Neither it nor the prayer itself speaks of commitment, mission or anything of the kind.

The prayer for the giving of the Spirit is ancient, coming from the Gelasian Sacramentary and reaching back perhaps to the time of St Ambrose. The intrusive *Amens*, a later feature, have been eliminated. It should be noted too that the gesture of the hands during the prayer is no longer spoken of as 'extending' them over the candidates, as the former pontifical did, but as a 'laying-on of hands' (*manus imponunt* – the rubric assumes that presbyters are going to concelebrate the sacrament with the bishop).

The Introduction (8) foresees that confirmation is going to be a concelebration of other non-episcopal ministers (vicars-general and other dignitaries but notably parish priests and those who have been concerned in the preparation of the candidates) with the bishop and while the clause in (8) seems restrictive, the ritual seems to envisage the concelebration of other ministers as normal. We may imagine that this will become usual practice. They are true concelebrants: with the bishop they lay hands on all the candidates together, they receive the chrism from the bishop (a sign of their delegation) and with him anoint those candidates allotted to them. The theological implications are interesting. Here is a concelebration for the giving of a sacrament that at least in the West has already been regarded as an episcopal prerogative; but more than that, the unity of the priesthood is made very plain. Presbyters are visibly, liturgically and sacramentally sharing in the one priesthood that ultimately is Christ's and of which the episcopate is the primary but by no means exclusive manifestation. It comes close to the vision of the Constitution on the Liturgy (41, 42) which sees the bishop as the president of the liturgy of the whole diocese which in turn 'manifests' the church. Given this experience, the people will understand all the more easily the role of the presbyter when, as in certain circumstances he may (7), he confirms alone in his own church.

Finally, a word must be said about the sign of peace that concludes the administration. The *alapa*, that thirteenth-century 'interpretation' of the gesture, has gone. It is no longer to be found in the rubrics and local conferences of bishops may decide how it is to be done. As the ancient texts show very clearly it was originally the kiss of peace exchanged in the eucharistic community and was given to the neophytes for the first time to show that they were now members of the community.[49] With the unique exception of the Roman rite this was the moment, i.e. just before the eucharistic action, when the kiss of peace was always given.

How and indeed when is it to be done? There is the practical difficulty that the celebrant, whose hand is covered with chrism, can hardly give the peace in the form of the handshake which is now widely accepted. And we may ask: is it necessary to give it precisely at this moment? It would seem best to delay it until the time of communion when the candidates could be brought before the celebrant to receive it. It would then be linked with the eucharist as it originally was. To save a further movement, there they could remain until they receive communion.

Where confirmation is given outside the Mass, candidates could be assembled after the Lord's Prayer when the sign of peace could appropriately be given.

Confirmation outside the Mass

There are few changes. There is an opening collect, the ministry of the word, the homily, the renewal of baptismal promises, the administration, the General Intercession, ending with the Lord's Prayer. There is finally the solemn blessing or the 'prayer over the people'.

Practical pastoral directives

These are to be found in the *Praenotanda* (here called the Introduction) (1–19).

Parents: As in the Order of Infant Baptism, the role of the parents is much enhanced. 'For the most part it is for the *parents* to see that their children are prepared for confirmation' and this they are to do 'by forming them gradually in the spirit of faith' and by supporting others who may instruct them. This duty will receive its proper liturgical expression by their active participation in the ceremony and notably when they present their own children to the bishop. The parents are naturally to be helped by others, the clergy and catechists, but 'the preparation of the baptized for confirmation concerns the whole people of God' though how this is to be carried out in practice is a question. However, the community at least can be asked to pray about the event and petitions can be inserted *before* the day of confirmation in the General Intercession of the Mass.

Sponsors: These are retained but the background of their function is again community. They are not Christians who merely lay a hand on the candidates. They are supposed to assist them before, during and after the celebration. That is, they are to have something to do with leading the candidates to confirmation, presumably by associating with them and giving informal instruction. In the course of the celebration, if the parents do not do so, they are to present the candidate to the bishop and, in doing so, they represent the local community. Afterwards they 'will help the candidates to keep the promises they have made in baptism' (5).[50]

To signify the link between baptism and confirmation the sponsors of the former may continue their function for confirmation and for the latter parents may stand. This may well be the best way to deal with the matter. Where parents are practising, they will be the children's best instructors and support and where they are weak, confirmation may well provide (another) occasion when their faith and practice may be strengthened.[51] Sponsors must be mature, must be Catholics, themselves have received the three sacraments of initiation and be free from canonical impediments.

No doubt it is a good and desirable thing that there should be sponsors and that they should have some part in the preparation of the candidates and continue to support them after confirmation. But this presupposes a parish that is a community where people know each other and that there is a large number capable of sustaining the role. Once again we meet the problem of community and also the need to form parents and other adults in a mature Christianity. As with so many matters that seem at first purely liturgical, here also we find that wider issues come into play. Until there is some recognized form of adult Christian education, it is improbable that the sort of sponsors envisaged by the Order will be found.

The minister(s) of confirmation: Taking up a term invented by Vatican II[52] the Introduction (7) states that the *minister originarius* of confirmation is a bishop and in the context of the Council document this can only mean the diocesan bishop with a pastoral charge. The term would seem to mean that the source of power for conferring confirmation resides in the bishop and the theological basis for this, to be found in the Constitution on the Church (28), is that bishop and priest share in the one priesthood of Jesus Christ. The 'power' therefore is not merely a legal one but a sacramental one. In the Eastern churches the bishop is clearly the 'originating minister' since it is he who blesses the chrism and the priest who regularly confirms. In the West this is true also though the priest receives a special delegation to confirm. According to the Introduction, the bishop is to be regarded as the *normal* minister of the sacrament since he is the successor of the apostles who received the Spirit at Pentecost and the power to transmit him.[53] yet, it is a marked feature of this Order, as well as that of adult initiation, that a variety of non-episcopal ministers may now, with proper authorization, confer the sacrament. The reason for this is undoubtedly the inability of the diocesan bishop to be present wherever and whenever he is needed. With this recognition of the practical difficulties, as well as an enhanced esteem of the importance of confirmation, Western practice is now beginning to approach that of Eastern Christians. If the plain implications of the Orders of confirmation and adult initiation are to be reduced to practice, that is, if the order of baptism, confirmation and the eucharist is to be observed *as a norm*, it will be necessary for priests to be regularly delegated to administer confirmation.

Apart from those who hold a special charge yet without the episcopal order (7a), priests who *ex officio* baptize an adult or a child not baptized in infancy or, as we have seen, admit a baptized person into the full communion of the church, may confirm and the power to do so is granted by this Order. The permission to confirm in danger of death, first restricted to parish priests and then to some others, is now extended to a wide variety of them (7c).

The co-operation of priests in the celebration of confirmation is expressed sacramentally in the rite itself. The bishop associates them with himself. With him they lay hands on the candidates and from him receive the chrism. The whole liturgy is a true sacramental concelebration.

The age of confirmation: As we have seen, the Order says that confirmation is delayed (*differtur*) until about the age of seven (or 'age of discretion'). Since first communion is given about the same time the Order seems to suggest that confirmation should *precede* it. This is the general sense of the whole Order: confirmation before communion. If that is so then this represents the ancient Roman tradition that has never varied. Yet there are or seem to be practical problems which the Order recognizes and leaves to local conferences of bishops the responsibility for setting a later age. There must be (good) pastoral reasons and these are suggested: they are to train the faithful to a fuller and enthusiastic devotion (*obtemperantiam*: lit. 'obedience') to Christ and to a greater capability to bear witness to him.

What age is this to be? The Order speaks of an *aetas maturior* and this could hardly be said to be eight, nine, ten or eleven. On the other hand there are few who would admit the age of early adolescence as suitable. Is anything as late as eighteen or nineteen envisaged? It seems bizarre. By that time some people are married. The question has been debated for over thirty years and it is pretty safe to say that no satisfactory conclusion has been reached.

The whole problem has come from (a) the separation of confirmation from baptism, which, as we have seen, was due to non-theological factors and (b) to the consequent association of this sacrament with adolescence. The notion too that confirmation was concerned with commitment to the work of the church ('mission', and in some places 'Catholic Action') also had much to do with the controversy which has raged until now.

If we look at the theology of confirmation as it is set out or is discernible in the liturgy, it is clear that it has nothing to do with adolescence.

If it had, there would be no point in confirming an adult convert. Secondly, if it speaks of the mission of the church, it does so in a very special way, as we have observed above. Thirdly, as we have also tried to show, there is a logic in the order of the three sacraments of initiation which carries its own weight. In the early church, even for children, the holy eucharist was seen as the perfecting of baptism and confirmation and to confer the latter after communion is to pervert the right order of things. We are forced or, before long, will be forced to re-unite confirmation with baptism and then the problem will be not the age at which confirmation is given but whether or not we baptize and confirm certain children at all. Infant confirmation or at least confirmation before communion will become the custom.

Celebration and community: There are the usual recommendations that the celebration should be festive, that normally it is to take place within the Mass and that the local community should be assembled for it. Since confirmation has always been a community celebration and usually sufficiently festive, there is no need to insist on these matters here.

Adaptation: Local conferences of bishops may adapt the formulas of the promises and profession of faith, as in baptism, and it is to be hoped that they will not be adapted in the direction of the soldier-of-Christ–defence-of-the-church mentality which is quite unsupported by the texts of the liturgy. Such conferences may however adapt the texts to the mentality of the candidates and this will be particularly important in the case of children.

As we have observed, the manner of giving the sign of peace is to be determined by the same local conferences of bishops.

The *celebrant* may adapt the address according to the psychological needs of the candidates as well as the invitatory to the prayer for the laying-on of hands and may insert brief commentaries (*monitiones*) where he thinks they may be needed. If he is not a bishop, he should mention that the bishop is the normal minister of the sacrament.

Further reflections

Since the promulgation of the Orders of Infant Baptism (1969) and Confirmation (1971) and especially since use of the RCIA became available in English in the mid-1980s the two strands of thinking about the sacraments of initiation involving confirmation have become clearer. Those who see confirmation as a sacrament of commitment and witness have tended towards an age that is later than formerly, namely about twelve or fourteen. They see no cogent reason why confirmation should precede first communion and presumably would be opposed to it as seven-year-olds are hardly able to bear witness.

They are supported by some theologians (but not I think by liturgists) who argue that the 'tradition' that is historical and liturgical is not what is meant by *theological* tradition, which allows of (demands?) development. Current practice of confirming after first communion, preferably about the age of fourteen, can be justified by a certain development that has been prompted by sociological changes and new psychological insights. These however do not provide a sufficient *theological* basis for a considerable change in sacramental practice.

The second trend of thought is concerned that the order of the three sacraments of initiation, baptism, confirmation and the eucharist, should be observed. Theologians and liturgists of this way of thinking maintain that this order is not just a matter of historical or liturgical tradition but that it is a theological matter. These three sacraments are so closely linked that to separate them is to deprive them of their true ecclesial significance. They invoke the Apostolic Constitution of Paul VI attached to the Order: 'Confirmation is so closely linked with the holy eucharist that the faithful, after being signed in holy baptism and confirmation, are *incorporated fully* into the body of Christ *by participation in the eucharist*' (p. 10, Latin text, emphasis mine). The Pope goes on to quote the Constitution on the Liturgy (71) where it refers to 'the intimate connection which this sacrament has with the whole process of Christian initiation'. One might also refer to no. 34 of the same document which requires that the rites shall be 'clear', within the people's powers of understanding and without the need of much explanation. That is, a liturgical rite or series of rites should have a certain visible coherence and when children of whatever age are confirmed *after* first communion 'the intimate connection' between confirmation, baptism and the eucharist is not clear.

It is for reasons such as this that bishops and priests, in Britain and the United States of America, have been devising patterns of practice that respect the teaching of the church documents.

In a certain parish in the diocese of St Paul–Minneapolis after prolonged catechesis of the people the clergy decided with their agreement that children ready for first communion should be confirmed before-hand. So 'On a Sunday morning in the Easter season . . . the bishop visited our parish and presided at our principal eucharistic assembly. All the children who were ready for first communion received the sacra-ment of confirmation and then first communion from the bishop at that Mass.'[54] Nothing very surprising in that, one may think, all very simple and understandable, yet how often is that way taken? The rest of Fr Moudry's essay is taken up with what went before and after, and it is not clear whether there were any imitators or what difficulties if any were encountered in the same diocese. Could the bishop cover the whole diocese in the Easter season (unlikely!) and if not, when was confirmation given in the rest of the year? It was not however the author's purpose to deal with such problems.

A more complete system, described[55] by Fr Geoffrey Steel of Ushaw College, was initiated in the diocese of Salford by Bishop Patrick Kelly. In outline it goes like this:

Advent: preparation, chiefly with parents.

Feast of Presentation of the Lord: enrolment: candidates presented by parents and sponsors.

Mass of Chrism (Holy Week): parents, catechists, sponsors etc. invited to attend.

Pentecost following: confirmation in every parish in diocese, parish priests and local clergy delegated to confirm. Bishop presides in cathedral.

Advent: children (and desirably their parents) celebrate the sacra-ment of penance in this season.

Easter Day: the confirmed children with their parents receive their first eucharist at a Mass of their choice. Later in the season there is a general celebration for the newly initiated in all the parishes.

The scheme (for which the bishop sought and received permission from the Holy See) has now been running for about four years. Although meeting with some opposition in the beginning, according to Fr Steel's and others' reports it has found a very wide measure of acceptance. It could be said to be a practical and visible expression of the teach-ing of the documents on Christian initiation. It was launched with a thoroughly worked-out catechesis given in gatherings and on tapes, often by the bishop himself. It was this that ensured success.

Difficulties, opposition, were understandable but both, given the 'revolution' in mentality it involved, were not great. Various objections have been brought against the scheme but they concern matters of detail: should children be confirmed at a service that is not the Mass? (One answer: they could not receive holy communion if it were.) Is the introduction to the sacrament of penance in Advent appropriate? Advent is not a penitential season (but penitential services are recommended for that season). What seems to be a more fundamental objection is that children of seven or eight should be made 'to go to confession' before receiving communion. Is it suggested that they can commit mortal sin? The Code of Canon Law (989) says that only those who have done so are obliged to go to confession at least once a year. In any case, long experience shows that children of seven to eight have a great difficulty in making a private confession in the 'box'. The removal of the apparent obligation would do much to simplify the preparation for confirmation and first communion. The whole matter can be dealt with more credibly at a later age, nine or ten, when children begin to be conscious of sin as they are not and cannot be at the age of seven.

With use and experience such difficulties as the Salford Scheme has encountered will be solved and they should not be allowed to hinder its continued use.[56]

One objection, long voiced even when children of eight, nine or ten are confirmed, is also brought against the Salford Scheme. No provision is made for adolescence! If those who make this objection would remember the scriptures they would see that holy communion is the essential support of the Christian life: 'Truly, truly, I say to you, unless you eat the flesh of the Son of man and drink his blood, you have no life in you' (John 6:53). However, it is perfectly possible to work out a service of commitment towards the end of secondary school age (about sixteen) that might be part of a youth rally over which the bishop could preside and receive the affirmations of the young. There is no need for a sacrament for that.

Notes

1 (Vatican Press, 1971).

2 About AD 215: **Ap. Trad.**, 21, p. 18.

3 Tertullian, **De Resurrectione carnis**, viii, 3.

4 E. C. Whitaker, **Documents of the Baptismal Liturgy**, 2nd ed. (London, 1970), p. xxxi.

5 St Ambrose, **De Sacr**. III, 5.

6 Text and trans., Whitaker, **op. cit.**, p. 130.

7 The rites of the catechumenate remained, somewhat adapted, and were 'practised' on infants for centuries and provided the basis for the rite of baptism in the old **Rituale Romanum**.

8 See J. D. C. Fisher, **Christian Initiation: Baptism in the Medieval West** (London, 1965), pp. 22-3. The evidence is not perhaps completely cogent but given Rome's age-old insistence on the order of the sacraments of initiation and the right of the bishop to confirm, any other arrangement is hardly conceivable.

9 See Fisher, **op. cit.**, p. 22. For the Latin text, see Gelasian Sacramentary, no. 451. For the text in English see Whitaker, **Documents**, p. 188.

10 See J. Tixeront, **Histoire des dogmes**, 3, 4th ed. (Paris, 1919), pp. 293ff. More recently doubt has been cast on Faustus's authorship of the sermon. It is thought that an unknown writer used one of his writings and produced what is described as a 'rather mediocre homily' where the term **confirmare** is constantly used. See Gabriele Winkler, 'Confirmation or Chrismation? A Study in Comparative Liturgy', **Worship**, 58/1 (January 1984), pp. 2-17. She also is of the opinion that the view found in this sermon is quite out of character with the 'Gallican' liturgical books, relevant to the issue, which she examines in this same article.

11 For all this see Fisher, **op. cit.**, pp. 59-65. It is interesting to note that Alcuin refers to holy communion given at the end of the (Gallican) rite as 'confirmation': 'he is confirmed with the Lord's body and blood', p. 61.

12 See Fisher, **op. cit.**, pp. 120 ff.

13 See J. D. C. Fisher, **Christian Initiation: The Reformation Period** (London, 1970), pp. 159 ff.

14 Fisher, **Christian Initiation: Baptism**, p. 137.

15 The language of the canon is remarkable: in the Latin church confirmation may be 'conveniently deferred' until seven, which would seem to indicate that confirmation at baptism is not ruled out. Moreover, it may be conferred even earlier, not merely on danger of death but 'for just and grave reasons', the judgement to be made by the minister (Code of 1917).

16 A comparatively recent example of Roman thinking can be found in the reply of Leo XIII to the Bishop of Marseilles who sought guidance about the order of confirmation and communion. The Pope replied that confirmation **after** communion was not in harmony either with the ancient and constant tradition of the church or with the good of the faithful (see A. Hamman, **Baptême et Confirmation**, Paris, 1969, p. 224).

17 **Constitutio Apostolica** of Paul VI, prefixed to the **Ordo Confirmationis** (1971), p. 8.

18 See above.

19 Hardly eight, nine or ten, one would think.

~

[20] See **Questions Liturgiques**, 1 (Mont-César, Louvain, 1972), pp. 5-8.

[21] The text of the Constitution seems to take the giving of the Spirit in Acts 2:38 as something separate from the baptism.

[22] Reference is made to 1 Peter 2:5 and 9.

[23] Cf. Const. on Church, II.

[24] Throughout references are made to the Council documents. This Constitution reflects the theology of the Council.

[25] The translation in JB 'sing the praise of God' is not generally endorsed by other versions: e.g. RSV 'that you may declare the wonderful deeds' of God, which seems to us the more accurate translation.

[26] See above, p. 102.

[27] B. Botte, **Questions Liturgiques**, 1 (1972), p. 7.

[28] St Ambrose, **De Sacr.**, III, 8; Whitaker, **Documents**, p. 131.

[29] The text does not say exactly 'more perfect members' though it may be thought that this is what it means, nor yet does it say that they are made 'fuller' members of the church. As we have seen, the Constitution says they are made 'fully' members of the church by the eucharist.

[30] Cyril of Jerusalem, **Cat. Myst.**, III, i, ed. Piédagnel, p. 121.

[31] Constitution on the Church, 12.

[32] E.g. St Ambrose, text quoted above.

[33] See Whitaker, **Documents**, p. 131.

[34] Perhaps the failure to realize that the Spirit is active wherever there is faith and sacrament has created difficulties for an understanding of confirmation. The Spirit is active in the holy eucharist. Too frequently, popular catechesis has given the impression that at confirmation the Spirit is given 'for the first time'!

[35] Fisher, **Christian Initiation: Baptism**, Appendix 1. He points out that in Ambrose **confirmavit** is related to **bebaiōn** of 2 Cor 1:21-2 which Ambrose refers to: 'It is God who **establishes** us' (RSV). The same use is found in John Chrysostom, in the **Apostolic Constitutions**, III, 117, and VII, 22, 'where it is clear that the editor of the **Apostolic Constitutions** understood **bebaiōsis** to mean sealing, or ratifying or completing', pp. 142-3.

[36] It seems to me that there are **two** theologies in this rite which are only imperfectly harmonized, if at all.

[37] Though there is nothing to stop local conferences of bishops from inserting such a commitment (cf. 17 (a)).

[38] Always 'hand' in the early and even the later liturgical documents.

[39] B. Botte, **Questions Liturgiques**, 1 (1972), pp. 3-4, who emphasizes the importance of retaining the anointing since it is a gesture common to both the Eastern and the Western church. B. Kleinheyer, **LMD**, 110 (1972), pp. 68-70. Cf. also the reply to this effect, **Notitiae**, 76 (September-October 1972), p. 281.

[40] Constitution, p. 14.

[41] It may be that the hand-laying plus chrismation was brought back because the theologians used Acts 8:15-17 and 19:5, 6, as 'proof-texts' for the existence of confirmation. As we see above (p. 87) these texts are not so straightforward as they might seem.

[42] Cf. Constitution, p. 14.

[43] '. . . reçois la marque de l'Esprit-Saint qui t'est donné'.

[44] Botte, **art. cit.**, p. 5.

[45] They remark that the **Filioque** is not in question since we are here dealing with the

~

external mission of the Holy Spirit and not the intra-trinitarian relationships.
[46] For an excellent study of the various theologies of the Spirit in the New Testament see Austin P. Milner, *The Theology of Confirmation* (Cork, 1972), pp. 90-9.
[47] A. Hamman in *Baptême et Confirmation*, p. 194, takes the same view as Milner though he deals with the matter much more summarily. Milner has made a contribution to the theology of confirmation of great importance. There does however remain the text of 1 Peter 2:4-9, which is presumably neither Pauline nor Lucan and attaches the preaching of the gospel to baptism and (probably) the eucharist. See Y. Congar, *Le Mystère du Temple* (Paris, 1958), pp. 208-15. All is not yet clear in this complicated matter.
[48] See Botte, *art. cit.*, pp. 6-7.
[49] Hippolytus *forbids* the exchange of the kiss of peace between catechumens and Christians until this moment (*Ap. Trad.* 18, p. 18).
[50] If this is meant to refer to children it is a little odd, for they have made no promises in baptism. One has to suppose that the revisers had adults in mind—or that Homer nodded. If for 'baptism' one read 'confirmation' the injunction would be comprehensible.
[51] If of course they have receded from the church so far that they can hardly be said to be members of it at all, other remedies will have to be sought and the question of the confirmation of the candidate, if very young, may have to be reviewed. It is the problem of infant baptism all over again.
[52] Constitution on the Church, 26.
[53] It is this last phrase that, presumably, in the mind of the Order distinguishes the apostles from the other Christians who were present in some numbers on the same occasion. They received the Spirit but not the power to transmit him.
[54] See Richard P. Moudry, 'The Initiation of Children: The Path one Parish Took', in *When Should We Confirm?*, ed. James A. Wilde (Liturgy Training Publications, Chicago, 1989), p. 73.
[55] *Ibid.*, pp. 33-52.
[56] For a powerful theologico-liturgical statement on confirmation and its rightful place in Christian initiation see Rinaldo Falsini, 'La cresima nel quadro della Iniziazione: rapporto con il battesimo', in *Mysterion* (LDC; Turin, 1981), pp. 441-56.

~

The Sacrament of Marriage[1]

~~~~~~~

HE DEVELOPMENT in more recent years of the theology of
marriage, in which secular factors (changing attitudes to sex
and love, the equality of women, etc.) have played their part,
has revealed or re-discovered new aspects of Christian marriage. The
Second Vatican Council both summarized and carried forward this
development, principally in its document, The Constitution on the
Church in the Modern World (47–52).[2]

Christian marriage is a union of *persons*: one is not the servant of
the other. Marriage which is entered into by the irrevocable consent
of the partners is a covenant in which they give themselves to each
other and their union becomes the sacrament-sign of the love with
which God has loved his people throughout the ages: 'Christ our Lord
abundantly blesses this manifold love which springs from the source
of divine charity and forms a union on the model of his own union with
the Church. For just as God once encountered his people in a covenant
of trust and love, so now, as the Saviour of the world and Spouse of
the Church, he encounters the faithful spouses in the sacrament of
Christian marriage.' Their love is taken up into the divine love and
enriched by the love of Christ (50). There is much more on the same
subject which it would be impossible to summarize here. Sufficient to
say that the Council teaches a deep and rich doctrine of marriage, much
of which is incorporated into the new marriage rite.

This doctrine was largely in possession before the Council opened
and although the Constitution on the Church in the Modern World
came along after the Constitution on the Liturgy, it is not surprising
that the Council Fathers decreed that 'the marriage rite now found in
the Roman Ritual is to be revised and enriched in such a way that the
grace of the sacrament is more clearly signified and the duties of spouses
are impressed on them' (77). If the last phrase seems a little over
moralistic and perhaps a bit condescending, one needs to remember
that the liturgy constitution was the first to be debated in the Council

~

and that later documents show a deeper understanding of the sacrament. The 'duties' and responsibilities are shown to arise from the nature of marriage itself and are not something externally imposed on the laity, unfortunately married, by a clerical church.

From a liturgical and even a human point of view, the marriage rite that was to be found in the then Roman Ritual was jejune in the extreme. In the deepest sense of the word it was an *insignificant* rite that hardly expressed the theology of marriage even as it was then known. Unless there was a wedding Mass (and until comparatively recently wedding Masses were rare) there was no ministry of the word, sometimes not even a sermon.[3] There were simply the expression of consent, a prayer for the blessing of the ring, a few versicles and responses and a not very inspiring collect. There was not even a blessing at the end.[4] The reason for this strange state of affairs was that when the rite was drawn up in the early seventeenth century, the compilers assumed that different countries and regions had their own rites and customs which it was intended should continue in use. In Europe this was indeed the case and some of them were rich and embedded in the national culture. Unfortunately no provision was made for the church in the new countries and since they could not plead customs of their own, they had perforce to use the austere rite of the Roman Ritual. Here in England we were protected from the rigours of that rite since both the Roman Catholic and the Anglican Churches (with one or two differences) retained the rite of Sarum. This, especially in the texts of the exchange of promises, has a warmth that is totally lacking in the Roman rite and, as is now well known, these texts, with but few changes, have been incorporated into the rite of the church.[5]

An examination of the texts of the marriage service, both those in the Order and those in the missal, shows that the church is now emphasizing two truths that have always been implicit in Christian marriage but which have never been so clearly expressed in the liturgy as they are in the new rite. The first is the importance of the human love of those about to be married, and the second is covenant.

The first must be said to be principally a contribution from modern society which very generally has repudiated arranged marriages and has come to a deeper understanding of what love can be between a man and a woman. The church's part in this matter has been largely one of reflection on the experience of married Christians, though an increasing tendency to put love (charity) at the centre of theological concerns has also helped Christians to integrate their sexual love into an authentic Christianity. None the less it may be said to be an interesting example of the influence of the laity on clerical thinking.[6] This development has a very great importance for, as we have said above,[7] marriage is a paradigm case of the interpenetration of the divine love with the human.

In the secularized, non-religious and non-sacral civilization in which we live, worship and religious practice seem to be a fringe activity indulged in either by the frightened to whom religion is a sort of fire insurance or by others for even less accountable reasons. Even Christians constantly experience the difficulty of relating their life to their worship and too often they are kept in separate compartments. There is no need to give examples, we are all aware of it and we all suffer from it. Marriage is important not merely for its own sake but because it involves a meeting of what is most ordinary and 'worldly' with Christ who gives it a divine dimension and depth.

Two young people love each other and, however imperfect their understanding of what love implies, however little they may know of its depths, its richness and its complexity, they also realize that it involves a mutual self-giving that is total. They are aware, of course, that their love becomes enfleshed in the union of bodies, that in a sense there is nothing more earthy than sexual union. But they realize in one way or another that this giving and even this giving-in-the-flesh transcends itself. There is a plus-value to their love and it is only the cynic who would say that they are not seeking it. It is *this* human love that 'becomes' the sacrament of marriage through which God transfuses it with his love. It is not merely that the human love of a couple is 'sanctified' as if it were left intact in all its secularity, much less is it just a 'blessing' that remains external to the 'real thing'. It is not even that this love is 'consecrated' so that in marriage it is redeemed from its earthiness. Sanctification and consecration do occur and both enable the partners to direct love away from self to the other for, as everyone knows, human love can be marred by selfishness and lust, even in marriage. The deepest truth seems to be that two people jointly bring their love to God in a spirit of self-giving to each other and to him and in the encounter that ensues, God's love meets theirs. As we have said, he transfuses it with his own. Henceforth they are able to love each other with a love in which God is present and active. Their love however remains human, it is not 'angelized', and is always limited by what the two personalities are and by what they will be throughout their lives. Their love for each other will undergo various vicissitudes, it will often be less than generous, sometimes self-seeking, but whenever they are truly loving each other, God is present to them and in their love. For *ubi caritas et amor, Deus ibi est* (Where is love and loving-kindness, there is God).

This view is at least implied in the first address of the minister of the sacrament: 'You have come together in this church so that the Lord may seal and strengthen your love . . . Christ abundantly blesses' it. The love already exists and will remain intact but it is going to be 'strengthened' by God, turning it, we may suppose, from the radical self-centredness that is in everyone to an other-centredness, precisely the partner who is the 'other'. And while 'blesses' is a rather vague word it would seem to indicate that the love is going to be transformed, as we can see from the texts that occur later in the rite.

But this love is not restricted in its expression to the exchange of promises before the altar nor yet to the more private and purely inter-personal relationships of the husband and wife. Young people today, with the recession of the high tide of romantic love, know very well that neither love nor marriage consists of murmured words or gestures of affection. They know that it is expressed in the most ordinary actions of human life, that marriage is not a romantic affair but that it is marked by a daunting ordinariness, by all the anxieties of forming a home, by the bringing up of children and the caring for each other in illness, depression and times of tension. All these vicissitudes offer opportunities of self-giving, of mutual love, and God is present to them in the stress and anxiety of their lives as well as in their joys. In all of them they meet God or rather God comes to them anew, animating their dedicated love and supporting them so that the process of mutual self-giving can continue. In this way, life in all its drabness and stress and joy is lifted up to God so that it is transformed. One is inclined to echo: *imma summis iunguntur*; the lowly is united with the Highest. Thus Christian marriage is able to play its part in the perfecting of this world until it too bears the image of Christ and at the end will be lifted up to the Father.

If the first address implies this view of love, other texts teach it explicitly and carry it further. Thus the second nuptial blessing asks that husband and wife 'may share the gifts of *your* (God's) love and become one in mind and heart'. Here it is clear that human and divine love are intended to interpenetrate one another and that the partners are meant to grow in a love which they share with God. In the same sense we read in the third group of blessings at the end of the service: 'May Jesus, who loved his church to the end, *always fill your hearts with his love*'. A collect, that of the third wedding Mass, shows the appropriateness of celebrating marriage within the eucharist: 'May the mystery of Christ's unselfish love, which we celebrate in the eucharist, *increase their love for you and for each other*'. But perhaps the most striking text is to be found in one of the prefaces which may be used for the wedding Mass. It sees the whole plan of salvation in the terms of love and marriage:

> You created all of us to share your divine life.
> We see the high destiny of the human race in the love of husband
> and wife,
> which bears the imprint of your own divine love.
> Love is our origin,
> Love is our constant calling, love is our fulfilment in heaven.
> The love of man and woman
> is made holy in the sacrament of marriage
> and becomes the mirror of your everlasting joy.[8]

The message these and other texts of the rite convey is a simple if profound one and there is no reason to suppose that it will not be clear to the participants. The somewhat bleak injunction of the Constitution on the Liturgy has been surpassed and in the new marriage rite we have a liturgy that will teach what Christian love is and indeed what love *tout court* is. In the world in which we live this is a very important matter. If romantic love has brought with it certain gifts of tenderness, of sensibility, or perceptiveness and *Innerlichkeit* so that modern people have been able to love each other with an intensity and awareness that seems to be foreign to civilizations that have not known it, it has too often been debased. Love has become *mere* emotion, mere feeling so that people can say, when this emotional love has disappeared, that the marriage has come to an end. What the new marriage rite is saying is that love is above all self-giving whose supreme model is the self-giving of the Persons of the Trinity. They give love to each other and then pour out that same love upon all mankind: 'love is our origin'. God created us because he wanted us to share his love and it is with love that God throughout the ages has called us to himself. This calling and this divine self-giving, to us, reached its climax in Christ who 'gave himself up' to death (Ephesians 5:2) so that he might call into existence a people who, in covenant, would be bound to him by love. Of this union, achieved by a sacrificial love, marriage is the sacrament showing forth and making that love present to husband and wife. Love is self-giving not self-seeking and it is in the self-giving that marriage has its origin and the sacrament provides the guarantee of its continuance. This is expressed at the high point of the whole marriage service when the partners give themselves to each other 'to have and to hold from this day forward, for better for worse, for richer for poorer, in sickness and in health, to love and to cherish, till death do us part'. Nothing could be more inclusive and nothing could better express in concrete fashion the truth of the scriptures that marriage is the sacrament of divine love.

If married love, as we have described it, binds husband and wife together and is a sharing in the love God has shown for mankind through the ages, that means that it is a sharing in the *covenanted* love of God for mankind and this is why in the new rite marriage is spoken of in terms of covenant. It has been pointed out[9] that the Constitution on the Church in the Modern World never speaks of the marriage *contract* but prefers the more biblical term 'covenant' (*foedus matrimonialis*). This is reflected in the new texts. The Introduction (2) refers to marriage as arising 'in the *covenant* of marriage or irrevocable consent' of the partners, the consent evidently being the means by which the pact or covenant is formed. But this covenant is not merely a legal thing, a contract in secular terms. The contract is no more than an external sign, one among others even if an indispensable one, of the more fundamental thing, namely the covenant. This in turn is a sacrament-sign of *the* Covenant. Thus in the second preface of the wedding Mass we read: '. . . through Jesus Christ our Lord . . . you entered into a new covenant with your people . . . This outpouring of love in the new covenant of grace is symbolised in the marriage covenant that seals the love of husband and wife and reflects the divine plan of love.'[10]

As the whole history of salvation shows, the covenant is the expression in both the Old and the New Testaments of God's steadfast love for man. In the Old Testament two words are always associated:

mercy and faithfulness. God is faithful to his promises to rescue and redeem, he will not go back on his promises, he is always *there* offering his love. This saving love and faithfulness reached its supreme expression in the obedience of Christ to his Father, an obedience that carried him to the self-giving and death of the cross. The faithful love of Christ was also supremely creative; it brought into existence 'the wonderful sacrament of the church', the people of God, and it is of this love that marriage is the sacrament-sign, declaring in all the ordinariness of married life the mystery of God's unfailing love for man. It is this love · that the partners are pledging to each other and to God and the fidelity of marriage is not simply something imposed by law for the good of the partners and society. It is an exigency that arises from the very nature of the love they pledge to each other and insofar as they live in faithful love, they will be making the sign to the world of God's steadfast love present and active among the men and women of today. It is not surprising then that the Introduction (1), quoting the Constitution on the Church (11), can say that married people have their own special gift (*charisma*) among the people of God and it is a matter of experience that the devoted life of a Christian family bears constant witness to the reality of God's love at work in mankind.

But if it is of this kind of love that marriage is the sacrament-sign, it is also clear that it is a sign of a love that gives itself to the point of sacrifice. This is the plain teaching of the Letter to the Ephesians,[11] part of which has for so long formed part of the formula of the wedding Mass. But though this passage, taken by itself, gives important teaching on Christian marriage, that teaching is greatly deepened if it is put into its context. The chapter begins with a statement about divine love and its issue: 'Try, then, to imitate God, as children of his that he loves, and *follow Christ by loving as he loved you, giving himself up in our place as a fragrant offering and a sacrifice to God*'.[12] The self-giving of Christ was total and issued into the suffering and death of the cross. It is with this sort of love that husbands are required to love their wives and we may add, that wives are required to love their husbands. It implies a giving that is self-sacrificial. Put this way, it may sound dramatic, or even over-dramatic, and married people may say that they do not recognize their marriage in it. Maybe that is because they are right in the situation and since self-giving involves self-forgetfulness, they do not remember the innumerable occasions, great and small, when they have given themselves to each other. The outsider can often see this, especially as husband and wife grow old together and are moved, it would seem, by but a single spirit. In any case, it is of this self-sacrificial love that marriage is the sacrament as the partners themselves declare when they say that they take each other for better for worse, in sickness and in health, until death shall part them. And as they declare it, God comes and makes that love possible and fruitful in their lives. For the sacrament is not merely a sign of this love; it is the efficacious sign of this love.

Married love, then, is a covenanted, pledged love involving self-sacrifice. But this immediately suggests permanence. Marriage is not simply a consent but a commitment to a way of life and the emphasis is now not merely on consent or contract but on relationship which has its origin in consent and is protected by contract: 'The Council's teaching is not concerned with the contract as such, but rather with the whole institution of marriage, the *communitas* (the common life) of man and woman that is initiated by the contract. Many theologians therefore see the whole marriage *relationship* as the grace-giving sign or sacrament, which is initiated by the marriage consent.' This fits in with what has been said above that marriage and married love is a life of which the consent and the contract are but the initiating signs. The 'graces of state' are not just so many *consequences* of the once-for-all contract. Rather, 'the key to the sacramental nature of marriage is to see it as a man-and-woman partnership directed to integrate and perfect the partners as persons and as Christians, and eventually to civilise and Christianise the world at large'.[13]

Relationship means not only the more intimate and interpersonal life of the partners but also their whole way of life and it is not new doctrine to call marriage a permanent sacrament. Pius XI, in *Casti Connubii* (116), citing a passage from the sixteenth-century Bellarmine, could state that the sacrament of marriage can be considered in the moment of its accomplishment and in its permanency afterwards: 'This sacrament, in fact, is similar to the eucharist, which, likewise, is a sacrament not only in the moment of its accomplishment but also as long as it remains. For as long as husband and wife live, their fellowship is always the sacrament of Christ and his church.' This means that no less than the sacrament of baptism that manifests and effects the regeneration of man through the passion and resurrection of Christ, marriage reveals and makes present Christ's redeeming power and love in the most ordinary life of the most ordinary Christians living in the world.

For the eye of faith, Christ with his love is here present and active showing that life in all its secularity or 'profaneness', with all its tragedy, its sufferings, its needs and its joys, is taken up into the loving purpose of God who, through it, works out his saving purpose for mankind and first of all for the men and women who in this way enter into his covenanted love.

If contract is less emphasized in the church's current teaching on marriage, it none the less remains essential to it because of the greater realities of marriage of which we have spoken. It is the necessary sign of what is inwardly intended and since marriage is a union that brings into existence a new community, both church and state need to take cognizance of it. Normally, marriage implies community, the family, and communities affect the life of society generally. As the church has said tirelessly in modern times, the well-being of the state as of the Christian community itself is dependent on the well-being of the institution of marriage and of the family that arises from it. Contract remains important since in the days in which we live, when marriage is becoming a temporary union, sometimes entered into with little thought or preparation and dissolved, it would seem, almost at will, it is necessary to emphasize the binding nature of marriage of which the public contract is the sign and evidence. By it the partners declare their intention before church and state to enter into a life-long union.

Contract too is the guarantee of freedom of consent: all contracts to be binding and valid must be freely entered into and the law of the church has always insisted on this freedom. Since marriages in our society are no longer 'arranged' it might seem that this is an unimportant element. Yet people are getting married nowadays at a very early age and it is necessary to ensure that they are fully aware that they are entering into a life-long contract and that they are doing so with a fully free consent. Perhaps young people are no longer carried away by emotion as they were (or were alleged to be) in the great days of romantic love. We may think that they are highly sophisticated about the whole business of love and marriage. They may be so about sex, but what do they know of love and indeed what experience have they had of life? How the gravity of the affair is to be brought home to them is another matter and there is at least one celibate priest who feels himself not a little handicapped in trying to do so.

All these—fidelity, contract and freedom of consent—are clearly set out in the new marriage rite.

In the first address the celebrant reminds the bride and bridegroom that Christ has provided them with a special sacrament which enables them to take up 'the duties of marriage in mutual and lasting fidelity'. This is put with more force in vows they make when they promise 'to love and to cherish each other' until death shall part them. Then, as the prayers for the blessing of the ring(s) and the formula for putting it on reveal, the ring is the outward sign of the partners' fidelity: 'the ring which you give' is 'a sign of your love and fidelity'; and, 'Take this ring as a sign of my love and fidelity' (27, 28). Finally, in the collect of the first formulary of the wedding Mass this doctrine is combined with that of the co-inherence of the divine love with the human:

Father,
you have made the bond of marriage
a holy mystery,
a symbol of Christ's love for his church.
Hear our prayers for N. and N.
With faith in you and in each other
they pledge their love today.
May their lives bear witness to the reality of that love.[14]

Contract and consent are inseparably bound up together in the various declarations and promises the partners make at the beginning of the marriage service. They freely undertake the obligations of marriage, they declare themselves ready to give themselves to each other without reserve and to accept lovingly such children as God may send them. Freedom is declared in the formula which has been taken over from the civil marriage rite and it and the contractual element can be seen in the questions and answers which (for England) have been retained from the former rite. The combination here of the civil and ecclesiastical formulas is a valuable indication of the importance that both church and state attribute to free consent and the permanence of the union. Likewise, it is a further sign that in marriage the 'sacred' and the 'secular', religion and life, are more closely associated than perhaps in any other area of Christian practice.

In the institution of marriage it has been realized very acutely in recent times that there is always the possibility of tension between the different ends of marriage. In the past the emphasis was rather that marriage was 'for' the procreation of children, what used to be called 'the primary end of marriage'. The Constitution on the Church in the Modern World refused to endorse this way of thinking and its views are found also in the new marriage rite, but rather more emphasized in the 1990 edition (10). Both documents teach that marriage is for the human and spiritual perfection of the husband and wife *and also* for the procreation of children and their education. Thus in the Introduction (3) there is the statement which is very close to a passage in the Constitution on the Church in the Modern World (48, 49): 'Christian couples nourish and develop their marriage by undivided affection, which wells up from the fountain of divine love, while in the merging of human and divine love, they remain faithful in body and mind, in good times and in bad'.[15] But married love, while destined for the perfecting and indeed salvation of the partners, is intended to issue into the procreation of children which is the sign not only of the human fruitfulness of the marriage but of God's love which in this way is revealed to be present in the marriage. As the Council put it: 'Authentic married love is caught up into divine love and is governed and enriched by Christ's redeeming power and the saving activity of the Church. Thus this love can lead the spouses to God with powerful effect and can aid and strengthen them in the sublime office of being a father or a mother.'[16]

But the Introduction (4) carefully repeats the teaching of the Constitution on the Church in the Modern World (50)[17] that procreation and the education of the children *together* constitute an end of marriage. The married couple are instructed (4) that 'by their very nature, the institution of matrimony and wedded love are ordained for the procreation and education of children and find in them their ultimate crown. Therefore, married Christians, while not considering the other purposes of marriage of less account, should be steadfast and ready to cooperate with the love of the Creator and Saviour, who through them will constantly enrich and enlarge his own family.'[18] Much has been written about this tension and there is no need to go into it here. The documents however do suggest that irresponsible procreation is not what is meant by this 'end of marriage' and that the sincere concern of husband and wife to produce a balanced family in which all the children will have their due meed of love and attention is also the sign of God's creative love in the marriage.

The acceptance of children is, as we have remarked, found in the first undertaking of the bride and bridegroom and while the doctrine mentioned above can hardly form the subject of a prayer, we find that three nuptial blessings pray that the marriage will be blessed with children, and their function as parents is underlined.

There is a final teaching which receives great emphasis in several parts of the service. The love of husband and wife, a love that is concretized in the gift of children, must be turned out from themselves and even from the family, first to the church and then the world:

> You are the loving Father of the world of nature;
> you are the loving Father of the new creation of grace.
> In Christian marriage you bring together the two orders of
> creation;
> nature's gift of children enriches the world
> and your grace enriches also your church.[19]

Elsewhere it is emphasized that Christian marriage is a witness in the world and to the world of God's ever-present love for mankind and the Christian community is conceived of as a community that is going to transmit that love to society around it. The theme is found in various places but notably in a blessing that will in fact be the last words the bride and bridegroom will hear before they leave the church:

> May you always bear witness to the love of God in this world
> so that the afflicted and the needy
> will find in you generous friends,
> and welcome you into the joys of heaven.[20]

The liturgy of marriage

Though profoundly rooted in the experience and customs of mankind, marriage has always had a rite that is basically simple, namely the exchange of consent and the giving of one partner to the other. This had been elaborated in the Catholic tradition by its association with the eucharist and in the Byzantine rite by the crowning of the spouses. Yet its simplicity remains. This is true, in spite of an appearance of complexity, in the new Order.

Like other sacramental rites, it takes place within the Mass, after the homily, and not before it as it did throughout the Middle Ages and until recently. Since marriage is now described as a covenant and a sign of the covenant between God and man and since the eucharist is

~

supremely the renewal of that covenant among men today, the appropriateness of this arrangement is obvious.

The first part of the marriage rite proper is concerned to secure an understanding of the obligations of marriage, the freedom of the partners and their mutual self-giving. Freedom to marry and intention to do so will already have been obtained before the marriage ceremony and these statements are to be seen as *public* declarations of the interior sentiments of the couple. In this sense they are sacramental signs.

It is worth pointing out that these texts are conflated from various sources. The declaration of freedom, to be used only in England and Wales, beginning 'I do solemnly declare . . .' is taken from the civil rite and the words are always to be recited exactly as they are with the full names of the bride and bridegroom. The words of consent 'A.B. will you take C.D. here present . . .' are from the former Roman Ritual[21] and were part of the rite of marriage in use in England until the new Order. The formula for the exchange of promises comes from three sources: 'I call upon these persons present . . .' (which must always be repeated exactly and with full names) comes from the civil rite; 'I A.B. do take thee, C.D. to be my lawful wedded wife, to have and to hold . . .' comes from the old Sarum rite; and the phrase 'to love and to cherish' comes apparently from the Book of Common Prayer.[22] The sentence by which the celebrant receives the consent of the bride and bridegroom replaces the very contentious one 'I join you together in matrimony, in the name of the Father . . .'. This did not appear in marriage rites before the fifteenth century but made a deep impression and its meaning was fiercely debated at the Council of Trent.[23] Some thought it was the 'form' of the sacrament and that the priest was the sacramental minister – a view which has been held since, but which in the West seems now to be abandoned.[24] Instead of this equivocal text a more general one is substituted in which the intervention of God is underlined. The last phrase, from the gospel (Matthew 19:6), which likewise does not seem to have been in marriage rites generally in the Middle Ages until the fifteenth century, has been retained.[25]

The blessing of the ring(s): The handing over of the ring(s) and its blessing ultimately derives from the *sponsalia* or engagement ceremony of the Middle Ages. It has long lost connection with it and the new Order merely recognizes the now age-long custom of giving a ring or rings during the marriage service. The first blessing given in the text of the rite is the shortest and is apparently new. The second is from the old rite and dates from as early as the eleventh century.[26] The third is notable for the fact that it is a blessing of the bride and bridegroom rather than of the ring. It may be seen as a text unfolding the meaning of the blessing of a ring or any other object. It is really a blessing of the people who will wear it or use it. The symbolism of the ring is again underlined in the formula for putting it on the finger of the bride: it is a sign of both love and fidelity.[27]

The intercessions ('Bidding Prayers') follow. The nuptial blessing is given immediately after the Lord's Prayer.

The wedding Mass: From very early times marriage has been associated with the eucharist. Tertullian saw the 'offering' (of the eucharist) as 'confirming' the marriage of Christians,[28] and the Roman tradition, as represented by the sacramentaries,[29] had a wedding Mass formula in which are to be found three separate versions of the nuptial blessing, as it was in the former Roman Missal. But a church wedding was not, it seems, obligatory[30] and it was not until the social order in Europe had broken down in the seventh and eighth centuries that the church, to protect freedom and prevent clandestine marriages, felt the need to intervene in an authoritative manner. Then the marriage came to be performed (literally) *in facie ecclesiae*, before the church doors, and in the presence of the parish priest and witnesses. From there the whole party moved into church for the Mass.[31] The last stage has been reached by the new Order which requires the marriage to be celebrated *within* the Mass.

In the new missal there are three formulas for the wedding Mass all of which are new and all the texts emphasize love and covenant.

The lectionary: This too provides a whole new range of texts for use at the wedding Mass and their selection for different marriages is a matter requiring tact and discernment. Most of the Old Testament readings will be appropriate only to a congregation that is sufficiently instructed in the Bible. It is not difficult to guess the effect of reading 'I hear my Beloved . . . leaping on the mountains . . .' though one supposes that the last part could be used: 'Love is strong as death . . .'. Genesis 1:26–28, 31 and 2:18–24 can be used in conjunction with Ephesians 5:2, 21–33 and Matthew 19:3–6. Jeremiah (31:31–34) with his reference to the covenant is usable and it is perhaps a pity that room was not found somewhere in the Mass-formulas for Jeremiah 31:3: 'I have loved you with an everlasting love . . .'.

Of the non-gospel New Testament readings the most appropriate will be Romans 12:1–2, 9–18, 1 Corinthians 12:31–13:8 (the song of love), Ephesians 5 and the two passages from 1 John 3:18–24 and 4:7–12. These, with the reading from 1 Corinthians, give the doctrine of love which in the marriage rite receives its particular and telling application. Of the psalms provided, 32, 33, 102, 127 and 144 combine most easily with texts speaking of love.

The gospel material is very various going from the beatitudes according to Matthew to the texts on love from St John. Experience shows that the Johannine texts make the deepest impact (15:9–12, perhaps the best of all with its reference to joy, 15:12–16, 17:20–26). All the scripture texts give plenty of scope but perhaps their chief contribution is the emphasis they give to love, thus echoing the marriage rite itself.

The intercessions ('Bidding Prayers') are to be used even when the marriage is celebrated apart from the Mass. The celebrant may compose them and it would be highly appropriate to work them out with the bride and bridegroom. To keep the marriage rite intact the creed, if it is to be said, should be recited *after* the intercessions.

As full a participation as is possible in the circumstances is urged for the bride and bridegroom and consequently the Order recommends that they should bring the offerings to the altar. This is not only the restoration of an ancient custom but is meant to be a symbol of their joint self-offering to God. In practice, it will mean that the bread and wine and other offerings they and the assembly may care to make will have to be placed near the sanctuary. Otherwise, the bride and bridegroom will have a long walk up and down the church.

For the eucharist proper three prefaces are provided (from two of which we have quoted above) which again give much the same teaching as is to be found elsewhere.

The nuptial blessing: A small change in the Order of Mass brings this prayer nearer communion and thus more clearly indicates that the covenant of marriage is sealed by the covenant of the eucharist. After the Lord's Prayer, the embolism is omitted, the nuptial blessing is said and then follow immediately the prayer for peace, the giving of the 'peace', which the bride and bridegroom exchange, and communion, usually in both kinds.

Of the three prayers said at this point and usually known as the nuptial blessing, the first has its origins in the old sacramentaries. The version in use until recently is to be found in the Gregorian Sacramentary. It is a fine prayer but, as the Fathers of Vatican II observed, it needed to be changed since it was addressed exclusively to the bride.[32] Occasion was taken to revise or rather re-write the prayer, some questionable remarks have been removed, the models of conjugal fidelity are subsumed under a general phrase and a blessing for the bridegroom is included. The substance of the prayer has been retained but some difficulties remain[33] and it is in any case a little long. It has had to be changed to include the blessing of the husband and has thus turned the prayer from its original sense. It was, as is well known, a blessing of the *bride* and it was *she* who figured the church. Adjustments have been made to show that it is the marriage of husband and wife that is the symbol of the union of Christ with his church. However, towards the end passages have been added concerning the witness that marriage should give and family life.

Of the two new texts, which are more specifically blessings, the second is the simpler, more moralistic in tone and makes no attempt to convey the symbolism of Christian marriage. The first expresses quite adequately that symbolism. Marriage has its origin in the beginning of the human race and it was God's plan to reveal his love through it for it is 'an image of the covenant between you and your people' and so, in the Christian dispensation, becomes 'a sign of the marriage between Christ and his Church'. Love, covenant, people, Christ and church, that is the order of the thought and though it is not without difficulty for catechetical purposes, it is clear and can be handled if care is given to the matter. This prayer, as well as speaking of witness and family, is much more concrete in its language: it asks in simple language all can understand that the bride may be a good wife and mother and that the bridegroom may be a faithful husband and father. When couples are helped to choose the texts of their own marriage liturgy, they almost always go for this one.[34]

The concluding blessings: These are particular examples of the more solemn blessings that may now be given at the end of every Mass, are for the most part good in quality[35] and in one way or another sum up most of the themes which have been prominent throughout the rite. For England and Wales there is an alternative taken from the Book of Common Prayer which seems to be remotely related to the final blessing of the Sarum rite.[36]

The Ordo Celebrandi Matrimonium (1990)

In response to requests and suggestions from bishops' conferences at one time or another the Congregation for Worship has drawn up the above-mentioned second edition. We may note the following.

The expanded *Praenotanda* cover the importance and dignity of marriage, preparation for marriage and who is responsible for it, the celebration of marriage and adaptation.

The first has been sufficiently expounded above, the second section is new and reveals the concern of the church about marriage and how often it is entered into without adequate preparation. The responsibility for it falls in the first place on the clergy, bishops and parish priests and their assistants. The local community should also be concerned and lay people are recommended as helpers (26) in the preparation of the couple.

The preparation falls under four heads: the general catechesis that is given by bishops and clergy through which the true meaning of marriage is made known as well as the duties of the married. Secondly, there is the all-important personal preparation of the couple themselves. Such preparation may need to go far beyond instruction about Christian marriage: it may be necessary to revive faith and encourage the couple to return to religious practice. It is a matter of experience that a couple often see marriage as the beginning of a renewed Christian life.

It is interesting to observe that the General Introduction sees the *celebration* of marriage as throwing light on the sacramental mystery of unity and fruitful love that is in fact Christian marriage. The sense is that good and joyful celebration of the sacrament of marriage conveys its own message and is an important formative event.

Finally, the introduction urges that there should be post-celebration care for the couples. This is not at all easy to ensure. Often they go away from their parish to live elsewhere and the local clergy lose touch with them, sometimes very soon.

There is of course much else in the General Introduction but space does not allow of a full account. One notes simply that the church urges once again that the celebration of Christian marriage should be regarded as a community event and not as simply a private one. The

~

celebrant should be mindful of those among the congregation, whether Catholics or not, who do not practise their religion. When there is a nuptial Mass it is assumed that the couple will receive communion in both kinds (unless of course one is not a Catholic). Of the chants or songs to be sung the introduction insists that they should be suitable (*apti*) to the rite of marriage and should express the faith of the church.

There are one or two small changes in the rite (e.g. an acclamation by the people present after the exchange of consent) which are very acceptable and a change of text in the first nuptial blessing invoking the grace of the Holy Spirit. To the three nuptial blessings another has been added which like the second and third in the baptismal rite has a response after each section, 'Blessed be God'.

As for adaptation(s), the wide faculty given to conferences of bishops to draw up local rites in accordance with their traditions is repeated (40–44). Such adapted rites have to be approved by the Apostolic See.

A marriage rite for England and Wales

Acting on the above permission the National Liturgy Commission has for some years been working out a rite that will be proper to England and Wales and that draws on the wealth of material to be found in medieval sources and on some of the modern rites of other churches.

It is impossible to give here a full account of this work, which is now complete but which has to be presented to the Conference of Bishops of England and Wales, criticized and accepted or rejected by them, and on acceptance sent to Rome for definitive approval. However, an outline will be of interest.

First, the principle adopted by the revisers is of the highest importance. They have aimed at providing a rite that can be celebrated *in stages*, as for instance in the RCIA. Marriage is a 'rite of passage', one of the most ancient known to the human race, and this should be restored to use. Thus there are rites and prayers for engagement and for the time of engagement–a restoration of the old *sponsalia*. They can of course be used during the period of preparation.

There is the celebration of marriage and the rite has been a little re-arranged, or added to (as indeed has the Roman revised rite). Thus there is a preliminary address, declaration of intent and affirmation by the congregation. The liturgy of the word follows and after it the

~

exchange of consent or promises (often called 'vows'). Then the people may sing an acclamation. The signing of the registers takes place now and the ring(s) is then blessed and given.

The exchange of gifts has been restored with alternative texts. A gift from the community may also be presented. After the nuptial blessing (several to choose from) the couple will be invited to voice their own prayer which they will have prepared previously (suggestions provided). The rest of the wedding Mass is as usual. Communion in both kinds will be recommended for all present. The post-marriage period is provided for with a series of blessings: over food and drink, of the new home, and prayers to be used by the couple. In addition and looking ahead there are rites and prayers for reconciliations and renewals of promises as also for anniversaries.

Mutatis mutandis the above rite of marriage can be used when there is no Mass.

Pastoral considerations

That the pastoral care of couples before and after marriage is one of the primary duties of the parish clergy goes without saying but it is a subject that goes beyond the scope of this book. We must restrict ourselves to the immediate preparation before marriage.

In more recent years, thanks to a deepening understanding of the importance of marriage on the part of both the clergy and the laity, interviews before marriage have become *de rigueur*. And the purpose of these interviews is not simply instruction to ensure that the couples understand that they cannot get divorced 'because the church says so' nor yet to dispel unacceptable notions of birth prevention. They are to be prepared mentally and spiritually for the marriage they have already decided to undertake. Where both partners are Catholics, they should be encouraged to intensify their prayer-life, to make a particularly thorough confession and, if they do not already do so, to receive communion as often as possible. Mentally, they need to be led to a deeper understanding of the sacrament of marriage and for this purpose far the best material is the texts of the marriage liturgy itself. Copies of the marriage rite should be made available to them and the talks will take the texts as the point of departure. In the course of such instruction, it seems important to deepen their understanding of human love for it is this, as the texts say, that is taken up by and into the love of God.

On the other hand, there are difficulties for a celibate priest in giving such instruction. Since he has had no experience of married life, it ill becomes him to be heavily moralistic about its duties. With people of normal intelligence, an exposition of the meaning of marriage will enable the couple to draw their own conclusions. Where there is serious intent and goodwill – and experience shows that this is nearly always present – they will readily take up points themselves and apply them to their own situation.[37]

Where one or both of the partners is of weak faith, there is of course more to be done but experience shows that on the occasion of marriage, people in this condition can be brought back to religious practice – at least for a time – and their faith can be revived. The attitude of the priest here is of the greatest importance. Such people need to be encouraged, they may need a little elementary instruction on certain aspects of religious practice which they have forgotten and the duties of worship and prayer will have to be brought before them. They too of course will need to go to confession and here great tact is necessary. It may well be that they choose not to have a wedding Mass and if they do so choose, it would seem to be unwise to press them. The congregation may be largely non-Christian and it does not seem wise to expose the 'holy mysteries' to them. The marriage service with its scripture readings, prayers, hymns and blessings is more than adequate to meet the situation.[38]

The situation is sometimes more difficult. People of little or apparently no faith present themselves for marriage and while this situation is fraught with difficulties of one sort or another, it seems necessary to confront such people with the fact that marriage, like all the sacraments, is a sacrament of faith, both requiring faith and, in its celebration, expressing it. The problem is similiar to that of 'delaying' baptism and the possible unpleasantness is as acute. But the question has to be asked: is it right to admit to a sacrament of faith those without the latter even if long ago they were baptized? The spiritual preparation of such people of course is immensely difficult and often little enough can be done.

The Exhortation *Familiaris consortio* (*On the Christian Family*, 68, 1981) is aware of this and similar problems. It stretches the charity of the church (which in effect means its ministers) to the limit. So long as there is a spark of faith and goodwill ministers must, after whatever preparation is possible, allow such people to marry in church. Yet the Pope recognizes that there are even more difficult cases when the couple 'reject explicitly and formally what the church intends to do when the marriage of baptized persons is celebrated'. In these cases the minister must refuse to admit them to marriage in church. One would add that consultation of the appropriate authority would be the most prudent course to take. The bishop or his delegate can make the necessary decision and his decision eliminates the appearance of any personal element in the minister's decision.

Then of course there are the mixed (religious) marriages. Some of the 'myth' that has surrounded such marriages in the past has disappeared. They no longer appear to be the 'evil' some thought them and the *Motu proprio* of 31 March 1970 has done much to ease the situation. However, it needs to be used in a human and pastoral and not a rigidly canonical way. In interview the attitude of the priest should be warm and welcoming and he should realize that often for the non-Catholic partner it will be the first time that he (or she) has ever had personal contact with a clergyman of any kind. The impressions such people carry away will be important in determining their attitude to religious practice (baptism of children, their first communion, etc.) in the future. But here too there is often, one would say usually, a chance to revive religious faith and to encourage a re-thinking of attitudes.[39] It goes without saying that the *celebration* of these marriages is a matter of the greatest importance. The non-Catholic partner must be made to feel at home in the church and the ceremony must be done with all the care that is possible. It should strike a note of joy and not gloom and the clergy should realize that it offers an opportunity to proclaim the gospel to people who hear it all too rarely.[40]

In the preparation of the marriage liturgy there are a number of matters to be attended to. In going over the texts the bride and bridegroom should be encouraged (and guided) to choose the texts, readings, collects, prefaces, nuptial blessing and final blessing that they think best meets their own case. Likewise, the hymns to be sung and where in the service they are to be sung will be a matter of discussion and again guidance. Not all that is wanted is appropriate.[41] Finally, there will be the rehearsal which (rightly) almost all people of today demand. In any case, it is the best tranquillizer in the world.

Marriage outside the Mass

The rite is exactly the same as within the Mass and no difference is made between fully Catholic marriages and mixed marriages. Both take place within a ministry of the word, including the homily. There is a greeting, prayer (one of the collects from the Mass-formulas will be appropriate), the scripture readings with a psalm or a hymn and the homily which is to be 'drawn from the sacred text' (42).

The rest is as above. 'The entire rite may be concluded with the Lord's prayer' and with the blessings (51).

In the case of marriage between a Catholic and an unbaptized person there is a modified service which however does not differ in pattern from the one given above (55–66).

Notes
~

[1] The Order of Marriage, 1st ed., was issued in 1969. The rite for England and Wales was approved in 1970, and there have been various editions of it. The Order of Marriage, 2nd rev. ed. (Latin), was promulgated in 1990. The **Praenotanda** (General Introduction) are much extended and are numbered from 1 to 44. For the new edition with commentary see **Notitiae**, 287 (June 1990), 6, pp. 300–27.

[2] Extracts from this and other Council documents will be found conveniently arranged in Clifford Howell, SJ, '**Companion to the New Order of Marriage** (Alcester/Dublin, 1970), pp. 29–40.

[3] In the **Ordo Administrandi Sacramenta**, originally edited by Bishop Richard Challoner, there was a homily written by him for use at the service. It survived until this century.

[4] **Rituale Romanum**, VII, ii. Was it merely an accident that the service was placed in the book immediately after the funeral rites? Certain it is that about a hundred years ago on the occasion of an uncle's wedding the celebrant—an ancient canon—began reading the funeral service over the bewildered pair until the bridegroom protested!

[5] That is of course with the exception of the Eastern churches which retain their own. In medieval England (and in other countries too) the liturgy of marriage was a gay and friendly affair. After the **Pax** in the wedding Mass the bridegroom kissed the bride. The Mass-formula was that of the votive Mass of the Holy Trinity with 'proper' readings and if it was not a very satisfactory text, it was one used in England for occasions of rejoicing and thanksgiving (see **The Church at Prayer**, III: **The Sacraments**, ed. A. G. Martimort (ET, Collegeville, MN/London, 1988), pp. 192–201; F. Procter and W. H. Frere, **A New History of the Book of Common Prayer** (1965 ed.), p. 611).

[6] There has almost certainly been an inter-reaction of both on each other though the literature on the subject, which is vast, going back to the early thirties, seems at

first to have been purely clerical. One remembers H. Dom's fruitful book which however authority suppressed at the time, at least *donec corrigatur*. In more recent years the laity have written a good deal on the subject. No attempt is made here to give a bibliography: it is too great.

[7] Chapter 1.

[8] ICEL translation. The Latin, in the last sentence, speaks of the 'mystery' of holy matrimony which is the **signum** of God's love. The ICEL translation is, I think, very good indeed and these two words give great difficulty in translation. You cannot say 'the mystery of marriage'! Nor I think would 'sacrament' for **signum** have conveyed that marriage is the 'sacrament-sign' of God's love. But perhaps it is worth while pointing out what the Latin actually says. I have ventured to retranslate the text into more inclusive terms.

[9] See D. O'Callaghan, 'Marriage as Sacrament', **Concilium**, 5 no. 6, pp. 101-10, quoted by R. L. Stewart, 'Marriage: the New Rite', **Life and Worship** (October 1970), p. 13.

[10] ICEL translation.

[11] Ephesians 5:21-33. It is still one of the readings that may be used though it needs to be used with discretion. In a 'mixed' congregation there will be many who cannot understand its relevance since they have not the background to do so.

[12] Ephesians 5:1, 2. This passage has been inserted into the Lectionary.

[13] Stewart, **art. cit.**, p. 14, the second quotation being from O'Callaghan, **art. cit.**, p. 104.

[14] ICEL translation.

[15] ICEL translation. 'Merging' comes from the translation of the Constitution in **Documents of Vatican II**, p. 253, and is perhaps a little strong for **sociantes**. A **socius** is one who 'goes with' another and is hardly 'merged' in the other. However, Lewis and Short, **s.v. sociare**, indicates that it can mean 'united', at least for abstract things.

[16] Constitution on the Church in the Modern World, 48, **ed. cit.**, p. 251.

[17] **Ed. cit.**, p. 254.

[18] ICEL translation.

[19] 115; first Preface of the wedding Mass; ICEL translation.

[20] 37; ICEL translation.

[21] VII, ii.

[22] The text from the Sarum Manual is given accessibly in Procter and Frere, **Book of Common Prayer**, 1905 ed., reprint 1965, p. 614. The phrase 'to love and to cherish' seems to replace the bride's 'to be bonere and buxum in bed and at board' of the Sarum text.

[23] See A. Duval, 'La formule "Ego vos coniungo" . . . au concile de Trente', **La Maison-Dieu**, 99 (1969).

[24] P. M. Gy, **LMD**, 99, p. 134, thinks that the expression 'ministers of the sacrament' as applied to the spouses is not very happy. He would prefer to say 'the spouses themselves form the sacrament'. The difficulty seems to lie in an understanding of what is meant by 'minister'. In a sense and whatever may be held as to who are the 'makers' of matrimony, the priest, apart from the most exceptional circumstances, is the indispensable minister and with the couple does celebrate the sacrament.

[25] R. Mouret, 'Le rituel français du Mariage', **LMD**, 99, p. 190.

[26] See Gy, **art. cit.**, p. 135.

[27] The French word for the wedding ring, *alliance*, expresses this and also recalls the covenant which marriage is. The same word is used in French for the covenant between God and his people.

[28] Cited in Gy, *art. cit.*, p. 135, n. 29. He refers to **Ad Uxorem**, II, 8. Tixeront sees in the *oblatio* of the text a reference to the eucharist, **Hist. des dogmes**, 1, p. 452.

[29] Verona, 1105–10 (pp. 139–40), Gelasian, 1443–55 (pp. 208–10), the Gregorian, 200 (pp. 110–12).

[30] Cf. E. Schillebeeckx, **Marriage, Secular Reality and Saving Mystery** (1965), pp. 18–56.

[31] The introit, sung during the procession, was the well-known Psalm 127(128), for long and for obvious reasons used on the occasion of marriage.

[32] CL 78.

[33] E.g. '(Marriage) . . . symbolises the marriage of Christ and his Church'. Put like that it will not be understood by those unfamiliar with the scriptures. The same teaching in more assimilable form is given elsewhere.

[34] It should be noted that local conferences of bishops may have others composed (cf. Introduction, 17).

[35] In the second set it is a pity that ICEL could think of nothing better than the phrase 'in good times and in bad'.

[36] Cf. Procter and Frere, **Book of Common Prayer**, 1905, p. 617, n. 1.

[37] Where it is a question of what has been conventionally called 'the use of marriage', lay help would seem to be a necessity. This can often be got at Marriage Guidance Centres but there are far too few Catholic ones and more ought to be founded in every part of every diocese.

[38] Clerics sometimes have an exaggerated notion of what the laity, especially those of weaker faith or none, look for in a church service. Provided it is done well and with sincerity, they do not look for any elaborate ceremonial. The 1990 Order approves of this view and states that sometimes a Mass should not be celebrated (29).

[39] Inter-church marriages are in a different category. For the preparation they present fewer difficulties though the subsequent pastoral care is both necessary and a matter calling for great tact. See **The Joint Care of Inter-Church Marriages**, the Joint Working Group of the British Council of Churches and the Roman Catholic Church (BCC, London).

[40] Needless to say, denunciatioris of divorce will hardly strike the right note and in the past some preachers have not been able to restrain themselves.

[41] Like the mother who insisted on a hymn paraphrase of the **De profundis** because, as the event proved, she was the only one who could sing it. Which she did in an ageing contralto. But this was years ago when things were less well ordered.

EIGHT

Holy Order[1]

~~~~~~~

S INCE THE liturgy of holy orders was revised and simplified in 1968 it is difficult to recall its former complexity. As you climbed up the sacred ladder so the complexity increased: vestings, anointings and the delivery of various cultic articles occurred at one point or another with a bewildering abandon. And if thirty or forty years ago you had asked lay people what was the essential rite they would almost certainly have answered that it was the anointing of the hands for the priest and of the head for the bishop. Likewise it was commonly thought by both priests and laity that the priesthood was the highest dignity or 'power' that could be given to a human being with the consequence that bishops appeared as a sort of sacramental afterthought. No doubt theology at this time was beginning to change or rather return to an older tradition but popular views remained the same. In other words the liturgy was putting the emphasis in the wrong place and popular theology and sentiment had got the proportions wrong. The Second Vatican Council, notably in the Constitution on the Church, reversed these notions and, taking up the theology that had been developing for some years, taught that the episcopate is the *primary* participation in the priesthood of Christ and that by it is conferred the fullness of the priesthood. The key passages are the following:

> In the bishops, therefore, for whom priests are assistants, our Lord Jesus Christ, the supreme High Priest, is present in the midst of those who believe. For sitting at the right hand of God the Father, he is not absent from the gathering of his high priests, but above all through their excellent service he is preaching the word of God to all nations, and constantly administering the sacraments of faith to those who believe.

> They are shepherds of the Lord's flock, they are servants of Christ, stewards of the mysteries of Christ and witnesses to the ministration of the Spirit to make men just. Thus

~

For the discharging of such great duties, the apostles were enriched by Christ with a special outpouring of the Holy Spirit, who came upon them. This spiritual gift they passed on to their helpers by the imposition of hands, and it has been transmitted down to us in episcopal consecration. This sacred synod teaches that by episcopal consecration is conferred the *fullness of the sacrament of orders*, that fullness which in the Church's liturgical practice and in the language of the holy Fathers of the Church is undoubtedly called the high priesthood, the apex of the sacred ministry.[2]

This decisively restored the episcopate to its ancient place in the hierarchy of holy order and presumably settles once for all this particular controversy. No doubt the Council does not solve all problems connected with papacy, episcopate and priesthood, for the relationships at least in practical terms between the papacy and the episcopate on the one hand and between the episcopate and the priesthood or presbyterate on the other still remain partially undefined. This much at least is clear: bishops are not delegates of the Pope nor are they, in the rude language used by some at one time or another, 'Pope's curates'. Their order is of divine institution and with him they share a common pastoral care over the whole church.[3] *Vis-à-vis* his clergy the bishop is not an overlord. With them he shares a community of sacrament and presbyters assume their role, with their liturgical and pastoral functions enhanced, as his counsellors, as his *consilium* of the sort we discern in the *Apostolic Tradition* of Hippolytus.[4] The episcopate and the presbyterate form a sacramental communion of which brotherly co-operation is the consequence, that is, not merely in the moral order. It is an exigency of what both *are*.[5]

A third change brought about by the Council is that the diaconate has been restored as a permanent ministry in the church.[6] For centuries merely a stage on the way to the priesthood, it can now once again play its part in the life of the church. It is for this reason that the functions of the deacon have been somewhat extended and although there has not yet been time to see exactly what his work is likely to be, there is no doubt that in principle he could be a most valuable aid to the pastoral clergy. The restored diaconate also envisages married deacons (there are some already at work in parishes) and these two factors, permanence and marriage, have made it necessary to modify the ordination rite.

In addition, the four minor orders, now to be called 'ministries', have been reduced to two; tonsure and the subdiaconate have been suppressed and two new elements have been added: admission to the clerical state and the public declaration of intention to observe celibacy for all but married deacons.

With the promulgation of the documents on 'ministries' and the other two rites, the revision of this part of the Roman Pontifical is now complete.

Ordination to the episcopate: the liturgy

The order of events as given in the *Pontificale Romanum* of 1968 is as follows: the ordination of deacons, secondly of priests and finally of bishops. But since the Council re-established the primacy of the episcopate it will be best to reverse the order of the Pontifical. Secondly, since the liturgy of holy orders is less familiar to the laity, a synopsis of the liturgy of each order will be given first and commentary on them will follow.

Like other sacramental acts, the ordination of a bishop takes place at the end of the ministry of the word.

1. Immediately after the gospel the *Veni, Creator Spiritus* or a similar hymn is sung.

2. The bishop-elect approaches the principal consecrator and is presented.

3. The homily by the principal consecrator.

4. The interrogatory, that is, the traditional questions concerning a bishop's obligations and duties.

5. Prayer of the assembly in the form of the Litany of the Saints.

6. The bishop-elect kneels before the principal consecrator who in silence lays hands on his head. The co-consecrators do likewise after him.

7. The principal consecrator places the gospel book on the elect's head and two deacons hold it there.

8. There follows the consecration prayer.

9. The principal consecrator anoints the elect's head with chrism.

10. He then gives him the gospel book, the ring, places the mitre on his head and puts the staff (crozier) in his hand.

11. If the elect is in his own cathedral he is now led to the episcopal chair (*cathedra*) and he and the consecrating bishops exchange the kiss of peace.

12. For the end of the Mass a special blessing is provided.

The theology of the episcopate

Perhaps 'theology' is too grand a word for what follows but, as is agreed by most scholars, it is possible to deduce a theology from a liturgy and the picture of the episcopate is clear in the new formulas for the ordination of a bishop.[7] There are two places where this theology may be discerned, first in the homily, the themes of which are suggested by the Pontifical, and second, the consecration prayer.

The homily is not a fixed text of the rite. It is no more than a suggestion to the consecrating bishop and it is difficult to determine what 'external' authority it may have. But here, and in most of the other Orders, the text is heavily dependent on the documents of Vatican II whose authority it will naturally enjoy. The homily is in fact not much more than a catena of texts from the Constitution on the Church which, as we have observed above, restored the episcopate to its earlier place in the sacrament of holy orders. The main lines of the homily then will be fairly familiar but it will be worth while to give a synopsis here.

Christ, sent by the Father into the world to redeem it, appointed the apostles to continue his work of preaching, sanctifying and ruling the flock entrusted to them. The bishops, who are the successors of the apostles, receive the gift of the Holy Spirit by the imposition of hands and thereby receive also 'the fulness of the sacrament of Order'. This 'tradition' has come down through the succession of bishops from the time of the apostles until now so that the redeeming work of Christ may be continued. Thus is expressed the Council teaching on the place of the episcopate in the structure of the ministry and it is interesting to observe that the order is spoken of in terms of 'gift', presumably *charisma*, which at once removes the whole notion of holy order out of the legal and juridical sphere. The term 'power' is nowhere used in the whole rite and yet it was largely in terms of power that the episcopate–presbyterate was discussed for many centuries.

In the next paragraph we have a strong suggestion of a mystery-theology of the sacrament. Christ, the high priest, is *present* in the bishop with his presbyters. The *presbyterium* or the *consilium*, as in the days of Hippolytus, is the *locus* of Christ. It is he who preaches in the bishop, he who is present in him when he celebrates the mysteries of faith and dispenses them to the people[8] and it is he who through the bishop adds new members to his body. Through him Christ leads the people in their earthly pilgrimage to their home in heaven. This teaching seems to be

~

a particular application of the Council's teaching that Christ is present in the liturgy which is 'an exercise of the priestly office of Jesus Christ'.[9] It is however a little surprising that the homily does not give expression to another truth of the Council that there is only one priesthood, that of Christ, of which holy orders are ministries.

Concluding the first part of the homily the consecrating bishop addresses the people and asks them to receive among them him 'whom we are co-opting (*cooptamus*) into our college'.

Then he turns to address the bishop-elect personally. He is taken from among men and is appointed to act for men in their relations with God (Hebrews 5:1). He is to be their servant, for the episcopate is not an honour but a responsibility (*nomen est operis non honoris*)[10] and his service is to be both liturgical and pastoral. Of the liturgy he is the president (*moderator*),[11] the minister (*dispensator*) and the guardian (*custos*). He is to preach and teach and in prayer and sacrifice he is to seek grace from God for the people. In his pastoral work the Good Shepherd is to be his model. He is to work *with* his fellows in the ministry (*in ministerio consortes*) and he is to have a special care for the poor, the oppressed and the stranger or exile. Those not of the flock also have claim on his care. But, a member of the college of bishops, he shares with them 'the care of all the churches', especially of those in need. 'Give your care to the whole flock in which the Holy Spirit has set you to rule the church of God[12] in the name of the Father whose image you show forth in the church,[13] in the name of his Son, Jesus Christ whose function of teacher, priest and pastor you perform and in the name of the Holy Spirit who gives life to the church and strength to you in your weakness.' A noble ending and a remarkable summary of the bishop's role in the church.

The second text that claims our attention is the consecration prayer itself. As is now well known, this is the prayer that is to be found in the *Apostolic Tradition* of Hippolytus dated about AD 215.[14] Just as few imagined that we should ever be able to use his eucharistic prayer, there were probably fewer who thought that his prayer for the consecration of bishops would oust the text that is found in the Leonine (or Verona) Sacramentary and that was the consecration prayer of the Roman rite from at least the sixth century. Yet this has now been done and we may adopt the view of a recent writer that in the whole history of the liturgy of ordination there has never been a reform comparable to this.[15]

Dom Bernard Botte, who played a principal part in the revision of the liturgy of ordination, reveals the motives that led to this change.[16] The former prayer was long and even so, as he says, 'short' on theology. To make up for its deficiencies, to the sacramentary texts a series of hortatory passages were added at a later date. These did little to relieve the essential poverty of the principal text and when the anointing of the head was introduced in the tenth century the prayer was divided into two parts. This threw the emphasis on the anointing, making it look more important than the laying-on of hands which in the earliest tradition of both East and West was always *the* rite of episcopal as of priestly ordination. Further, since the prayer of Hippolytus underlies all the rites of ordination of the Eastern church, it was clear that its restoration to the Roman rite would be a notable ecumenical gesture. So it was done and the prayer appears in the Roman Pontifical of 1968–1990 with only quite minor verbal changes. It is clear, simple and significant and its restoration to use must be regarded with satisfaction.

After a preliminary recalling of Old Testament arrangements the prayer goes on: 'Pour out now on this your Elect that strength (*virtutem*) which is from you, the sovereign Spirit, whom you gave to your beloved Son (Child = Servant) Jesus Christ, the Spirit he himself gave to the holy apostles who established the church in different places to the unceasing praise and glory of your name'. Although Dom Botte did not think it necessary or even desirable, the decision was made that all the consecrating bishops should pronounce this part together. It is to be regarded as the 'form', though such notions were foreign to the church of the time, as Dom Botte states. The whole prayer is consecratory. However, it was a compromise which some judged to be necessary.

The last part of the prayer lays out the functions of the bishop and in so doing reveals what he is. He is the shepherd of the holy flock of God, he exercises the high priesthood (*summum sacerdotium*), serving God night and day, and by 'offering the gifts of your holy church' he is to propitiate God unceasingly. By the power of the Holy Spirit he has the authority of the high priesthood to remit sins. Likewise he enjoys the authority once given to the apostles to order the offices concerning pastoral care. He is to be gentle and clean of heart, offering (by his life) a sweet savour (to the Father) through the Son 'through whom is given glory and power and honour, with the Holy Spirit in holy church, now and throughout endless ages'.

Short though this prayer is, expert commentary[17] reveals the depth and richness of its content. Among other things it consists of a tissue of scripture texts and references that it would take too long to draw out here. We can give no more than the main lines of interpretation. There is a very close correlation between the baptism of Christ with the illapse of the Spirit on him, the Pentecost event and the liturgical celebration when that same Spirit who came upon Christ and through him was given to the apostles is, now by the laying-on of hands, conceived to be given to the bishop: 'Pour out *now* the power of that Spirit whom *you* (the Father) gave to your Son and whom *he* gave to his apostles'. This Spirit is the sovereign Spirit (*pneuma hegemonikon*), the *spiritus principalis* of Psalm 50:14 (LXX and Vulg.) and signifies the 'power of ruling' or government though the style of government is given in the rest of the prayer (e.g. *mansuetudine et mundo corde*). But it is important to realize that this is the *specific* gift of the Holy Spirit for the bishop whose office is *primarily* pastoral though not exclusive of liturgical functions through which he in fact exercises the 'high priesthood'.[18] The liturgy itself, the offering of the eucharist, the forgiving of sins, prayer, is a pastoral service of God's people.

It is this realization that the episcopate is a pastoral charge, in this sense, that made it possible for Vatican II to get rid of the topsy-turvy theology of orders which had been current since the early Middle Ages and re-establish the right relationship between the episcopate and the presbyterate. No longer is it a question of the presbyter possessing certain 'powers', e.g. that of consecrating the eucharist ('than which there is no higher') and, as it was said, making him 'equal' to the bishop so that the latter appeared as some sort of sacred appendage. The bishop is the chief pastor of his diocese and in him principally are vested all the functions, both the purely pastoral and the liturgical, that belong to the priestly office.[19]

The next part of the prayer that merits some commentary is that which speaks of the functions of the bishop. 'Father, *knower of hearts*, grant to this your servant whom you *have chosen* for the episcopate'; this recalls the context of Acts 1:15–26 when Matthias was elected to the apostolic body and thus relates the election of a bishop to the election of an apostle.[20] All this is a much more profound way of expressing the notion of apostolic succession than that of a merely tactile continuity by the laying-on of hands from the beginning till now.

~

The apostolic succession, as was made clear as early as Irenaeus,[21] is wider and deeper than that. To understand episcopacy we have to see it as existing in the apostolic context which involves a succession of *doctrine*, the preservation of the unity of the faith and the *koinonia* of the local church which in turn is an indispensable link in the *communion* of the great church. The bishop's liturgy, that is, the liturgy he presides over, surrounded by the *presbyterium* or counsel of priests and the deacons, who are his and the community's servants, a celebration at which he proclaims the word of God for the building up of the body of Christ, is the sacrament-sign of this *koinonia* or communion. This in miniature *is* the church and the bishop's key position in its structure and his necessary role in its action are very clear.

Even in the statements defining the functions of the bishop the background of the prayer remains richly scriptural. He is to be the Good Shepherd and the whole world of the biblical teaching on shepherd is immediately evoked. Peter was given the supreme pastorate over the flock of Christ (John 21:15ff.), the heads of the local communities are called shepherds (Ephesians 4:11), in Acts (20:28) Paul tells the *episkopoi* that they are to 'shepherd' the church of God and in 1 Peter 5:2 the 'elders', whoever they were, are exhorted to 'be shepherds of the flock of God that is entrusted to you'.[22]

He is 'to exercise the high priesthood'. The Latin is odd: '*exhibeat tibi summum sacerdotium*'; presumably the translator had difficulty in rendering the Greek which means precisely 'to act as high priest' (*archierateuein*). But what is surprising is that the office is called a 'priesthood' and even a 'high priesthood', terms restricted in the New Testament and in sub-apostolic literature generally, to Christ himself. However, if we are to judge by Cyprian's use of them, they had become general less than fifty years after Hippolytus.[23] At any rate, if the prayer of Hippolytus seems to be less 'sacerdotal' than subsequent prayers and theological statements, this term is sufficient to show that he thought of the bishop as not only a priest but the chief priest of his diocese.

This priest serves (*leitourgounta*) God night and day, and presumably prayer is intended here, but it is also his function 'to offer the gifts of your holy church' (*prospherein dora*) and thus gain God's favour for his people. This is clearly a eucharistic expression and refers to the bishop's role as the (principal) offerer of the eucharist and it is interesting to recall that the 'prayer of offering', which appears in the *Apostolic Tradition* and has now (with additions) become the second Eucharistic Prayer, follows on immediately after the ordination of the bishop as a model for his use. Thus, while there is but this single reference to the eucharist in the whole prayer, it says all that is necessary and if the whole liturgy is taken together, as it is in the *Apostolic Tradition*, the bishop's function in this regard is made amply clear.

In the perspective of the prayer, the function of remitting sins is an action of this same priesthood and here again, as the Greek text makes clearer, these few phrases recall the New Testament at almost every step (cf. Matthew 9:6; John 20:23 and for the giving of the Spirit, the same place, verse 21).[24]

In the same way, what might be called the administrative duties of the bishop, the supervision of the clergy, and the quality of his own life which is to be marked by gentleness and purity of heart, are exercises of his priestly function and the latter, in accordance with New Testament teaching, is to be a sacrifice (*offerens tibi odorem suavitatis*) which is combined with the offering of the eucharist.[25] Even this brief examination of the prayer will have revealed its depths and scriptural richness and we may conclude with A. Rose that 'a comparison of the vocabulary and style of this prayer with the New Testament and the writings of the earliest Fathers reveals the profound unity that exists between it and the sources of revelation'.

The other texts, e.g. the interrogatory, and rites add nothing of substance to what is contained in the homily and the prayer and this is all as it should be. The prayer is the climax of the rite and all that follows are what they should be, namely *ritus explicativi*, gestures and accompanying texts which unfold the meaning of the prayer. In the questions we need here note only the one that clearly reflects Vatican II theology: 'Is it your will to build up the body of Christ, his church and to remain united with it along with the order of bishops under the authority of the successor of blessed Peter, the apostle?' To this of course he answers that it is.

Among the rites subsequent to the prayer, the formula for the anointing of the head deserves brief attention. In the former liturgy this rite appeared as the climax and the formula was: 'Let your head be anointed and consecrated with heavenly blessing (to incorporate you) into the pontifical order'.[26] The new formula clearly indicates that the anointing is no more than the explicitation of what has already been done in and by the consecration prayer: 'May God who *has* made

148

you a sharer in the high priesthood of Christ, fill you with the grace of (this) mystical anointing and by the richness of (his) spiritual blessing make you fruitful'. The gesture and the substance (chrism) are a symbol of the fullness of the Spirit which has been given by the laying-on of hands. Here symbolism is performing its proper role.

The rite: a brief commentary

The former rite of consecration was one of the most complicated of the Roman liturgy and except to the connoisseur of ceremonial (and there were such), wearisome and largely incomprehensible. It will already have been noticed that the new rite is comparatively simple. Of course even this can be 'built up' if anyone is disposed to do so but in structure it is simple and all the signs are that it is meant to be presented as such. In what follows we attempt to isolate the most significant moments and to indicate some of the changes.

First, it will be as well to dispel an illusion that is still common. It has been thought for a long time that two assistant bishops to the principal consecrator were necessary for validity. As we see in the early centuries of the church, it was the bishops of a province or region who presided at the election of a bishop and who proceeded to 'order' him, that is incorporate him into the episcopal order. In the course of time and as the collegiality of the episcopate began to be forgotten, they were reduced to two, the smallest number to express the notion that a man *was* added to the episcopal college. Validity is a quite modern notion. The new Order returns to the older custom: at least two bishops must assist and lay-on hands but it is recommended that *all* the bishops present (and these will normally be the bishops of the province at least) 'ordain' (*sic*) the elect.

Formerly, two bishops introduced the elect – as if only bishops could introduce a bishop even if he was only *in fieri*. Now two priests (*presbyteri*) present him to the principal consecrator. There follows the reading of the Apostolic Commission and the homily.

Formerly the interrogatory (which took place at the beginning of the Mass) was a formidable affair. There was a long oath-formula in which the elect promised among other things to 'pursue' (*persequar!*) and fight (*impugnabo*) heretics, schismatics and those who had rebelled against the Lord. For all its bloodcurdling solemnity, bishops seem to have taken little notice of the content of this oath for several hundreds of years. There followed a long interrogatory in which the elect was required to profess his faith in detail and to reject an amazing number of heresies. All of course was in Latin, no doubt to the edification of the admiring multitudes who heard their bishops talking Latin for the first and only time in their lives.[27] In the new rite, in response to the questions (nine), the elect promises to proclaim the gospel, to guard the faith handed down from the apostles, to act in union with the college of bishops, to give due obedience to the successor of St Peter, to care for the people and clergy (*comministris*) entrusted to him and to exercise the pastoral ministry for the good of all. All very reasonable and simple.

The Litany of Saints that follows calls for no special mention though we may note that the collect concluding it has been salvaged from the former rite where it appeared as the introductory prayer to the prayer of consecration.

The *ceremonial* of the central part of the rite that comes next deserves more attention. The bishops stand together with the principal con-secrator in the midst of them; the elect comes forward and kneels before them. The principal consecrator then in silence lays hands on the elect's head and then the other bishops do likewise. So far this is exactly the ceremonial of the *Apostolic Tradition* and its symbolism is as rich as it is profound. Here the gesture of the laying-on of hands, which always means the giving of the Spirit, appears in its most significant form: the gesture alone, without words, is sufficiently strong to convey its message.

Then comes a rite that is first found in the East (fourth century?), the imposition of the gospel book on the head of the elect. Formerly it was held by two bishops (no less!); now by two deacons who were the original ministers. What is its meaning? It is not wholly clear. One view is that it signifies the giving of the fullness of the Spirit and one could point to Luke 4:16–21 as its possible source. The other is that it signifies that the bishop is to live under the yoke of the gospel and this view finds support in the gesture itself: the book is laid on and then held over the elect's head (not as formerly on his neck). Of the two I prefer the former though the second is better supported by the documents.[28] In the rite of 1990 the imposition of the book of the gospel *and* the handing of it to the bishop later is a sign to show that the preaching of God's word is a principal duty (*praecipuum munus*) (no. 28).

The consecration prayer proceeds and, apart from the section *Effunde super hunc electum . . . nominis tui*, is said (sung) by the principal consecrator alone. The book is removed and the anointing of the head, now seen as signifying participation in the priesthood of Christ, follows immediately. After the handing of the gospel book to the bishop he receives the ring, symbol of his 'marriage' (a very ancient notion) to his diocese. The mitre, a sign that the bishop is to seek holiness of life, is now placed on his head with a (new) formula: 'Receive the mitre and may the light of holiness shine in you . . .'. Lastly, he is handed the pastoral staff, a symbol of his task to rule and care for the flock of Christ committed to his charge. (It may be noted here that if it is desired to bless these insignia, this is to be done before the service.) The rite concludes with the kiss of peace exchanged between the new bishop and the other bishops. This has the special significance on this occasion that the new bishop is welcomed among the bishops as one of them. Finally, if the new bishop is consecrated in his own cathedral it is he who is the principal celebrant of the eucharist that follows.

The priesthood or presbyterate[29]
~

If the revision of the liturgy of the episcopate is the greatest reformation of it since the third century, that of the presbyterate is hardly less so though the revision has taken a rather different line. The former liturgy of the presbyterate, which has been described as a *maquis presque impénétrable,*[30] has been very considerably simplified and it would serve no good purpose either to detail the rite as it was or to note every change in the new one. The first thing that is important is that the revisers have adopted the same pattern for all three orders: laying-on of hands and prayer of consecration/ordination, the subsidiary rites (anointing) and the delivery of insignia. This alone shows, as it has been observed,[31] that they are three degrees of one and the same sacrament. It is a point worth making since people have been asking: 'Is, then, the episcopate an eighth sacrament?'

Ordination to the presbyterate: the liturgy

1. After the gospel the candidates are called by a deacon (not by a bogus archdeacon).
2. They are presented by a priest delegated for the purpose.
3. The homily.

4. The interrogatory (new).

5. Litany of Saints.

6. The act of ordination. The candidates approach the bishop one by one who lays hands on them in silence. The priests who are present do likewise and then form a half circle round the bishop though the rubrics do not say that they continue to hold their hands raised. The prayer of ordination follows.

7. The anointing of the hands. First, priests, without ceremony or formula, arrange the candidates' stoles and invest them with chasubles. (Formerly this was a more elaborate ceremony done by the bishop.) The bishop then anoints the hands of each (on the palms) with chrism (formerly oil of catechumens!) while Psalm 109 with the antiphon 'Christ the Lord, high priest for ever in the line of Melchizedek, offered bread and wine' may be sung.[32]

8. Bread (in communion dish) and the chalice containing wine (mixed with water as usual) are brought in procession by lay people to the bishop who then delivers them to the newly ordained.

9. The kiss of peace ends the ordination rite and the ordained con-celebrate Mass with the bishop. The Order urges that other priests should be invited to celebrate with them.

Commentary

From this brief synopsis of the rite it is clear that it is simple and straightforward. There is the laying-on of hands, the ordination prayer and the anointing of the candidates' hands which clearly appears as a subsidiary rite. The 'tradition of the instruments' which played so large a part in the ordination of priests for so many centuries has been transformed and the heavy emphasis on the priesthood as a cult-ministry has disappeared. Likewise, other subsidiary rites such as the commissioning of the priest to forgive sins after communion (which got there by accident) have been suppressed.[33] It is however on the quality of the ordination prayer that the whole rite must be judged and it is this that we will consider in a moment. As in the liturgy of the ordination of a bishop, so here the prayer is preceded by a specimen homily which merits consideration.

It must be emphasized that it is no more than a specimen and the ordaining bishop will want to adapt it to the circumstances of the time and place and speak more directly to the people than this sample indicates. It is not without importance however since it is heavily dependent on the documents of Vatican II.[34]

The whole people of God is a royal priesthood,[35] but Christ, the high priest, chose disciples to perform the priestly office for the people. As the Father sent the Son, so are they sent into the world to continue Christ's work. These are the bishops who share the teaching, priestly and pastoral functions of Christ. Presbyters are their co-operators sharing with them those same functions in the service of the people. More particularly, they are ministers of Christ's priesthood (*inserviant*) and through their ministry the church, that is the people of God, is built up and grows.

Here the total dependence of the earthly ministry on the priesthood of Christ is made very plain, as is also the truth that the priesthood is *for* the service of the people.

The image of Christ is to be formed in them (*configurandi*), they are to be united to the priesthood of bishops (so there is a *sacramental* and not merely a *juridical* union between priest and bishop) and they will be consecrated to preach the gospel, to care for the people and to celebrate the Lord's sacrifice. The order of the functions is noteworthy and their implications are then spelt out. They are to meditate on the word of God, to believe what they read, to teach what they believe and to imitate in their lives what they preach. In this way their word and their lives will help to build up the people of God.

Likewise, their liturgical ministry is not to be that of a mere functionary. Christ's sacrifice which they celebrate is to be the pattern of their lives which will be the expression of the paschal mystery of Christ's passion and resurrection. Their personal lives will be fused with their liturgical function: they are to realize what they are doing and to imitate (in their lives) what they celebrate. Thus is salvaged the phrase found in the address of Durandus of Mende in the thirteenth-century Pontifical. But this liturgical function too must be orientated to the service of the people: it is through it that the people are able effectively to make their 'spiritual sacrifice',[36] now united with Christ's, to the Father.

The ministry of the other sacraments, baptism, penance and the anointing of the sick, is recalled and the candidates are reminded that prayer too is a ministry. They are to praise and thank God in the Divine Office and pray not only for the people of God but for the whole world.

~

Finally, there is the pastoral care of the people committed to their charge and here their model is to be the Good Shepherd who came to seek and save that which was lost, to serve and not to be served. Caring for their people in all these ways, priests are to lead them 'through Christ in the Holy Spirit to God the Father'.

Of its nature a model address like this can hardly be very specific or concrete though it may be thought to mention at least all that is important. The priest's liturgical role which was so heavily emphasized for so many centuries is at least put in the context of life and service. It is to be seen as the sacramental expression of *both* and the demands that view of the priesthood makes are very great. But perhaps there is still not sufficient emphasis on mission. There are few, if any, countries in the world where the church is not in a missionary posture and vast numbers of priests are looking for inspiration and help to enable them to carry out the mission they believe is theirs. Here above all the episcopal celebrant of the sacrament will need to speak out of his knowledge and experience of his local church and see ordination as a unique occasion to give both priests and people a new vision of their missionary role.

The ordination prayer

This is of course the key text of the whole rite and the revisers had difficult decisions to make. Having adopted the Hippolytus text for the ordination of bishops, they will naturally have thought about his text for the ordination of priests. But first, it is rather short and *at first sight* remarkably unexplicit about the nature and role of the presbyterate. Secondly, in the *Apostolic Tradition* the prayer runs straight on from that for the ordination of a bishop and one gathers the impression that in the mind of the author the ordination of presbyters regularly took place on the occasion of the ordination of bishops. Since presbyters share in the priestly office of the bishop, the specifically priestly roles are indicated in the prayer for the ordination of bishops. Nowadays however a presbyter is rarely ordained at the same time as a bishop and the prayer would be evidently inadequate. The revisers, then, chose the old Roman prayer[37] in a slightly shortened and revised edition.

A brief summary of the Hippolytus prayer will provide a useful term of comparison with the present text.

The prayer asks that as God of old looked on his chosen people and commanded Moses to appoint 'elders', whom he filled with the Spirit which he had given to Moses, so may God look upon this servant (here present) and grant him the Spirit of grace and of counsel that belongs to the *presbyterium*. By the Spirit may he help and govern the people of God with a pure heart. The prayer ends with petitions that 'we' (bishops and priests) may, by the gift of God, never lose this Spirit and may serve him, praising him through his Child Jesus Christ through whom is glory and power with the Holy Spirit in the Church now and for endless ages. That is all. There is no mention of the presbyters' liturgical function if only perhaps because at this time they did not celebrate the eucharist independently but always celebrated with the bishop.[38] The proper functions of the presbyter are counsel and government and this is wholly in accord with the thinking of the ancient world on the 'council of elders'.[39] Hippolytus seems to witness to a very primitive arrangement, close to the New Testament, and suggests the situation thought by many scholars to be that of the famous First Letter of Clement to the Corinthians: it was sent by the Roman presbytery. We note however that it is the *same* Spirit that is given to both bishop and presbyter and, as the theology of orders developed, it was seen that the presbyter shared certain functions with the bishop. The reference to Moses makes this certain.[40] In Numbers 11:16, 17 we read 'I will take some of the spirit which is on you and put it on them', that is the seventy elders whom Moses appointed to help him in ruling the people. The Hippolytus prayer interprets this 'spirit' as the Holy Spirit of the New Testament and it is this same spirit who is given to both bishops and priests. But the ruling function, and we may add the counselling and judging functions, of the presbyterate are also made clear.

This exegesis helps us to understand the Moses-typology which is retained in the Roman prayer which we will now consider. The pattern of the prayer is similar to the Hippolytan one though more explicit even if by later medieval standards insufficiently so. After an introduction which speaks of hierarchy, and growth and order in nature, the prayer speaks of the growth of the degrees of the priesthood and of sacramental institutions. God has set bishops (here called *pontifices*, a Roman pagan word) in the church to rule over the people and *they* have elected others 'of second rank' to help them. At this point Moses is evoked and also the institution of the seventy elders through whom God 'propagated the spirit' (a curious phrase) and who were the helpers of Moses in ruling the people. But to this is added at this point mention of the Aaronic priesthood which is a foreshadowing of the Christian priesthood. Priests are ordained so that there may be a sufficiency to 'offer saving sacrifices and to provide a more frequent celebration of the sacraments'. The prayer has become more 'sacerdotal'. Yet, as the text goes on to indicate, presbyters share with the bishop in the government of the people and in his teaching office and as a recent commentator has observed,[41] the spirit of the bishop animates the whole *presbyterium*. The prayer ends with a passage which has been re-written in the interests of mission: 'May they (the presbyters) prove to be trustworthy co-operators with our Order so that the words of the Gospel may, by the grace of the Holy Spirit and their preaching, bear fruit in human hearts even to the ends of the earth'. (For an account of the changes made in the prayer of ordination by the revision of 1990 see Appendix at end of chapter.)

Priests, then, are clearly subordinate to the bishop but they are also his co-workers enjoying, as we have observed, a sacramental union with him. They share in his work, whether that is liturgical or pastoral or teaching. It is not for a liturgical text to give a theological elaboration of its themes but there is sufficient here to show that the *lex orandi* (the rule of prayer) provides a sound basis for the *lex credendi* (the rule of faith). *This* is what the priest is even if it is not all that he is.

This prayer with the laying-on of hands by bishop and presbyters is the climax of the rite and in the revised liturgy stands out as such. In the old rite it was overshadowed by the anointing of the hands which was solemnly inaugurated with the singing of the *Veni, Creator Spiritus*. At this point everyone felt that the real business was beginning. In the new rite the anointing is clearly explicative: it unfolds the meaning of the ordination prayer and of the laying-on of hands, which is the principal sign of the giving of the Spirit, that precedes it. The formula used for the anointing shows that the rite is the continuation of the thought in the prayer: 'May our Lord Jesus Christ whom the Father anointed with the power and the Holy Spirit keep you that you may sanctify the Christian people and offer sacrifice to God'. It is in this way that 'the portion of the spirit' who descended on the seventy elders from Moses now descends through Christ, the Anointed of God, on the presbyter by the laying-on of hands. And his function to sanctify, or as I suppose we should say, to be the means of sanctification of the people and of offering sacrifices, is also made plain.[42]

The cultic function of the priesthood has been sufficiently emphasized by the foregoing gestures and texts and for this reason it was possible to modify others. The solemn clothing with the sacerdotal vestments
by the bishop has given way to a simpler action: members of the clergy
present re-arrange the stole and put on the chasuble. The famous *traditio
instrumentorum* (the giving of the paten and chalice) with its emphatic
formula 'Receive the power to offer sacrifice to God for both the living
and the dead', which in all the later Middle Ages was regarded as essential to the rite, has been reduced to a giving of the *people*'s offering of
bread and wine (in paten and chalice) which are to be used in the Mass
that follows. This is made plain by the accompanying formula: 'Receive
the offering of the holy people which is to be offered to God. Realize
what you are to do, imitate the mystery you are going to handle and conform your life to the mystery of the Lord's cross.' Apart from other considerations, the reason for the change is that the priest has *already*, by
virtue of the ordination prayer, received the power to offer the eucharist.

The ordination rite concludes with the giving of the kiss of peace
by the bishop and the attendant priests to the newly ordained. Meanwhile, during the giving of the offering and the kiss of peace either the
well known *Iam non dicam servos* ('I will no longer call you servants . . .')
or the thanksgiving psalm (99) *Iubilate*, with the antiphon 'You are my
friends . . .', may be sung. The newly ordained then concelebrate with
the bishop. The giving of the kiss of peace is of course, as in the ordination of the bishop, the sign that the newly ordained are incorporated
into the *presbyterium*.

One or two other matters call for comment. After the homily and
before the Litany there comes an interrogatory, which is new, and the
promise of obedience which has been moved from the end of the
ordination Mass to this place. Obviously a great improvement. The five
questions the bishop asks the candidates sum up the five great themes
of the ordination rite. Put positively they run like this: The priest, as
the co-worker with the bishop, under the guidance of the Holy Spirit,
has a pastoral care of the people of God. He has a ministry of the word,
the duty to proclaim and expound the Catholic faith. He is commissioned to celebrate the mysteries of Christ, i.e. the sacraments, especially
the eucharist and the sacrament of reconciliation (this last an addition).
Finally, he promises with the help of God to enter day by day into an
ever closer union with Christ and with him to consecrate himself to

God for the salvation of the people. The union of personal life with pastoral function is emphasized throughout the rite and an attempt is thus made to close the gap between truly priestly work, whether in liturgy, preaching or care of people, and the *fonctionnairisme* which was the plague of the priesthood for so long.

The promise of obedience formerly came at the end of the ordination Mass along with a clutter of other rites, the final unfolding of the chasuble, the commissioning to forgive sins and the famous 'penance' which was imposed for being ordained! The promise looked very much like an afterthought and yet it is one of the most important and difficult duties of the priest's life. It is wholly appropriate that it should be brought forward and placed with the undertakings which we have considered above. It should be noted that the gesture of laying the hands in the bishop's folded hands comes from feudal custom and the church does not wish any longer to insist on it. Bishops' conferences may decide on some other gesture.

The Diaconate

Along with the episcopate and the presbyterate the diaconate is one of the primitive ministries of the church. It is the first degree of the sacrament of holy order and its importance has always been realized even if the addition of the subdiaconate to major orders by Innocent III in the thirteenth century did something to overshadow it. Since the early Middle Ages it has too been no more *in fact* than a stage on the way to the priesthood. Recently the church has made two changes of considerable importance. The Second Vatican Council envisaged the setting up of a *permanent* diaconate and the subdiaconate has finally been suppressed.[43]

The first change is of considerable pastoral importance and has brought with it some minor modifications of the rite. Canonically speaking, it means that the obligations of celibacy and recitation of the Divine Office have now been attached to the diaconate. Furthermore, admission to the clergy is now delayed until the diaconate, the rite of tonsure being abolished, and a special rite of commitment to celibacy for non-married candidates is attached to the diaconate. These changes hardly affect the rite of the diaconate and something will be said about them lower down.

In the revision of 1990, to accomodate the event of unmarried and married deacons being ordained in the same service, certain adjustments have been made in the (optional) homily that comes before the questions. Likewise religious are required to make a public commitment to celibacy.

A synopsis of the rite

1. After the gospel of the Mass the candidates are presented to the bishop by a priest appointed for the purpose.
2. The homily.
3. The interrogatory and promise of obedience.
4. Prayer, the Litany of Saints.
5. The bishop (alone) lays on hands in silence.
There follows the ordination prayer.
6. The vesting with stole and dalmatic by other deacons or presbyters.
7. The delivery of the book of the gospels.

Fundamentally, it is a very simple rite and like that for the episcopate and the presbyterate has been pruned of much later medieval accretion.

The theology of the diaconate

This is to be found principally in the homily and the prayer of ordination.

The homily is largely an extract from the Constitution on the Church but like those proposed for the ordination of bishops and priests, it is in no way obligatory and the celebrant may compose his own. However, it does provide a useful summary.

The deacon has a threefold ministry, of liturgy, of the word and of charity. In the liturgy he assists the bishop and/or presbyter in the eucharist, reading the gospel, preparing the offerings and administering communion. In addition, he administers baptism, assists at and blesses marriages, takes communion to the sick and dying and presides at funeral services. As for the ministry of the word, he preaches at liturgical and non-liturgical services and he teaches the faithful and non-faithful alike. All these are by no means radical changes though there is some extension of their powers both in what they may do and in the source of their power. As we have observed in the matter of baptism, they are now no longer 'extraordinary' ministers of it and their presiding at marriages and funerals is new. Evidently the giving of blessings, at marriages for instance, is not (or no longer) a sacerdotal privilege.

While his liturgical ministry is clear, the ministry of charity he is said to have for the assistance of bishop and priest remains vague. Emphasis on it no doubt represents an attempt to restore this ancient function. Deacons, who in Rome became archdeacons and often eventually Popes, were very important persons at a time when the church had large numbers of dependants, widows, virgins, the sick, on its 'pay roll' and they came to control considerable amounts of property. Presumably this situation is not envisaged! Even where in the modern church priests are often administrators of diocesan charities of some size, there would seem to be but a poor case for making deacons such administrators. In any case, it would seem that only permanent deacons are envisaged here. Where they are married and remain substantially members of the lay community, they might well become useful ministers of the less fortunate members of society and through the knowledge and experience gained in this work, they could bring to bishop and priest valuable information about the needs of people who do not normally come across the notice of the parish clergy. Perhaps it will be a case of *solvitur ambulando* but it does mean that permanent deacons should not be looked on as just clerical assistants.

Charity is a broad term and almost anything might be brought under its umbrella but the deacon's function as teacher might well be thought of in this light. Given the widespread need for instruction to various groups of Christians both young and older ones, it would seem that the permanent deacon could offer most valuable assistance if he were trained in catechetics. With this knowledge and expertise he could instruct groups here and there and become the means of forming them into authentic Christian communities who in turn would help the neighbourhoods in which they live.

The last part of the address is directed to the candidates themselves and they are bidden to live a sincere Christian life, to be strong in faith and to reproduce in their living the lessons they teach to others.

Of the questions and promise that follow, which do not add anything of substance to the above, we need to note that there are two new elements of the rite. The first is evidence of the church's concern that candidates for major orders should have a clear and firm determination about what they are doing. They are left in no doubt about this and, even without the new rite of commitment to celibacy, they are being asked to consecrate themselves to the ministry. This will take different forms with the permanent and married deacon and with the 'temporary' deacon but the reality remains the same. The promise of obedience too has a new importance since deacons are now for the first time entering the clerical state, a moment when it is opportune to declare the necessary obedience publicly. In fact it highlights an aspect of the diaconate that elsewhere in the rite is not emphasized. In all the early literature the deacon is the assistant of the *bishop*: he serves him at the eucharist and he acts at his bequest. Things have changed somewhat since then and his work will in fact be with the presbyter but his primary relationship will be to the bishop.

The prayer of ordination

The first change here is in line with the ordination of bishops and priests. Formerly, the bishop simply began reciting the prayer of ordination at the end of which he laid his right hand on the candidate saying, 'Receive the Holy Spirit for strength to resist the devil and his temptations' – not a very inspiring thought anyway! The laying-on of one hand only was presumably a childish medieval way of showing that the deacon was not quite a priest. Now the bishop lays both hands on the candidate, in silence and before the beginning of the prayer. The ancient order is thus restored and the symbolism of the hands-laying is given full prominence.

The prayer itself, basically the old Roman one, has been corrected and considerably changed in the last part. The long exordium remains: God, the giver of honours, arranges orders and distributes functions, renews all things and through Jesus Christ his Son who is Word, Power and Wisdom, dispenses everything harmoniously in time and place. This variety is reflected in the church, which is his body, by the variety of graces which all make for the unity and growth of the body and by the threefold ministry of bishop, priest and deacon. Of this last the ministry of the Levites in the Old Testament who served in the Tabernacle is a foreshadowing. Up to this point the text is corrected only in minor ways. Then comes an almost entirely new section that runs on to the end and gives a much more Christian and a fuller notion of the diaconate.

The text recalls the institution of the seven deacons of Acts 6:1–6:

in the beginning of the church the apostles of the Son chose out seven men who were to help them in their daily ministry so that they (the apostles) could give themselves more effectively to prayer and the ministry of the word. By prayer and the laying-on of hands they committed them to the 'ministry of tables'. While this emphasis on service is to be welcomed, it should be said that by no means all scripture experts regard this incident of Acts 6 as the institution of the diaconate.[44] However it does connect the diaconate with the New Testament ministry, which the old version failed to do, and by its reference to 'the service of tables', even if that is not a very happy phrase in the context, relates the diaconate to the ministry of charity, also wanting in the old rather clerical version.

The next part of the prayer was given over to more or less appropriate common-places and ended with the unsatisfactory formula 'Receive the Holy Spirit . . .' which had been interpolated into the text. That formula, which formed a duplicate with what followed, is now suppressed and the prayer runs on asking God to look graciously on the candidates whom the bishop is dedicating to the ministry of the altar. Then comes the solemn invocation of the Holy Spirit: 'Send, Lord, your Holy Spirit on these (candidates) that they may be strengthened by the gift of your sevenfold grace for the faithful execution of their ministry'. This is not only more pertinent but emphasizes that the diaconate like the other orders confers a *charisma* (and not merely a 'power' to do something) for the building up of the body of Christ. The theme of the prayer is now quite consistent.

The last part of the prayer, which, as in the other rites, is addressed to the candidates, is only slightly revised. The deacon is to be conspicuous by his sincere love and care for the sick and the poor (there is the ministry of charity), he is to bear himself modestly (and we remember the acid comments of St Jerome on the Roman deacons who gave themselves airs) and he is to lead a life of innocence and purity. The attachment of celibacy to the diaconate, though it was mentioned in the former version, becomes particularly important as this is the moment of total commitment. However 'chastity' has been replaced by *conversationis* (behaviour), in view of the ordination of married deacons. The prayer ends on the note of service: the deacon is to be like Christ who came not to be served but to serve.

Whatever may be the difficulties of working out the implications of the diaconate in the terms of pastoral action, the prayer makes abundantly clear what it is.

The explanatory rites

In the former rite there was at this point the solemn 'delivery' (*traditio*) of the diaconal vestments, stole and dalmatic, and the clothing of the candidates with them to the accompaniment of formulae. Deacons (or presbyters) now put them on without formulae while Psalm 83 or some other chant is sung. The delivery of the gospel book which follows was formerly made with the formula: 'Receive the *power* to read the Gospel in (the) church for *both the living and the dead*'! This was obviously an imitation of the 'power' given to the priest by the tradition of the paten and chalice. The formula now says: 'Receive the *Gospel of Christ* whose herald you now are; believe what you read, teach what you believe and imitate (in your life) what you teach'. A concise phrase that sums up much of the meaning of the order the candidate has received. While this is being done Psalm 145 which speaks of the service of the poor and sick may be sung and its significance for the rite is underlined by the antiphon: 'If anyone serves me, my Father who is in heaven will honour him'. These simple rites do in fact unfold the meaning of the diaconate as a ministry: the deacon is a minister of the liturgy, of the word and of charity.

Commentary

The revised order for the diaconate is so clear that it hardly calls for further commentary. As with the other orders one feels that it would have been better if the homily followed immediately upon the gospel. The rite would then continue in unbroken succession: the introduction of the candidates, the questions, the homily, the prayer of the assembled community, the ordination prayer and the performance of the explanatory rites.

It is questionable too whether the psalms or other chants provided to accompany these rites are really necessary. Presumably the revisers envisaged a large number of deacons and the continual repetition of the same formula would be boring. However, it would seem highly desirable that the people should hear the formula for the giving of the gospel more than once. The words are worth pondering on. True, these psalms remain optional and those in charge of the celebration will arrange for their singing or the singing of other chants as they think best. What 'other chants' are to be used is a problem. In the English language at least none as yet exist and there is a case for composing some though the authors and the composers will have to be filled with a sense of what holy orders are if they are going to be appropriate. One does not envisage with equanimity the singing of 'Sweet Sacrament Divine' or of anything from the epoch to which it belongs.

The lesser ministries

Since the *Motu proprio, Ministeria quaedam* of 15 August 1972 made a number of changes in what used to be called 'minor orders', it will be as well to set them out here.

1. Tonsure has been suppressed and replaced by 'Admission to the Clerical State' which is an action to be combined with the diaconate. A man becomes a cleric with all the consequences (e.g. incardination into a diocese) only on receiving the diaconate.

2. Only two minor orders remain now, to be called 'ministries', the offices of reader or lector and acolyte.

3. The subdiaconate is suppressed, the obligations of this ministry (celibacy and the recitation of the Divine Office) being attached to the diaconate. Other functions are divided between the ministries of reader and acolyte.[45]

4. These ministries may be committed (*committi possunt*) to laymen but, 'in accordance with the venerable tradition of the church', not to women.

We are not concerned here with the canonical side of institution to these ministries. It is sufficient to note that candidates must ask in writing for institution and it rests with the Ordinary to accept the petition or not. They must have a firm purpose to serve God and the Christian people and must be endowed with the right qualities of personality.

The reason for the change of name is not merely negative–to distinguish more adequately major or sacred orders from minor–but is positive. These ministries are means of *serving* the people whether within or outside the liturgy and as the needs of the people change, so can the ministries.[46] The institution of these ministries brings to mind such passages as Romans 12:6–8 and 1 Corinthians 12:4–11 and they may not unfairly be described as more or less permanent *charismata* for the building up of the body, the church. The *Motu proprio* even envisages that these ministries may be multiplied if the needs of the people require and local conferences of bishops so ordain. The ministry of catechists is among those mentioned.

The functions of the lesser ministries

The reader

Quite obviously his function is to read the lessons, except the gospel, whether at Mass or at any other service, but the document remarks that he may perform the duties of cantor (*psalmista*) mentioned in the *Ordo Missae* of 1969 (64). He is to support and lead the people in singing and in general participation in the liturgy. If trained, he could render valuable service. In the absence of a deacon he will lead the people in the General Intercessions of the Mass.

According to the *Motu proprio* (V), the reader may be given other duties too though the document is remarkably laconic: 'He may instruct the faithful in the worthy reception of the sacraments'. He evidently has a teaching function and it is for the local church to make as much of his function as possible. He may also train those who 'temporarily' act as readers at the liturgy, though some of these will perform for life!

For his personal life the reader is exhorted to meditate on the scriptures and live by their message.

The rite: The rite, which is short and simple, begins after the gospel of the Mass (or a Bible Service). There is the homily and, in the sample given, we note that the reader has an additional function: to proclaim the good news of salvation to those who are ignorant of it. There follows an invitatory, the collect by which the reader is blessed and then the delivery of the Bible with the charge to hand on the word of God faithfully 'so that it may be active in men's hearts'.

The acolyte[47]

His function is essentially liturgical. He is appointed for the service of the altar, in particular of the presbyter and deacon in the eucharist.

However, his function has been extended and in cases of necessity he may assist in the giving of communion 'even to the sick'. In the liturgy he will make administration of holy communion a great deal easier and since he may take it to the sick, he could be of considerable assistance to the parish clergy. If he intends to proceed to holy orders this would be valuable experience and if not, he could become a regular 'minister' of the parish. In addition, he may expose the Blessed Sacrament (but not give the blessing) and instruct those who serve at the altar.

The rite: This is the same as for the reader: homily, invitatory, prayer of blessing and the delivery of the sign of office, namely a vessel containing bread or wine. Acolytes receive communion immediately after the deacon and may be allowed to assist in the distribution of communion.

Pastoral observations

Even if it is agreed that the whole business of 'minor orders' needed reform, it is unlikely that anyone will get very excited about the institution of these new 'ministries'. Yet, one of the effects of the reform is to smudge the distinctions between clergy and laity and since laymen may be instituted to these ministries, it will be here that their value will chiefly lie. Much will depend on what local conferences of bishops choose to make of these ministers but they could be very useful assistants in the parish. It may be asked whether it was necessary to institutionalize such functions. There is a case for it. A recognized body of lay readers, who could also be authorized as 'acolytes', would mean that structures could be set up for their training and parishes would have available sufficiently educated men to carry out a great variety of tasks.

When young men who are candidates for the priesthood receive these ministries, they should be authorized to exercise them in parishes as often as possible. Not only should they read at the liturgy but they should, we think, be regularly authorized to give communion to the sick during vacations. In this way the whole purpose of the document would be realized.

Admission to the clerical state

Formerly tonsure admitted men to the clergy and we remember the bitter battles that were fought over the issue in the Middle Ages. Then there was a 'clerisy' which had become a separate caste. With the abolition of the tonsure which had become almost meaningless and the reformation of the 'minor orders' whose members are *not* clerics, it was thought necessary to transfer the admission to the clerical state to the time when men are ordained. It could very well have been dispensed with altogether but the church authorities have an understandable anxiety about the determination and good will of candidates for major orders. Admission to the clerical state is then to be seen primarily as a commitment to the service of the church whether in the diaconate or the priesthood.

The rite: It may take place at a time to be determined by local authority but in connection with the diaconate.

There is the homily after the gospel which is followed by a short interrogatory to secure the candidates' commitment. This is followed by an invitatory, intercessions and the collect which asks that the candidates may persevere in their vocation.

The public declaration on celibacy

Celibacy, formerly attached to the subdiaconate, was never mentioned in the ordination rite. With the growing concern about this matter, the church authorities have for years sought to secure from candidates an understanding of what they were taking on themselves. It has been thought good to make the whole matter explicit at a liturgical and public level and a rite is now provided which is to be inserted into the ordination service of deacons. The words of commitment take their place among the other promises the candidate makes.

Celibacy is seen as a sign of charity which enables a man to give himself to the pastoral ministry with freedom and 'undivided heart'. Accordingly the question put to him is: 'Is it your intention to keep perpetual celibacy on account of the kingdom of heaven, as a sign of your dedication and for the service of God and man?' To which he replies 'Yes'.

Married candidates then come forward and to both groups is committed the obligation of reciting the Divine Office.

In the 1990 edition the Rite of Admission to Holy Order is added as an Appendix in the Pontifical.[48]

Appendix

The prayer of the ordination of presbyters

The prayer in the rite of 1968 was already a revision of the prayer as it stood in the Verona Sacramentary, perhaps of the sixth century. It retained certain terms that are now less acceptable; these have now been changed. Thus the old prayer spoke of God as the 'author of honours' and the 'giver of dignities'. These have been christianized, as it were, and they read 'author of *human dignity*' and 'giver of all *graces*'. In addition to general statements about the divine order we now have an explicit New Testament statement: (God) arranges in different orders, by the power of the Holy Spirit, the ministers who are to form a priestly people (ref. to *Lumen gentium* 28 to which might have been added 1 Peter 2:5).

The typology of Aaron (whose place in this prayer was always somewhat questionable; Christian priesthood derives from Christ whose 'type' was Melchizedek) is set more clearly in the New Testament context: the sons of Aaron were appointed to offer the sacrifices of the Tabernacle 'which were the foreshadowing of the good things to come' (Hebrews 8:5). Next, a thoroughly New Testament passage is added: 'Holy Father in the appointed time (*novissime*) you sent your Son into the world (John 3:17), the Apostle and High Priest of our faith (Hebrews 3:1). By the Holy Spirit he offered himself to you, an unblemished sacrifice (Hebrews 9:14), and made his apostles, consecrated in truth (John 17:19), sharers in his mission. To them he added co-operators (*comites*) to proclaim and celebrate the work of salvation (*opus salutis*; cf. CL 6) throughout the whole world.'

Among other changes one notes that the passage about presbyters being the co-operators of bishops is expanded to include the duty of proclaiming the gospel to all, to be faithful ministers of the mysteries, viz. baptism, the eucharist, but also the sacrament of reconciliation and the sacraments of the sick. Priests are also reminded that they must pray for their people and for the whole world. This is intended to refer to the Liturgy of the Hours or the Divine Office; a necessary reminder though neither here nor in the injunctions to the bishop are they told to pray *with* their people using the Prayer of the Church *par excellence*, precisely the Divine Office.

The prayer ends on an eschatological note: the church gathered here below is destined to be one people in the kingdom or reign of God to come.

What is a considerable re-writing of this ancient prayer must be said to be the fruitful result of long reflection on priesthood as it is shared by presbyters with Christ. For ordination to the presbyterate we now have a worthy prayer that is apt and fitted for its high purpose.

(For the above information about the rites of ordination in the revised Pontifical see *Notitiae*, 283 (February 1990), 2. Other changes may be noted here: the 1968 edition had no *Praenotanda* or Pastoral Instruction. This has now been supplied. In the earlier edition the order was diaconate, presbyterate and episcopate. In accordance with the theology of *Lumen gentium* (the Constitution on the Church), the order is now episcopate, presbyterate and diaconate, as was suggested in the first edition of this book (p. 139) in 1973! The above-mentioned issue of *Notitiae* also carries commentaries in Italian and Spanish. The main texts are given, of course, in Latin.)

Notes

~

[1] The revision of the liturgy of holy order, episcopate, presbyterate and diaconate, appeared in 1968: **Pontificale Romanum: De Ordinatione Diaconi, Presbyteri et Episcopi** (Vatican Press). The institution of the minor ministries with the rites, the form of admission to the clerical state and the declaration on celibacy were promulgated by a **Motu proprio** of Paul VI, **Ministeria quaedam** (Vatican Press, 1972). See above, p. 164.

[2] Constitution on the Church, 21 (**Documents of Vatican II**, pp. 40-1).

[3] This settles in principle the long and sometimes unpleasant controversy that raged in the centuries after the Council of Trent. See J. D. Crichton, 'Church and Ministry from the Council of Trent to the First Vatican Council', in **The Christian Priesthood**, ed. N. Lash and J. Rhymer (London, 1970), pp. 117-39.

[4] *Ap. Trad.* 7, p. 12.

[5] The relationship to bishops of religious engaged in pastoral work in a diocese has been clarified by a change of text in the questions to presbyters in their ordination. Religious are now required to promise obedience to a (the?) diocesan bishop and their own superiors.

[6] See Constitution on the Church, 29, pp. 55-6.

[7] This is the term the Pontifical, in accordance with ancient usage, uses for the rite in general though it speaks of the 'consecration' of a bishop in the texts. Its significance is that a bishop is raised to or incorporated into the 'rank' or 'order' of bishops who together form the 'college'. The notions underlying these terms go back to Hippolytus and probably beyond.

8 It is not quite clear whether **mysteria fidei** refers to teaching, **expounding** the mysteries of faith, or as above, celebrating them in the liturgy. I think the latter.

9 Constitution on the Liturgy, 7.

10 An ancient phrase.

11 Cf. CL 41.

12 Cf. Acts 20:28.

13 Cf. St Ignatius of Antioch, **Ep. ad Trall.**, 3.

14 **Ap. Trad.** 3, p. 9.

15 B. Kleinheyer , 'L'ordination des prêtres', **LMD**, 98 (1969) p. 94.

16 **Ibid.**, pp. 113ff.

17 A. Rose, 'Le prière consécratoire de l'évêque', **ibid.**, pp. 127ff.

18 As Rose points out, **art. cit.**, p. 133, the prayers for the ordination of priests and deacons ask for 'the Spirit of grace and counsel' for the presbyters and 'the Spirit of grace and zeal (in service)' for the deacons.

19 This at least is the vision of Vatican II and of Hippolytus. It is another question whether this is all to be said and the New Testament experts seem to endorse nowadays the high likelihood of a plurality of ministries, on a rather different pattern, in New Testament times. Still, holy order in the terms of bishop–presbyter–deacon goes back beyond Hippolytus to Ignatius of Antioch and, probably, to Clement of Rome.

20 Rose, **art. cit.**, p. 135. This is Lécuyer's view too.

21 **Adv. Haer.**, III, ii–iii (ET, H. Bettenson, **The Early Church Fathers**, 1956, pp. 122–6).

22 Cf. Rose, **art. cit.**, p. 137.

23 See P. Gy, 'Vocabulaire antique du sacerdoce', in **Etudes sur le sacrement de l'Ordre** (Paris, 1957) pp. 141–4 (ET, 1962, pp. 98–115).

24 Cf. Rose, **art. cit.**, p. 138.

25 Further scriptural references will be found in **ibid.**, pp. 139–41.

26 The Latin is odd and needs interpretation! **Ungatur et consecretur caput tuum, caelesti benedictione, in ordine pontificali.**

27 In my edition of the **Pontificale Romanum** this procedure occupies six pages, not counting the rubrics!

28 See **Etudes sur le sacrement de l'Ordre**, discussion between B. Botte and J. Lécuyer, pp. 36–7; Botte holds for the first view and Lécuyer for the second. Apparently the original meaning was already lost by the time of St John Chrysostom (died 407).

29 There is a question of terminology. 'Priesthood' applies primarily to Christ, secondly to the episcopate which is the primary participation in it and for centuries **sacerdos** meant 'bishop'. On the other hand, the term priest has become so common for the one who has the second rank in the priesthood that it seems somewhat artificial to use the term 'presbyter'. I have used it whenever I have wished to point the contrast between the episcopate and the presbyterate.

30 An 'almost impenetrable thicket'; cf. Kleinheyer, **LMD**, 98, (1969), p. 95.

31 **Ibid.**, p. 68.

32 Other **suitable** chants may be used.

33 The explanation is that in the Romano-German Pontifical of the tenth century the rite ended with the mention of the participation of the new priests in the eucharist. When in the twelfth–thirteenth century a formula for the laying-on of hands was added a copyist finding a space at the end of the rite inserted the phrase 'Whose

sins you shall forgive . . .' in that place. Hence the rite after communion! See Kleinheyer, **LMD**, 98 (1969), p. 102 and also his long study **Die Priesterweihe im römischen Ritus** (Trier, 1962), pp. 208–11.

[34] Especially that on the Church and the Decree on the Ministry and Life of Priests (ed. Abbott, pp. 532–76).

[35] Cf. 1 Peter 2:9; Rev 1:6; 5:10.

[36] 1 Peter 2:5 and cf. Rom 12:1. This teaching is from the Decree on Priests.

[37] **Sacram. Veron.**, pp. 121–2.

[38] Text of **Ap. Trad.**, p. 12.

[39] Cf. A. Lemaire, **Les Ministères aux origines de l'Eglise** (Paris, 1971).

[40] The reference to Moses is interesting not only as testimony of a quite advanced typology but because it is found in the later Roman prayer and has remained throughout.

[41] P. Jounel, in **The Church at Prayer**, III: **The Sacraments**, ed. A.G. Martimort (ET, Collegeville, MN/London, 1988), p. 155.

[42] The Latin word **custodiat**, 'keep' or 'guard' you, is a little odd. Something like 'appoint' would have been more to be expected. Perhaps, however, the revisers see the 'appointing' as done in the ordination prayer itself. Anyway, it is difficult to translate **custodiat** in this place!

[43] Constitution on the Church, 29; **Motu proprio, Ministeria quaedam**, of Paul VI, 1972.

[44] Cf. **inter alios** J. Colson, **La Fonction diaconale**, pp. 39–46 (quoted in Ludwig Ott, **Le sacrement de l'Ordre**, Paris, 1971, p. 24). Colson writes: 'If the "Seven" were not perhaps the first deacons, they were at least probably at the origin of the diaconate in the church'. He sees the event as an early case of differentiation of function in what he calls 'la fonction épiscopo-presbytérale'.

[45] The document says that if local conferences of bishops wish, the acolyte can be called a subdeacon!

[46] **Motu proprio**, p. 8.

[47] A Greek word meaning 'follower'. We could do with an English one.

[48] For further reading on the role of the deacon see **The Deacon's Ministry**, ed. Christine Hall (Gracewing, Fowler Wright Books, 1991).

NINE

The Anointing and Care
of the Sick[1]

~~~~~~

S INCE THIS Order contains a great deal more than the rite of
the anointing of the sick it is necessary to detail its contents.
Apart from the decree of promulgation, there is first the
Apostolic Constitution *Sacram Unctionem* which gives the official background to the revision. This is followed, as usual, by the *Praenotanda*,
divided into 41 paragraphs and referred to hereafter as the 'introduction'. The Order is divided into seven chapters:

I   Visitation and communion of the sick, comprising recommenda-
     tions for (a) the care of the sick and (b) the rite of communion.
II   The Order of anointing, the 'ordinary' one, the one as celebrated
     within the Mass and a third for celebration with a great gathering
     of people.
III *Viaticum* both within and outside the Mass.
IV   The Order for the administration of these sacraments to people
     in proximate danger of death, the continuous rite (penance,
     anointing and *Viaticum*); anointing without communion.
V   Confirmation in the danger of death.
VI   The Order for the commendation of the dying.
VII A collection of texts, prayers, suggested lists of scripture readings
     for use *ad libitum*.

In view of the importance of the anointing of the sick from many
points of view, it will receive first consideration here.[2]
With it we shall of course consider the various styles of celebrating
it (chapters II and IV), then the visitation and communion of the sick
which will be followed by a commentary on *Viaticum*. Confirmation in
danger of death calls for no special comment and the whole treatment
will end with the commendation of the dying.

The anointing of the sick

In view of what has been said in Chapter 1 of this book[3] it is interesting to note that the introduction sets the sacrament firmly in the life-situation of ordinary people, envisaging at first non-Christians. Disease, suffering are part of the experience of every man and present peculiar difficulties for all. The Christian faith however does help those who believe. It enables them to understand something of the mystery of suffering and to bear it more bravely. But illness is (for the most part) not to be thought of as a punishment for sin;[4] it is a *natural* phenomenon as is also, under divine providence, man's struggle against it and his desire for healing. To this the introduction adds that doctors, nurses and all who serve the sick are co-operating with the divine order of things. They are fulfilling Christ's command that we should care for the sick and, the text goes on, it is as if Christ committed the whole person (*totum hominem*) to their care so that they may restore the sick person by means of both physical and spiritual remedies. We may add that this is true even if the doctors and nurses do not know Christ but are striving according to the rules and art of their profession to restore health.

All this, it seems to us, is a sane, realistic and ultimately Christian view and, although the text does not refer to it, it reflects teaching to be found in the Constitution on the Church in the Modern World (18, 22). Illness and the suffering that comes with it are purely natural phenomena and it is wholly right and proper that we should have recourse to medical science to be healed. Although there is a mystery of suffering which we can never hope fully to understand, our first approach to it must be realistic and practical even if the mysteriousness with which doctors sometimes like to surround their craft does not always make this easy.

Yet this approach is not the end of the matter. It is little more than a beginning and it is a common experience that serious illness and suffering, especially when prolonged, can almost destroy a personality. Not only is there the erosion of the body by disease, there is all the mental and psychological stress that goes with it. There is the difficulty of understanding the mystery of suffering experienced in one's own personality and there are the questionings that inevitably arise. It is well known that some people do experience temptation in illness. They lack, they say, trust in God's goodness and as their mind gets weary, they may have temptations against faith in God altogether.

It is not surprising, then, that the introduction sketches out a spiritual theology of suffering. It will be best to make an approach to the matter rather different from that of the introduction, which puts the difficult text of Colossians 1:24 in the forefront of its thought.[5] The best approach is through the great baptismal text of Romans 6:3–5. By baptism we are committed to a life of 'imitation' of Christ. Interiorly we have to be conformed to him in his passion as well as in his resurrection; his life has to become the pattern of our own and even if we feel we shall never achieve 'crucifixion' with Christ so that we are able to say 'I live no longer I but Christ in me' (Galatians 2:19, 20), yet this must be our aim. Without succumbing to fatalism (even of a Christian kind) or passivity, our attitude must be one of acceptance of what life brings which includes illness and pain. Granted this, illness and suffering can become participations in the sufferings of Christ for the sake and the good of 'the church which is his body'.[6]

Mysteriously in Christ there is a communion in sufferings as there is in faith and love and it is this that it is possible for us to experience in illness. Possible, because for most it is very difficult to rise to this height when we are in pain. Our ability to 'handle' suffering is conditioned by our whole life and if we live outside Christ instead of in him, we cannot hope to rise to the mystical heights of consciously suffering with him.

This is in line with the use the introduction makes of Isaiah 53:4, 5 first to show that illness is not a punishment for sin but, secondly and more importantly, to indicate the solidarity there is between Christ and those who suffer: 'Christ, who is without sin, took upon himself all our "sickness and pains"[7] and shared the sufferings of all men. Indeed, in those of his members who are conformed to him he is crucified and suffers (*angitur*) when we suffer pain.' We are reminded of St Leo's saying: 'The passion of Christ is prolonged until the end of the world . . . it is he who suffers in and with all who bear adversity for righteousness.'[8]

This, broadly, is the Christian teaching on illness and suffering. Both remain ultimately mysteries but for the Christian there is here light and help. Light, because he is better able to see suffering in the whole context of Christianity, and help, because Christ comes to our aid. If suffering, whether our own or that of others, is a puzzle, at least we can see that God has not left us to ourselves. He in Christ has taken upon himself all the suffering of mankind, he has involved himself in the human condition at its weakest and most anguished, and by his love and his power he redeems this condition, at least for those who believe in him. In all the sacraments we meet the suffering and the risen Christ, that is, we are able to share in his paschal mystery, but in illness we are called in a special way to share in the sufferings of Christ and through the sacrament of anointing, as well as in communion, he reaches out to us, or rather reaches into the innermost places of our being, to raise us up in hope, to dispel anxiety and despair and to heal that condition so that we can return to the community of men and the community of the church, there to serve our fellow-men and to give praise to God.

Another element the introduction sees in the experience of illness is a sense of proportion about the meaning of life. It helps us to see that this life is not everything, that our sufferings, compared to the glory to come, seem light and of little weight and the text refers to 2 Corinthians 4:17. If this consideration seems a little light-hearted to one who is weighed down by pain, later on the text refers to Romans 8:19–21 and sees illness and pain as part of the whole process which the world is undergoing until it achieves deliverance. The world 'groans' and we literally groan with it. We experience something of the tragedy of things and we bring that experience to Christ in the sacrament where he works 'alleviation'. As the introduction says further on (5), in the sacrament of anointing Christ brings to his faithful ones who suffer a most certain help.

The existence of the sacrament and its effect[9]

Although there is in the Letter of St James (5:14–16) what seems to be a clear enough reference to the sacrament, it is not in fact heard of again until the beginning of the third century. It is one of the many puzzles of the history of sacramental theology. In James there are already all the elements of the sacrament. There is the assembly of the presbyters (as still in the Byzantine rite), prayer, the anointing with oil and the twofold effect, the 'raising up' of the sick man and, if necessary, the forgiveness of sins. The introduction sees in this passage the 'promulgation' of the sacrament which was 'instituted' in the gospels (the Apostolic Constitution refers to Mark 6:13).[10] The introduction goes on, 'From that time it has been the custom of the church to celebrate the sacrament with the anointing and prayer of the presbyters, commending the sick to the suffering and glorified Lord that he may raise them up and save them' (5). The reference to 'the suffering and glorified Lord' is interesting: the sacrament is a means of sharing in the paschal mystery. The words 'save' and 'raise up' however need a little further explanation especially as both now come in the new formula of anointing.

The text of James 5:14–16 is not at all as clear as our traditional understanding of it has made it seem. What does 'save' mean? In contexts referring to judgement and eternal death, it can mean 'salvation' which consists in eternal life. But, apparently in contexts concerning sickness (Matthew 9:21, Mark 5:28, etc.) this is not so. Similarly, 'raise up', *egeirein*, 'which occurs only here in James' can refer both to resurrection from the dead (which is not in question here) or to 'raising up from sickness' (Matthew 9:5–7; Mark 1:31, etc.). A modern Catholic exegete writes 'Here in the present context the most obvious meaning of the words seems to be that the sick man will be "saved" from death and "raised up" to life and health'.[11] If this exegesis is sound, then anointing is certainly a sacrament of healing and not a preparation for death. It also follows that the words in the formula of administration must be translated 'save' and 'raise up' though one hopes that someone will have the courage to translate the latter as 'raise you up to health' or even 'restore your health'.

After the text in St James we hear nothing about an anointing of the sick until the *Apostolic Tradition* (5) of Hippolytus. There the oil is blessed after the eucharistic prayer and is clearly intended for healing whether by external application or by drinking. In the Sacramentary of Serapion (*c.* 350) oil for healing is blessed in much the same place.[12] There is the well-known letter (28) of Pope Innocent I (died 417) who, interpreting the James text, says that there is no doubt that the faithful who are sick can be anointed and the oil used is chrism.[13] Not to take the matter any further, there is the prayer of blessing, found in the Gelasian Sacramentary,[14] later in the Roman Pontifical, where it still is, though in slightly revised form. All these texts, referred to in a general way in the Apostolic Constitution (pp. 7, 8), stress the healing property of the sacrament but nowhere more strongly than in the prayer of the Gelasian book. Since it may be used, in cases of necessity, in the administration of the rite itself, it will be useful to give a translation of it.

God, Father of all consolation,
it was your will that the sick in their weakness should be healed
    by your Son;
hear the prayer of faith;
send from heaven your Holy Spirit, our advocate, upon the
    richness of this oil
which by your kindly providence is produced by the olive tree
for the restoration of the body.
Through your blessing may it be
a source of strength for the body, mind and spirit
of all who are anointed with it.
May it dispel all their pains, weakness and sickness.
May it be a holy oil, Lord, blessed by you in the name of our Lord
Jesus Christ who lives and reigns with you through endless
    ages.[15]

The first thing that is notable is the heavy emphasis on healing. What is more, it is a healing of the whole personality, body, mind and spirit, and in this sense the prayer is astonishingly modern. We note too that the forgiveness of sin is not mentioned, nor is it in the letter of Innocent. What the formula was in the fifth and sixth centuries we simply do not know though we do know that 'patients' drank the oil and, a little later, we find that it was applied to those places where the pain was greatest. What is clear is that the symbolism of oil as a healing element was dominant, and as far as we can discern, gave the 'tone' to the whole sacrament. It was later, in the tenth century, that it came to be associated with penitence and death.[16]

When we turn to the statement of the introduction on the effect of the sacrament we find that it is very elaborate.[17] In the sacrament of anointing the grace of the Holy Spirit brings help to the sick person for the salvation of his whole personality (*qua* totus homo *ad salutem adiuvatur*); his trust in God is raised up, he is strengthened against temptations and the anxiety that the thought of death brings; he is enabled to bear his sufferings more patiently and, if it is expedient for his spiritual salvation, his health is restored. Finally, if he is in need of forgiveness, his sins will be pardoned and the sacrament is described as the consummation of penance (6). In the next article the sacrament is spoken of as 'a pledge of the kingdom to come'.

There is a great deal here, too much perhaps, and the statement is to be regarded rather as a description of the effects of the sacrament than as a definition. On the one hand, the revisers seem to have been practising a certain theological concordism taking up into their description all that has been said by theologians since about the time of St Thomas who saw anointing as the sacrament that '*immediately* disposes a man for glory *since it is given to those who are dying*'.[18] Hence we get the statements that the sacrament is a 'consummation of penance' and 'a pledge of the kingdom to come'. They also make rather too much of the *tentationes maligni*, the temptations of the Evil One, and the struggle against illness or pain (it is not clear which) which psychologically may be a bad thing. And 'health' is slipped in as if it were unimportant. This is odd since the rite itself is much more emphatic.[19] On the other hand, the great positive contribution of this statement is that it refuses to accept any sharp division between body and soul. In this it is in line with the psychosomatic views of modern medicine. The dispelling of anxieties can help physical health and alleviation of pain can bring a more tranquil state of mind to the patient. This view is also in accordance with biblical teaching which did not distinguish body and soul as they have been since Scholasticism became the prevalent philosophy of the church. The Bible, especially the Old Testament, saw sickness and sin as closely connected.[20] 'And just as the miraculous healing by Jesus (in Matthew 9:1–8 and par.) operated first on the body and then on the soul, so here the ritual of the priests works not only on the body but, when necessary, on the soul.' The object of the sacrament is the whole personality (*totus homo*) which it seeks to heal. It is against this background that we should see the apparently difficult statement that in this sacrament 'the grace of the Holy Spirit brings help to the sick person for the salvation of his whole personality'. Here *salutem* is, I think, to be taken in its widest possible sense: health for the body and salvation for the soul, or rather, a salvation that means health, the reintegration of the vital forces which are disorientated by disease for the body, and a spiritual renewal of the whole personality.

The forgiveness of sin of course assumes repentance on the part of the patient and the introduction on the point is laconic, much less explicit than the Council of Trent whose doctrine it is summarizing throughout this paragraph (6). Trent put the taking away of sin first (in line with Aquinas's teaching) and speaks (again in the language of St Thomas) of the removing of the 'remains (*reliquiae*) of sin'. The introduction simply uses the expression *veniam peccati*, pardon of sin, which the sacrament can effect.[21] It is more difficult to understand why anointing is called 'the consummation of penance' (or perhaps, as the text has it, 'Christian penitence'). This seems to be a relic of the medieval situation when the sacrament was all mixed up with the discipline of penance. As we have seen, in the fifth and sixth centuries this was not so though we can see from the letter of Innocent that the recipient of the sacrament must be repentant. One must suppose then the phrase means that if patients accept their illnesses and the sufferings they involve as reparation for sin and in union with the passion of Christ, such acceptance will be a significant expression of their life-long penitence.

As we have observed often enough, we are saved by faith and the sacraments of faith and the introduction underlines this (7), as well as connecting faith with prayer. As in St James, it is the prayer of faith that will save the sick man. So, says the introduction, *both* the celebrant and the patient must have faith and it is a faith that is at once the faith of the individual and the faith of the church. It looks to the person of Christ in his passion and resurrection, the Christ who shared human suffering, who by his resurrection radically overcame death, sin and disease, and whose power is the source of the sacrament. It is a faith too that looks to his second coming (*futurum prospicit regnum*) when all tears and mourning and suffering will be done away. Anointing is both a participation in the paschal mystery of Christ and an anticipation of the final consummation.

Who may be anointed?

This too has been a contentious matter in the past, especially when the sacrament was associated with death. The priest felt that there must be some grounded expectation of death before he was justified in administering it. In more recent years practice has tended to be more flexible and now the Order comes along to say that it is not danger of death that is the condition of reception but '*a serious illness*' (8) and

~
179

judgement on its gravity need only be 'probable' though doctors may usefully be consulted. No doubt the casuists, as they have done in the past, will try to define more closely what 'gravity' is but it would seem that it is hardly necessary. The introduction is speaking of the normal judgement priest or patient will make on the matter. Once the emphasis on death is removed, judgement becomes all the easier.

Anointing may be given to the same person as often as there is serious illness and also during the *same* illness when there is a new and more serious crisis, as is usually the case. A monthly anointing in cases of prolonged illness, as some expected, is not allowed for. On the other hand, where an operation becomes necessary on account of a dangerous disease (*morbus*), the patient may be anointed beforehand. This has long been requested and is now officially granted. Again, the old, even if not dangerously ill, but suffering the debility that often accompanies old age, may be anointed. This too is new but in practice it is not at all an easy matter to find the right moment for this, especially as it is often the old who think of anointing as a prelude to death.[22] Likewise, children who have a sufficient use of reason to understand the sacrament and 'to receive comfort from it' may also be anointed. This is a rather more liberal permission than the former *Rituale Romanum* (V, i, 8) which seems to say that the use of reason must already have been achieved. In practice, young children seem rarely to have been anointed though after they have made their first communion, however young they may be, they can certainly 'appreciate' the sacrament of anointing. As before, the unconscious may be anointed on the assumption that they have had a desire for it. If a person is dead, however, the priest is to pray that God may forgive him his sins and admit him to his kingdom. If there is doubt about the actuality of death, he may anoint conditionally. There is nothing new here although surprisingly the text does not mention conditional absolution which is common practice in these circumstances.

Finally (13), the laity are to be instructed to ask for the sacrament and, it goes without saying, receive it devoutly 'and with full faith'. They are not to conform to 'the bad custom' of procrastination. In the new atmosphere created by this Order, an atmosphere that in fact is already widely prevalent, it will be all the easier to persuade people to ask to be anointed. The death-nexus has certainly done ill service to pastoral work in the matter.

The ministers of the sacrament

Little need be said here. Everyone from bishops to parish priests, their assistants and hospital chaplains are the ordinary ministers of this sacrament and in cases of necessity, all priests with the presumed permission of the parish priest.

The oil of the sick

As we have seen, the oil used in the anointing of the sick in the fifth and sixth centuries was called chrism which on account of its richness and perfume was regarded as the symbol of the Holy Spirit. But since at this time and until much later it was the custom for the people to bring oil for the use of the sick to Mass to be blessed, it will have been the ordinary oil used in the house. Either *chrisma* in the texts means simply 'holy oil' or perhaps it means oil blessed by the bishop more solemnly. However, no distinction seems to have been made between chrism and the oil of the sick until the ninth century.[23] However that may be, until now the oil to be used in the sacrament has always been olive oil but the Order (20) now says that it may be any oil so long as it comes from a plant. The Apostolic Constitution (p. 10) explains that this has been allowed at the request of many bishops who have made known that olive oil cannot be obtained in certain regions or only with difficulty. It is a plain example of the 'adaptations' mentioned in the Constitution on the Liturgy (40) and witnesses to a gratifying flexibility about symbolism. It is to be the oil of a plant since it is 'more like' that of the olive and can, as easily, carry its symbolism.

The oil must still be blessed by a diocesan bishop (or by one who is 'equiparated' to him) unless, for urgent reasons, it is blessed by a priest. This he will do during the administration of the sacrament. The reasons for this are fairly obvious: on account of distance he may not be able to renew his supply, communication lines may have been broken down by flood or some other natural disaster. The regulation witnesses to a right sense of proportion: it is more important for a sick man to be anointed than it is that the bishop should bless the oil.

The manner of administration

This too has been changed. Only the forehead and the hands are anointed though more numerous anointings may be allowed if local custom requires (24). The first part of the formula is said while the forehead is anointed and the second part while the hands are anointed. A rather complicated affair! In cases of necessity only one place need be anointed, as in the former rite.

The liturgy of the sacrament

1. The greeting and the blessing of the patient and the room (with holy water, if desired).
2. Brief introductory remarks which include the recitation of James 5:14–16.
3. The penitential act or sacramental confession of the patient if this has not been done beforehand.
4. A scripture reading and brief homily if possible.
5. Intercessions for the patient and his attendants.
6. The laying-on of hands in silence.
7. The blessing of the oil (in case of necessity); otherwise a prayer of Jewish pattern, blessing God for his compassion shown in this sacrament.
8. The administration. The formula is said once, the patient is anointed in two places, the forehead and the hands.
9. The rite ends with the saying of a collect (a selection is given to be used according to circumstances), the Lord's Prayer, and a special form of blessing.

Commentary

Those who are familiar with the former rite will see that there are considerable differences. The first three prayers of that rite were really a blessing of the house and those in it with no special mention of the patient. There was not even a proper laying-on of hands. The rubric instructed the celebrant to 'extend' his right hand over the patient while he said a long and unmanageable prayer. After the anointing there were three collects, the first of which mentioned the James text for the first time, all asking for the restoration of health even when the patient was visibly dying. The new rite conforms to what is now the set pattern for sacramental celebration. There is first a ministry of the word, prayer and finally the administration of the sacrament. The whole rite is visibly more personal, directed to the patient and engaging his and the attendants' participation. Finally, it may be noted here that for almost every part of the rite alternative texts are given which together build up a powerful impression of the healing power of the sacrament.

The preliminary rites: The blessing with holy water is interpreted by a formula saying that the sprinkling is a reminder of baptism and recalls Christ who by his passion and resurrection redeemed us. Anointing is a celebration of the paschal mystery which for the Christian begins with his baptism.

The address (or invitatory), which may be replaced by a collect, again emphasizes that we have to do with a sacrament of healing: in the gospel the people approached Jesus asking for health and he is amongst the company now commanding (present tense) that 'if any one is sick among you, let him call in the priests of the church' and the rest.

The penitential rite may be the same as that in the Mass but the second alternative is worth looking at: 'By your paschal mystery you gained for us salvation; By the wonderful works of your passion, you do not cease to renew us; By our partaking of your Body you make us sharers in your paschal sacrifice' and to all these sentences the people reply either 'Lord have mercy' or 'Christ have mercy'. There is liveliness and sound teaching in all this.

The ministry of the word: A very large selection of scripture readings is provided for the sick and the dying and they are to be used at the discretion of the minister. They are intended to be used in *all* the eventualities of ministering to the sick and the dying both in church and at home and they provide material for the construction of services of the sick. They are drawn from the Old Testament, the epistles and the gospels and their content is so various that it would be impossible even to summarize them here. The reading in the text of the rite is Matthew 8:5–10, 13, the incident of the centurion's servant with the words 'Lord, I am not worthy . . .'. All the scripture readings are provided in the *Pastoral Care of the Sick.*

The intercessions that come normally after the reading (though they may be said after the anointing or even in some other place) represent one of the oldest and most important elements of the rite: 'The prayer of faith shall save the sick man . . .' and there was much praying in the medieval rites. This situation is summed up in the former Roman Ritual (V, ii, 7) where the attendants were enjoined to recite the Litany of the Saints, the seven penitential psalms (a relic of the connection with penance) or other prayers *while* the minister anointed the patient. Apart from the undesirability of having a paraliturgy going on, it in fact never worked. The family was too concerned to indulge in a self-directed liturgy. Still, the principle was preserved and, as we have remarked elsewhere, the prayer-element in the celebration of sacraments in all the early church was seen to be most important. If it had been adequately maintained, the charge of sacramental automatism or even magic would never have been made.

The style of the intercessions, of which three forms are given, is litanic, of the kind we have become used to. They ask that God will come to the patient and strengthen him with the anointing, that the sufferings of all the sick may be alleviated and that those in charge of the patient may receive help from God. The response is 'Hear us (Lord), we beseech you'. Two further points may be noted: (1) the introduction explicitly takes up the James text: the assembly is praying the prayer of faith; (2) the last petition leads to the laying-on of hands: 'May he in whose name we lay on our hands give life and salvation (*salutem* = health?) to the patient'.

The other two forms are worth looking at. The second (240) is shorter and more scriptural: (The Lord) took upon himself our sickness and bore our sufferings; he had compassion on the multitude and went about doing good and healing the sick; and (finally) he sent out the apostles and bade them lay hands on the sick, a petition that leads to the laying-on of hands. The response is 'Lord have mercy' or 'Christ have mercy'. The third form (241) has shorter petitions but these are rather more numerous though covering the same ground. It ends with the petition about the laying-on of hands as the first form does. In certain circumstances, e.g. when the patient is in pain, this will be the best form to use. The petitions are short and are likely to be more easily grasped by the patient.

The rite, though simple, moves to an impressive climax from the

184

readings and through the prayers to the laying-on of hands and the anointing. The restoration of a proper laying-on of hands is welcome not merely for its liturgical appropriateness but for its theological implications. The sacramental action is now visibly the extension in time of Christ's gestures of healing in the gospel. In recent years we have heard often enough the Augustinian tag 'When the church baptizes, it is Christ who baptizes' and we are justified in saying 'When the church anoints, it is Christ who anoints'. As so many of the texts of the rite say, Christ is present with his power of healing and comfort.

After the hand-laying there is either the blessing of the oil or the 'blessing' of God for his compassion shown in the sacrament. Clearly it draws attention to the oil and this is no doubt intended. It is a Jewish form of prayer, blessing God for his gifts: 'Blessed be God, Father almighty, for us and for our salvation you sent your Son into the world'. The response is 'Blessed be God'. The second is addressed to the Son and the third to the Holy Spirit. The litany ends 'May your servant who is in pain, Lord, be restored (to health), may your power strengthen him (*confortari*) in his weakness (or illness) as in faith he is anointed with this holy oil'. It might have been the 'form' of the sacrament!

The administration

The 'form' of the sacrament is much changed. The chief change is that while the former one (no older than the tenth century) seemed to be wholly concerned with *sin* ('May the Lord forgive you whatever sins you have committed by sight'),[24] the new one suggests by its position that it is the secondary effect of the sacrament. Since the Latin, which is very packed, provides some difficulties of translation, it will be best to give it in Latin:

Per istam sanctam unctionem
et suam piissimam misericordiam,
adiuvet te Dominus gratia Spiritus Sancti (℞ Amen);
ut a peccatis liberatum
te salvet atque *propitius* allevet (℞ Amen).[25]

The first two lines are from the old formula and the last three are new. It is the last three that require commentary and provide difficulties in translation.

(a) *Adiuvet te gratia Spiritus Sancti* is based on the *teaching* of the Council of Trent and refers back to the prayer of blessing of (thanksgiving over) the oil.

Once again we note the link between *prayer* and the action of the sacrament. This phrase, then, introduced into the formula of administration, reminds us that the effect of the sacrament is the work of the Holy Spirit, as the prayer of blessing says it is, and if the Roman Church in the past could be accused of neglecting the Holy Spirit in its liturgy, this can no longer be said!

(b) The last two lines echo the James text with its message of 'deliverance from sin' and the healing effect (*salvet . . . allevet*) though precisely what the former word means is not clear. In verb or noun form it occurs elsewhere in the service (intercessions, blessing) and yet its meaning remains unclear. If it means 'save' or 'salvation' it is odd for we never speak in that way of the effect of any other sacrament. It is a deliberate reference to the 'save' (*sosei*) of James 5:15 and will have the same interpretation as that text bears.[26] '*Raise up*' can only mean 'raise up to health', restoration to health, as the collect after the administration says: 'Restore to him full health, interiorly and externally'.[27]

The conclusion

Six collects in all (243–246) are provided for use after the anointing, the last four adapted to the condition of the patient: for one weak from old age, for one in great danger, for use when anointing and *Viaticum* are given together and for one in his (last) agony. This directly responds to the request of the Council Fathers in the Constitution on the Liturgy (75) and relieves one of having to pray for the recovery of one who is certainly dying. The first collect (77), phrases of which are to be found in the Gelasian Sacramentary (1539), is ancient.[28] An examination of all these collects would be profitable. They underline the healing properties of the sacrament very strongly. Thus the alternative under no. 77: (grant that) by this anointing his strength may be restored, he may be consoled by (your) help, his powers be renewed (*vires erigat*) and all evil be dispelled. In addition, these prayers are filled with a truly Christian compassion.

Even the blessing deserves mention. It runs:

May God our Father bless you (℞ Amen, and so throughout).
May the Son of God heal you.
May the Holy Spirit shed his light on you.
May he guard your body and save your soul.
May he enlighten your heart and bring you everlasting life.

And then the usual form of blessing follows.

The communal celebration of the sacrament

In recent years there has been a growing practice of anointing people at Mass, sometimes in considerable numbers, as at Lourdes. This is the direct result of separating anointing from death and it is certain that if this sacrament is to appear for what it is in the eyes of ordinary people, such public celebrations are necessary. They will do more than any instruction to show them that anointing is a sacrament of healing and they will readily ask for it.

Anointing, then, may be celebrated within the Mass for one or two sick people (80–82), for a large number of the sick (83–85) and outside the Mass in a service that takes the form of the ministry of the word.

There is no variation in the rite itself which is fitted into the structure of the Mass (or the service) in what is now the accustomed place, namely after the homily. The minister(s) will receive the sick at the beginning of the Mass immediately after the greeting, and except for days of the highest liturgical rank (81), the readings may be taken from those provided for the sick in the lectionary and the other texts are to be taken from the Mass-formula 'For the Sick'. Thus after centuries the sacrament of the sick is united with the eucharist. The vestments, it is interesting to note, are no longer to be violet (a sign of penitence) but white.

The sacrament is administered after the gospel and its homily, which is to take the scripture texts as its basis (82), showing the significance of human suffering and disease in the divine plan of salvation, though the celebrant is to have regard for the condition of the sick. Brevity will be the keynote. There follow the intercessions (which however may be deferred until after the administration), the blessing of the oil (if necessary) or the 'blessing prayer' for the oil and finally the anointing itself. If many priests are taking part each one lays hands on one of the sick persons and then anoints (19).[29] Otherwise, the various actions of the service may be distributed among the ministers (*ibid.*). What is evidently to be avoided is the administration of the anointing by two ministers. The intercessions may take place at this point and if they do, they conclude with the collect of the rite. The Mass then proceeds as usual though we note that the sick and their attendants may receive communion in both kinds (82, c).

Celebration of the sacrament outside the Mass hardly differs though the arrangements may be more flexible. The sick are to be given opportunity to confess beforehand, they are received at the beginning, there is an act of penitence. There may be one or more readings, there is to be a homily after which silence may be kept. During the administration suitable chants may be sung though the text (90) says that the words of administration should be heard at least once. After the administration, either a collect from the rite or the Lord's Prayer may be used, and the latter may suitably be sung. The service concludes with the blessing.

These communal celebrations may take place not only in churches but in hospitals or other suitable places though the bishop remains the judge and is in any case responsible for their proper organization.

The visitation of the sick

Probably the least-used part of the former *Rituale Romanum* was that called 'The Visitation and Care of the Sick' (V, iv). The reasons for this were that it was very long and rarely translated into English. The Irish *Collectio Rituum* (1960) showed what could be done. The compilers, as well as translating the text into English (and Irish), divided the material into three parts which could be used on successive visits.

The revisers of the new Order have taken a different way. They have subsumed under the heading 'Visitation' the communion of the sick and other pastoral care, including of course confession. But they have not seen fit to provide a service. They recommend however a pattern which follows the now familiar lines. There will be a reading of the scriptures 'which will be prepared with the patient in a friendly and informal way'. This will lead to prayer from the psalms or other sources and the visit will conclude, if circumstances indicate, with a blessing and a laying-on of hands. This latter was featured in the previous form and is very important. It continues the gesture of Christ and, without being a sacrament in the strict sense, must be conceived of as at least a prayer for Christ's healing. The alternative blessing after the anointing would seem to be an appropriate text to use: 'The Lord Jesus Christ be present with you and defend you; / May he go before you and lead you and follow you and protect you; / May he look upon you, preserve you and bless you.'

It is probably a very good thing that the pattern has been left free. Sick people differ enormously and if they are really ill, they cannot manage formal services. It is the familiar and very simple prayers that count at this time and the priest has to find out what they know and like. But this does not exclude other material and as the people are becoming more familiar with the psalms, phrases from these too, as the introduction suggests, will be helpful. Certainly passages from the gospels about Christ's healing and compassion are acceptable. And the 'sentences' provided for the commendation of the dying offer another suggestion for those who are sick. No doubt each priest will make up his own anthology and use it according to circumstances.

But there is something else of even greater practical importance. Right at the beginning the Order establishes that it is not just the clergy who are to visit the sick. It is a duty incumbent upon all the faithful. They are to 'share the care and love of Christ for the sick, they are to visit them, to comfort them and where there is necessity, to provide for their material needs'.[30] Everyone knows, and this goes for the clergy too, that a 'sick visit' can be nothing much more than an enquiry after the patient's health, a brief prayer and a blessing. The bunch of grapes (rarely eaten by the patient) and the glossy magazine (on the assumption that you can get one that is respectable) are hardly adequate to express one's Christian care for the patient. What, then, is required is small booklets with collections of texts (including the most familiar prayers) for use by the laity and by the sick.[31] Alongside the scripture texts there should be short, simple and direct prayers that will 'speak to the condition' of the sick person. Given a new outlook and this simple instrument, the visitation of the sick by the laity could become a permanent activity. One of the 'seven corporal works of mercy' *and* the fulfilment of the gospel injunction would become a reality in the lives of many Christians.

Communion of the sick

In the former Ritual this was a very jejune rite which one felt compelled to 'nourish'. The new rite follows the now familiar pattern: introduction, blessing of the house and sick person, the penitential rite, the reading of the scriptures, the Lord's Prayer, the administration, the final collect and blessing.

Even this is not a great deal and the scripture passages could well be extended. The revisers did not think to include 1 Corinthians 10:15, 16, nor 1 Corinthians 11:23–26, nor any of the narratives of the Last Supper from the synoptists. Yet the sick often need to be reminded where the communion they are receiving originated. There would seem to be no reason why the readings of the day (from the lectionary) should not be used if appropriate. After the (brief) homily intercessions may be made though no texts are given. The minister may like to ask the patient and those present whom they wish to pray for. However this may have to be adapted to circumstances. See the section 'Communion in a hospital or institution' (*Pastoral Care*, p. 119).

Viaticum

This follows the same pattern as that of the communion of the sick though there are one or two differences. (a) The 'Last Blessing' is neatly included in the penitential rite. (b) After the reading of scripture there is a profession of faith (in the terms of the Apostles' Creed). This is a restoration of an old practice which survived, I believe, only in the administration of *Viaticum* to a bishop. It is a valuable feature. (c) Intercessions, of very good quality, are provided. (d) The problem of pronouncing the old and rather frightening formula at communion has been eliminated. The minister says 'The Body (or Blood) of Christ', the patient says 'Amen' and the minister continues 'May he guard you and bring you to everlasting life'. Discreet but sufficient.

The Ritus Continuus *for those near to death*

There is no fundamental change here. The omissions are predictable: duplications are eliminated. What *is* important is that *Viaticum* has been restored to its original place, the *last* sacrament before dying. It was ousted from this place when anointing came to be regarded as a preparation for death and in the twelfth century acquired the name of 'Extreme Unction', the last anointing—before death. It was in fact restored to its original place in some of the vernacular rituals of the pre-conciliar days, notably in the German *Collectio Rituum* (1950), which here and elsewhere has exercised a certain influence on this new Order.[32]

It should be noted that *Viaticum* may be given during the Mass and the Order (26) recommends this on account of the special significance of the eucharist as a participation in 'the death of the Lord and his passage (*transitus*) to his Father'. This means in practice that bishops should readily give permission for the Mass to be celebrated in the homes of the dying. It should be noted too that where there is a lack of priests, authorized lay people, whether men or women, may give *Viaticum* to the dying (29), as indeed they may do to the sick once they have received authorization. The extension of this permission is much desired, especially in parishes where there is only one priest. Finally, both the sick and the dying may receive communion in the form of wine alone if they cannot take it in the form of bread.

The commendation of the dying

Assistance of the dying is one of the greatest and, at the same time, one of the most difficult, of charities. The Order is aware of this and urges both clergy and laity to do all they can to help the dying. The aim should be to help the patient to overcome the natural fear of death by arousing his hope in the power of the resurrection of Christ through whom he will enter into eternal life. He is to be led to accept his death in imitation of the suffering and dying Christ.

The Order is to be seen as a collection of 'sentences', scripture readings and prayers of various kinds which may be freely used according to circumstances. The condition of the dying is to be closely observed and the minister is to recite slowly and in such a voice as may help him. As well as the texts suggested, others may be used and short prayers ('ejaculations'), which as is well known are most acceptable at such a time, should be used. Simple gestures, like signing the patient with the cross, are also recommended. The minister should also remember that those present will also profit from the prayers and other texts used on this occasion. They will strengthen them for what is always a very great ordeal and they will learn to see death as a participation in the paschal mystery of Christ.

The 'order' breaks down into four parts: (a) 'sentences' all from holy scripture and of course to be used at choice; (b) scripture readings (some obviously from the passion narratives); (c) prayers of various kinds; (d) the commendation proper which includes the famous *Proficiscere* (shorter and much improved), another similar prayer, a litany (similar to the one in the former ritual though much shorter and better) and another commendation. Immediately after the expiry the *Subvenite* is said. The text suggests that before the *Subvenite* the *Salve Regina* may be *sung*. A lot will depend on circumstances but one recalls the Canadian chaplain who on the death of Maurice Baring stood up and recited the *Magnificat*.[33]

Pastoral considerations

Further comment is almost superfluous. The new Order is a thoroughly pastoral document and has only to be read to be appreciated. In all the discussion about the role of the priest in modern society it rarely seems to be understood that, apart from him, there is no one else always available to give the spiritual help and comfort that are necessary to the dying. It is true that, as the Order urges, the laity too must play their part. Care of the sick and dying is not the exclusive duty of the clergy but it is he who will be the leader if others are to take it up.

It is however very arduous work and both clergy and, when they take it up, the laity need a good deal of help if it is to be done effectively. There are four categories of patient one can think of right away: (a) those ill at home, perhaps seriously but not fatally; (b) there are those who are terminally ill and most likely in hospital; (c) there is the problem of the old; (d) finally, there are the mentally ill.

(a) It is easier to minister to *those ill at home* than to anyone else. There is time and there is privacy. Although illness can have devastating effects it often provides time for reflection and the patient becomes open to God and to his word. Much can be done but much more could be done with the informed and willing help of the laity. It is now usual for lay people to be authorized to give holy communion to the sick and housebound. The publication of booklets containing at least a summary of the teaching of the Order and essential texts for the participants would be very helpful to both patients and ministers. In these booklets the introduction or at least a summary of its main teaching should be printed. With this material familiar prayers (even the Hail Mary which some have forgotten!) should be included.[34]

(b) The difficulties of the care of *the sick in hospitals* are considerable and the greatest is lack of privacy. Chaplains overcome this difficulty and others in a remarkable way but it would seem that some formal approach to hospital authorities is sometimes necessary to secure the necessary conditions. For the terminally ill, both clergy and laity are in need of information and help from doctors and psychiatrists though even here the situation is improving. Courses of one sort or another are being made available.[35]

(c) *The old.* Perhaps a good deal is known on the subject but it has hardly filtered down to parish level. How do you give spiritual comfort to those who are 'hard of hearing' in a hospital ward or an old people's home common room? How do you get people to return to Christ after forty or more years of lapsation? What are the phases through which old people go? Are they better off in a 'home' or at home and if the latter (which seems more desirable), could not something more be done to look after them? These are some of the questions that need asking. There is here a whole new and very difficult field for which the pastoral clergy need help. If sight is faint and hearing all but gone, no amount of new 'orders' will help them. The clergy of course must play their part, but it is here one feels that laity, trained in some measure for the task and with leisure to talk to the old for quite long periods, would be of the greatest assistance. A small but practical and very important 'instrument' would be a booklet for communion and the other rites printed in large type. I do not know of even a New Testament so printed.

(d) The greatest defect of the new Order is that nowhere does it mention those who are *mentally ill.* At times they can be very ill indeed and the mental illness can affect their physical health.[36] Even apart from that, it is now recognized that mental trouble is an *illness.* In this condition people suffer from great anxieties, apparent denial of the faith and a whole range of troubles which anointing, in the terms of the Order (6), could alleviate. Yet the matter is not mentioned.[37] This is inconsistent with the general line of the introduction and the rite which makes no sharp distinction between body and soul. In the opinion of the present writer, the clergy would be justified in making up their own minds on the matter though it would be better if the church authorities recognized that this situation exists and that the remedy of the sacrament is readily available. The pastoral care of such patients is extremely difficult and a great deal of help and information is necessary if the pastoral clergy are to perform their task adequately. It is yet another field which, from the standpoint of pastoral care, is insufficiently explored.

Notes

[1] *Ordo Unctionis Infirmorum eorumque Pastoralis Curae* (Vatican Press, 1972). It was actually promulgated on 7 December 1972 but was not available until 1973. The authorized text for England and Wales is *Pastoral Care of the Sick* (ICEL translation, 1982). It has extra pastoral notes that change the numbers of the paragraphs in the Latin edition.

[2] In what follows, the sacrament will be referred to as 'the anointing' as the whole phrase is cumbersome and 'unction', apart from being very Latin, has unhappy associations.

[3] Pp. 6-10.

[4] The Order refers to John 9:3 though not all scripture experts interpret the passage in so simple a way.

[5] Difficult for many reasons but among others because there can be no 'addition' to or 'making up for' (JB) the sufferings of Christ which in verses 19, 20 St Paul has already made clear are all-sufficient.

[6] For an excellent treatment of Col 1:24 see J. H. Houlden, *Paul's Letters from Prison* (Penguin, 1970), pp. 176-8.

[7] RSV, *in loc.* margin.

[8] *De Pass.*, XIX: PL 54, c. 383.

[9] A recent study is that of B. Sesboüé, *L'Onction des malades* (Lyon, 1971).

[10] A modern exegete has this to say about the Marcan text: 'The fact that healing by unction was practised by the early Church (James 5:14f.) is no ground for denying that the disciples, or even Jesus himself, may have practised it': D. E. Nineham, *Saint Mark* (Penguin Books, 1963), p. 171.

[11] Kevin Condon, 'The Sacrament of Healing', in *Sacraments in Scripture*, ed. T. Worden (London, 1966), pp. 179-82. The same author goes on to say that if this is not the right interpretation of the words, we are involved in insuperable difficulties. The above paragraph is dependent on this essay.

[12] *Sacramentarium Serapionis*, XVII, ed. Funk, *Constitutiones Apostolicae*, 2, pp. 178-81.

[13] Text in Denz., 17th ed. (1928), no. 99.

[14] No. 382, p. 61, where the oil is again called chrism. For a brief summary of the history of the sacrament see the present writer's article 'Unction', in *A New Dictionary of Liturgy and Worship*, ed. J. G. Davies (London, 1986).

[15] The last sentence is new.

[16] For a convenient summary of Chavasse's research on this sacrament see Dom Placid Murray's article 'The Liturgical History of Extreme Unction', in *Studies in Pastoral Liturgy*, 2 (Dublin, 1963), pp. 18–38. The revised text of the prayer of blessing does not differ substantially from that in the Gelasian Sacramentary. The reference to drinking the oil is removed and the famous phrase about the oil being a chrism with which priests, kings, prophets and martyrs were anointed (a phrase that has its origins in the **Apostolic Tradition** of Hippolytus) has been removed.

[17] It is heavily dependent on the Council of Trent: Denz., 909.

[18] ST III (Supp.) xxix, a.1, ad 2. His theology (which may not have been his final thought) is clearly conditioned by the practice of his time.

[19] One hopes that the reasons for this are not that introductions matter and the liturgical texts do not.

[20] See Condon, *art. cit.*, p. 184, and other articles in the same book on 'Sin'.

[21] Aquinas saw the sacrament as principally aimed at spiritual infirmity brought about by the sin-ridden condition of mankind and the **reliquiae peccati** are 'the defects (or weaknesses) left in man' by sin. It is **these** that the sacrament is concerned with, strengthening the patient against their consequences. Cf. ST III (Supp.) xxx, a.1. The revisers evidently did not wish to concern themselves with this theology which must be regarded as coming out of a now obsolete situation.

[22] However, I find that the old when they are unwell, even if not seriously, are willing to ask for the sacrament if the priest is attentive to them.

[23] See B. Poschmann, **Penance and the Anointing of the Sick** (ET, London, 1964), p. 247.

[24] Perhaps this English translation was rather more explicit than the Latin: **indulgeat . . . deliquisti** which might be rendered 'your delinquencies'. Still, the meaning was plain.

[25] In a handout to recommend the new Order by no less a body than the Secretariat of State a translation is given: 'Through this holy anointing and his most loving mercy, may the Lord assist you by the grace of the Holy Spirit, so that when you have been freed from your sins he may save you and in his goodness raise you up'. The purpose of the handout is to undercut the critics of the revised liturgy. The full weight of the church's authority that is behind the Order is indicated.

[26] See above, p. 176.

[27] The provenance of the second part of the formula is unknown to me. There were many formulas current until the thirteenth century. See **The Church at Prayer**, III: **The Sacraments**, ed. A. G. Martimort (ET, Collegeville, MN/London, 1988), pp. 129–30.

[28] The second collect of the former Ritual is not repeated though it is found in so respectable a source as the Gregorian Sacramentary (208).

[29] The text says **possunt**. The individual hand-laying is not obligatory but seems highly appropriate.

[30] This is an echo of the **Rituale Romanum** in its excellent pastoral notes before the Visitation of the Sick but there the obligation of material help is laid on the clergy!

[31] See **Care of the Sick** (CTS, 1978), by the present writer.

[32] Which is not surprising as Dr Baltasar Fischer of Trier has been concerned with both. It is also a good example of how liturgical reform has been going on since the late forties, and represents work on which the Council was able to build.

~

Unhappily, there were some in this country who were either indifferent or hostile to such efforts. It was a case of 'those dotty foreigners'.

[33] Laura Lovat, *Maurice Baring: A Memoir* (1947), p. 33.

[34] See now *Prayer of the Sick* (Geoffrey Chapman, 1984); also *Care of the Sick, op. cit.*

[35] For literature see H. Guntrip, *Psychology for Social Workers* (1971); Heije Faber, *Pastoral Care in the Modern Hospital* (1971), with review in *Clergy Review* (February 1973) by Peter Hocken.

[36] Years ago I anointed a woman (who had to be held down) who was very seriously ill from mental trouble which eventually killed her.

[37] The *Pastoral Care of the Sick* (1982) has inserted a paragraph on the mentally ill: 'Some types of mental illness are now classified as serious. Those who are judged to have a serious mental illness and who would be strengthened by the sacrament may be anointed' (p. 27).

The Order of Christian Funerals

~~~~~~

I N RECENT years it has become a common-place to say that the modern world no longer believes in death. It is the supreme non-event. Before its onset it is disguised in certain ways and after it the corpse is swept away to be buried or cremated as soon as possible. Even expressions of grief are for the most part suppressed for it is not regarded as the proper thing to indulge them. It is indeed difficult to discern what people, sometimes even Christians, believe about death and what, if anything, is to come after it. Among others, Catholics are affected by this attitude though they have at their disposal a more clearly articulated belief in heaven, hell and purgatory than any others. But this belief is often held in an almost crudely materialistic form and we can agree with a recent writer that 'perhaps no area of Christian theology is in more need of a responsible *demythologization* than eschatology, that is, the theology of the last things, of death, judgement, heaven and hell'.[1] The demythologization should cover the whole range of events that concern both the individual and the end of the cosmos but for our purposes here it will be sufficient to concentrate on death, judgement and the time-model that most of us use to think of the other world.

For Christians death should not be the mere cessation of biological life even though with them the ending and the severance are usually uppermost in their minds and sentiments. However paradoxical it may seem, death is a part of life. All through our lives we are dying. We die to childhood or if we do not, we remain infantile. We die to youth as the price of maturity. We die to family that we may enter into a totally committed love for another or for another kind of life, the priesthood, the religious life or some form of dedication to the service of others. But all these dyings are the seed of a newer, richer kind of life. You could say that we die *into* a new life and the condition of entry into it is death.

This means that we are continually making assents to life, and however obscurely, we are saying that life has a purpose that is worth living

~

for. If we are Christians it means that we are continually assenting to Christ, doing what he wants of us. Work, an avocation, a vocation – and that covers almost every human activity – and all the effort that goes into them, all the strivings, all the prayer, every kind of service we do for others, are so many attempts to say Yes to God – in conventional language, to do his will.

Or, to put it another way, God has made himself known to us in his Word who has given us his word in the gospels. He calls us to accept it – and him – and this we do or try to do throughout our lives. Whether we celebrate the sacraments, whether we pray, listen to God's word in the Bible, we are responding to the call of God, we are trying to give ourselves to him. Then comes the final call of death. Is all that self-giving that has gone before, no doubt imperfectly, throughout our lives of no account when we come to die? The conventional answer, which is true but insufficient, is that we shall be 'rewarded' though often enough the implication is that the 'reward' has nothing to do with what has gone before – like giving a boy a book on mathematics for winning the cross-country race. If it is true that we are constantly 'dying into' a new and richer kind of life here below, it is at least intelligible that our death at the end of our life is a dying into eternal life which is promised to us by the word of God. It is at least intelligible that death, instead of being the supreme negative, is the supreme and all-embracing affirmation of our life by which, with all our being, we are able, through the mercy of God, to say Yes to his love.

All this may seem a little speculative and *a priori* but if we turn to the death of Christ we find the same pattern. And the first thing we notice is that the death is not the end. As the liturgy has always had it and as a renewed reflection on holy scripture has shown, the passion–death–resurrection are *together* the saving work of Christ. As he himself made clear (John 13:1ff.), his death was a passing over from this world through the suffering and the supreme self-giving it involved to the glory that was his before the world began. He 'died into' the resurrection and the glory. As St Paul would say, he 'emptied' himself and the results of that emptying were seen in the mysterious cry of abandonment on the cross: 'My God, my God, why have you forsaken me?' He gave all and the self-giving that went on all through his life reached its culmination in the Last Supper when he said 'I dedicate myself for their sake' (John 17:19), I am giving myself over to sacrifice for them and all who shall believe in me through them. Further, St John uses the strong and rich word *tetelestai* to describe the final and complete giving of Jesus on the cross: 'It is finished, it is accomplished', the whole life of obedience, the life of self-giving here reaches its supreme expression and because that self-giving was borne up by and permeated with Jesus' love for his Father, his saving work could be redemptive of the whole human race. In the terms we used above, the death of Jesus was the supreme affirmation of his life.

There was the giving, the affirmation, and this was 'answered' by the resurrection, the exaltation and the glory: 'Therefore God has highly exalted him and bestowed on him the name which is above every name' (Phil 2:9). Through his death Jesus acceded to the full life of the resurrection when his human nature became totally permeated by the Holy Spirit and became total gift to the Father.

It is in this sense that the death of Jesus is the model or type of all human dying. Always we are dying, that is trying to give ourselves, so that we may live more fully, and then comes the final death through which we enter into a new and richer kind of life. It is at this point that the words St John records of Jesus speaking of his own death become relevant: 'Unless a grain of wheat falls into the earth and dies, it remains alone; but if it dies, it bears much fruit'.[2] Jesus is the grain of wheat and by dying he became 'the source of life to all who believe in him'. All proportions kept, if we die into the Lord, if we make our passage through death, accepting it, we too shall pass into the fuller life that is called eternal and shall become, under Christ, a channel of life to others. For that is what the communion of saints means.

Understandably, then, the church sets the funeral rite in the framework of the paschal mystery, thus emphasizing the truth that in death the faithful Christian shares in the death of Christ and passes over into eternal life. Thus in the first collect of the funeral Mass we ask that as in this life the deceased has believed in the death and resurrection of Christ, so by that same mystery (the paschal mystery) he may be brought to the resurrection. This is typical of a great number of other texts, prayers, antiphons and readings which we will examine later.

There is, I think, a change of emphasis of another sort. Catholic funeral rites were for a very long time dominated by the thought of purgatory and while there is no reason to believe that we are in less need of purgation than our forefathers were, the reason for that point of view is probably a defective understanding of the next world. Here almost all is mysterious but at least we can say that clock-time does not apply there. To recall the adage of Aristotle, time is the measure of motion, itself thought of as a measurable quantity. Clearly it belongs only to this material world and can have no place in the next. Likewise, eternity is thought of as unending duration and understandably people think of it as rather boring. Admittedly, the matter is difficult, not least because the industrialized world lives by clock-time as the condition of its continued existence. Yet, we are not wholly conditioned by it. We experience moments of *intensity* when we are unconscious of the passage of time and the more intense the experience the less revelant measured time becomes. The lover takes no account of time. As he says, the world stands still. The saint who is caught up in prayer is even less conscious of the passage of time but the intensity is the greater as it is less time-conditioned.

This would seem to provide a basis for understanding a world that is without clock-time. What happens when we die is a mystery, we can have no experience of it but it is credible that at that moment when, in Christ and by the power of Christ, we sum up our life, we make the supreme affirmation, we are also 'living' at the greatest moment of intensity. Its only parallel is the highest mystical experience. At this same moment we are confronted with God *for* whom we make the final choice and yet at the same time in our personalities there remains much that has resisted him in this life. In this encounter and in the intensity of the experience, all that is imperfect is purged away and we are able to enter into the joy of the Lord. Whatever may have been Newman's picture-world of purgatory, judgement and heaven, he seems to have a glimpse of this notion in his *Dream of Gerontius* where the Angel speaking to the Soul just dead says, 'Learn that the flame of Everlasting Love/Doth burn ere it transform'. Death is an encounter with the Everlasting Love and we have no need to look elsewhere for a cleansing or a means of purgation. But it is a Love that transforms and must be thought of in terms of intensity rather than time.

This view also provides a background for a consideration of judgement. The 'Grand Assize' parable has sometimes been interpreted as literal fact and medieval people seem to have thought of God as some sort of earthly judge, only more terrible. Yet the whole point of the parable is in the words 'As you did it to one of the least of these my brethren, you did it to me' (Matthew 25:40). In so far as we have

~

responded in life to Christ in his and our brethren, we have been responding to him and the contrary is also true. Then there is all the sense of St John's gospel that judgement, *krisis*, decision and so separation are *now* (3:19; 9:39; 12:31; 16:11). The responses whether positive or negative we make in life are going to be of literally supreme importance in the moment of death. We hope and strive to respond positively to Christ in life, we pray that these responses are constantly cancelling out the negative ones and that the main thrust of our life is ever Godward. The judgement will simply be a confrontation with God when by his grace we shall be able to embrace his will for us with all the energy of our being or, on the other hand, there remains the awful possibility of the final refusal. But because our responses have often been feeble, because there have been refusals in our life and our motives have often been impure, there is the need for cleansing, for being perfected so that we may come to the vision of God.

But it does not seem possible to postulate time for that cleansing and perfecting process. We must think of it then in terms of intensity and it is a matter of experience that a person can undergo a spiritual growth that is quite incommensurable with time. Why then should we pray for the dead, why go on praying for them perhaps and indeed usually for years? The reason again is that there is no time with God. Our prayers are necessarily spread out in time but with him they exist in a single undivided moment and he, at the death of an individual, takes account, so to say, of all the prayer that has been made or will be made for him.

These considerations may well be elementary but there seem to be people almost hopelessly puzzled about death and the after-life and perhaps for this reason they turn away from it with dismay. In any case, in one way or another these notions underlie much of the new liturgy of the dead which we must now consider in detail.

The funeral rite

The first *Ordo Exsequiarum*[3] was issued in 1969 (the text of which can be found in the last pages of the *Order of Christian Funerals*) but since then a considerable work of revision and addition has been undertaken by the Congregation for Worship in Rome, by the International Commission on English in the Liturgy (ICEL) and by the national Liturgy Commissions of England and Wales, and, for this text, Scotland. The *Order of Christian Funerals* that appeared in 1990 is the only official text for the countries named and consequently no other may be used. It has certain features proper to these countries such as extended rites of committal and two good texts from the Anglican Book of Common Prayer.

A notable feature of the new edition is the extended General Introduction, much longer than that of the original *Ordo*, and additional pastoral instructions.

The General Introduction spells out at greater length the meaning of Christian death as a participation in the paschal mystery of Jesus Christ: 'In the face of death, the Church confidently proclaims that God has created each person for eternal life and that Jesus, the Son of God, by his death and resurrection, has broken the chains of sin and death . . . (He) achieved his task of redeeming humanity and giving perfect glory to God principally by the paschal mystery of his blessed passion, resurrection from the dead and glorious ascension' (1 and cf. CL 5). The effects of the paschal mystery are mediated to Christians through the church, through the proclaimed word of God and above all by the liturgy: 'The Church's liturgical and sacramental life and the proclamation of the gospel make this mystery present in the life of the faithful' who through baptism, confirmation and the eucharist were initiated into the mystery; there follows the text from Romans 6:3–5.

This is the basis of the church's intercession for the dead: 'At the death of a Christian, whose life of faith was begun in the waters of baptism and strengthened at the eucharistic table, the Church intercedes on behalf of the deceased because of its confident belief that death is not the end nor does it break the bonds forged in life'. As indeed we proclaim in the funeral liturgy, for the Christian 'life is changed not ended' (Preface I) and like Christ himself we pass through death to the new life that is a share in his risen life.

In its funeral rites the church does indeed 'offer worship, praise and thanksgiving to God for the gift of a life which has now been returned' to him but it is also aware that Christians sin and so 'through its funeral rites commends the dead to God's merciful love and pleads for the forgiveness of their sins'. Especially in celebrating the eucharist the church joins the Church in heaven, the one great communion of saints from whom the dead as the living, still united after death, receive the help of their intercession.

Finally, as the various rites amply show, the 'celebration of the Christian funeral brings hope and consolation to the living' and this

~
202

as we know is becoming ever more needed even by Christians, whose faith in life with Christ after death (or less christianly 'life after death') is weakening. It seems that people, even Christians, are finding it more and more difficult to come to terms with death which, as we have said above, is too often swept under the carpet. Perhaps there are slight signs of change in this attitude; death is being discussed a little more than it was but when one is confronted with it personally it is still difficult to cope with. It is not surprising that the Order of Christian Funerals so often stresses the need for faith and urges us constantly to pray, on the occasion of death and throughout our lives, for a strengthening of faith in Jesus Christ who suffered, died and rose again for us so that we can enter into a life with God that is everlasting.

The emphasis in the rites on the need to pray for the dead and the awareness they show that most of us are sinners also seem necessary in our time when one would think that at times the celebration of the death of someone is a sort of premature canonization. It is true that the ambience of the old funeral rites was heavily sin-laden, death was presented as a terrifying appearance before a harsh Judge and the 'fires' of purgatory seemed already to be licking round the coffin. If we have got rid of that mythology it would be foolish and detrimental to the departed to cease to pray that God may be merciful to them and remove all traces of sin.

Rites, symbols and gestures

Funeral rites have varied greatly in the past and still do in different cultures. One reason is that death and mourning are profoundly human experiences and at the same time point to something beyond this world. Few people at any time have been willing to neglect their dead and they realized that the body must at least be treated with respect (a respect that seems to be disappearing in our harsh, irreverent culture). The Order (21) is aware of cultural differences; they must be accommodated and purified if necessary. It goes on to say that 'Since liturgical celebration involves the whole person it requires attentiveness to all that affects the senses'. The message of Christian death is communicated not only by words, above all by the word of God, but by rites, actions, symbols and gestures.

The word of God

The church sees this as peculiarly important for 'the readings proclaim to the assembly the paschal mystery, teach remembrance of the dead (and) convey the hope of being gathered together again in God's kingdom'. But readings must be carefully and sensitively chosen to meet the needs and feelings of the mourners. If the selection can be made with them these are all the more likely 'to speak to their condition'.

The Order makes a particular point of the psalms which it sees as providing material to help the bereaved to mourn: 'they enable the assembly to pray in the words that Jesus himself used during his life on earth'. This is true in a special way when they are used more extensively in Vigils and the Divine Office.

Under the heading 'The Word of God' is included the homily. The Order repeats the injunction of the former edition that this is not to be a eulogy of the deceased. There has been a tendency (particularly at priests' funerals) to eulogize the deceased. The mind of the church as expressed with force in this Order and its predecessor is that the theme of the homily is the paschal mystery, the passion, death and resurrection of Christ as lived out by human beings in this world. This is the basis of the Christian hope that is sounded again and again in the texts of the liturgy. But this does not mean that the homily should be an impersonal disquisition on a theological theme! The preacher will speak to the mourners who are before him, he will recall aspects of the deceased's life or character to show that he/she did strive to live out the paschal mystery and he will try to strengthen their faith and hope. Sometimes however, the less said about the deceased the better and in any case the preacher needs to be sparing of discourses about the dead.

Under the term 'Symbols' the Order details with brief commentary things that are or may be used in the funeral liturgy.

The Paschal Candle

This is a symbol 'of Christ's undying presence, of his victory over sin and death, of (our) share in that victory by virtue of' our baptism and the other sacraments of Christian initiation. To those who have taken part in the Easter Vigil it recalls the procession through the dark church and is a reminder of the journey in faith we all make from this world to the next. (Other candles may be placed round the coffin but there is much to be said for using the Paschal Candle alone.)

Holy water

For long enough holy water has been understood as a symbol of baptism. This is made explicit in the Order: 'In the waters of baptism N. died with Christ and rose with him to new life. May he/she now share with him eternal glory.' This rite takes place at the reception of the body into church and during the commendation.

Incense

In the funeral rites the body of the deceased is honoured and treated with reverence. One signal mark of this is the censing of the body during the final commendation. As the Order says (37) the body 'through baptism became the temple of the Holy Spirit'. However the use of incense is ill-understood nowadays and discretion is needed.

The pall

In the distant past most churches had a pall (in black or purple) but for reasons unknown it fell out of use. In more recent years the coffin has been piled high with flowers and 'Mass cards'. Its use is now recommended again and is to be seen as a reminder of the baptismal robe with which the deceased was clothed after baptism and as a sign of his/her Christian dignity. Although the Order does not say so, most commentators think that its colour should be white to emphasize the link between it and the baptismal garment. On the pall may be placed a book of the gospels or a Bible for 'Christians live by the word of God', and a cross since the Christian is marked by the cross in baptism and 'through Jesus' suffering on the cross is brought to the victory of his resurrection'.

These symbols may be placed on the coffin as it is brought into the church and it is the relatives or friends of the deceased who, it is desired, should reverently place them. The pall should be folded in such as way as to make its unfolding easy and the undertaker will no doubt assist. Flowers may be placed round the coffin but no insignia, whether national or honorific, may be put on it. The pall, as the Order says, is a sign that we are all equal in the sight of God.

The colour of vestments

This is dealt with under 39. White, expressive of Christian hope 'in the light of the paschal mystery', may be used. Violet recalls the expectation of the Lord at the end of time and the penitential preparation in Lent for the celebration of the paschal mystery. Both *may* be used but due regard must be paid to the feelings of the bereaved, who should be consulted in the matter. Black vestments, 'increasingly without the associations of Christian hope', are not recommended.

Music

By what one can gather from a certain amount of published comment many funerals are taking place without any music or singing of any kind. This, it seems, is true not just of a committal in a dreary cemetery chapel but of church funerals. There may of course be reasons for this but if it is regular practice it is clearly against the regulations of the Order: 'Music is integral to the Funeral rites. It allows the community to express convictions and feelings that words alone may fail to convey' (30). There is much that might be said about the matter but lack of space forbids. All one can say is that there is now available sufficient material for singing that should be within the capacity of most congregations. If the Mass is sung throughout the year many of the texts and hymns familiar to the people can be used at funerals.

Silence

As in all celebration silence is conducive to prayer and places for it can be during the final commendation and after the homily.

Gestures and movement

That on the occasion of a funeral the celebrant, his assistants, the choir (if any) should do all that is incumbent on them with gravity and sensitivity hardly needs saying (yet one still hears from undertakers that some Catholic priests say the prayers, even the Lord's Prayer, 'so fast'). An unhurried style of celebration is prayerful and helps the assembly to make the message their own.

The Order (40–42) makes much of processions during the funeral rites and indeed they formed an important part in the funeral rites of the early church. But with the increasing urbanization of the church, at least in Western Europe, processions whether to the church from the house or from the church to the cemetery are now all but impossible. All that is left to us is the procession into the church when a suitable hymn or chant may be sung and the procession at the end for which the Order provides among other things a metrical version (in English) of the famous *In paradisum*. If however (e.g. in a rural setting) a procession to the grave is possible a selection of psalms is provided.

A synopsis of the rites

When confronted with the *Order of Christian Funerals,* either in the two-volume edition (to be used in celebration) or the Study Edition, a reader may be somewhat overwhelmed by the abundance of its contents. A summary guide may not be out of place.

All can be held together by the understanding that the death of a Christian is a journey, a passing over, from this world to the next, to God. This is symbolized by the journey of the body from the home or funeral chapel to the church and by the final journey from the church to the place of committal. The wealth of rites and services is there to ensure or to make it possible that the whole period from the moment of death to committal is a time of prayer, of consideration of the meaning of Christian death and, through a strengthened faith, coming to terms with it. This, if possible, is done by the local Christian community who have their part to play at this time; by prayer and presence they support the bereaved.

The whole of the period then is punctuated by the first gathering of the family after death, by the Vigil (Wake) or the singing of the church's Evening Prayer, by the reception of the body in church, by the funeral liturgy (the Mass) with the final commendation, all of which lead to the committal.

Some of this material may not seem usable in the circumstances of parish life but it is available and a long process of education of both the laity and the clergy would seem to be necessary if we are to come to a deeper understanding in faith of Christian death.

Here comment will (perforce) be restricted to the three principal 'stations': the home, the church and the cemetery (cremation chapel).

~

The home

Either on the day before the funeral liturgy or on the day itself family and friends gather at the home (or funeral chapel) of the deceased. The short service that is provided consisting of prayer, scripture reading and blessing may well help to calm the emotions of the mourners.

The Vigil

This has two forms: a separate service in church (or even the home) or the same service combined with the reception of the body which is likely to be the most practical and acceptable. The main elements are the sprinkling with holy water, the entrance procession, the placing of pall and Christian symbols, an opening prayer, a first reading, a psalm, a reading from a gospel, a (brief) homily, intercessions, the Lord's Prayer, the concluding prayer and the blessing.

This is likely to be the best way of celebrating a Vigil service. It will take place on the evening before the funeral liturgy when relatives can assemble with members of the local parish community. It fills out the very brief and inadequate rite of the reception of the body and gives a mental space for prayer and reflection. It could of course be led by a deacon or a lay person.

The Divine Office

According to circumstances either Morning Prayer or Evening Prayer from the Divine Office may be sung. (See below.)

The funeral liturgy (i.e. the Mass and the final commendation)

'The funeral liturgy is the central liturgical celebration of the Christian community for the deceased . . .' (137). This is readily understood by Catholics even if cemetery or cremation chapels are, according to some reports, being used to the exclusion of the church. Since however the funeral Mass is familiar to most Catholics there is little need to say much about it here.

If we are to follow the injunctions of the Order there should be some singing for the reasons given above. The readings, if possible selected with the relatives, and the homily *based on the readings* (and not a eulogy or a mini-biography), attention to alternative collects etc. and to the intercessions (which may need to be adapted): all need careful consideration if the funeral liturgy is to convey its message of comfort and hope.

There are however deeper considerations. At the heart of the funeral liturgy is the eucharist when the church, represented by the local community, pleads the eternal sacrifice of Christ for the deceased and for all who have died 'marked with the sign of faith' they received in baptism. The assembly enters into union with him and also with the deceased. Through the eucharist the redeeming love of Christ is made available to them and ushers them into the presence of God. No doubt the sense of final severance remains for those left behind but the strength to bear the loss is found in the funeral liturgy.

Two moments in the Mass call for a word or two. The presentation of the gifts was one of the oldest surviving processions of the former Roman rite and it should be kept in the funeral Mass. If relatives feel that they cannot undertake it members of the parish community can do it in their place. Some mourners are so overcome with grief that they feel they cannot receive holy communion. If possible they should be gently persuaded beforehand that in holy communion they will find the strength they need from Jesus Christ who is the pledge of the everlasting life they will share with the deceased.

The final commendation

The celebrant with servers and/or ministers goes to the place where the coffin is and addresses the people. The Order (146) suggests the themes of his remarks. It is a moment of separation and the community, led by the celebrant, is commending the deceased to the loving mercy of God. Baptized into the one body of Christ all share in the promise of resurrection in him and will be gathered together one day with Christ into the joy of the new and eternal Jerusalem. Forms of words are indeed given (182, A–E) but the celebrant may use his own words and as it is a very personal moment it is better that he should do so. While speaking he can include a few words about the meaning of holy water and its sprinkling and about incense (if used).

There follows a silence and during the sprinkling of the coffin the silence may continue or a chant sung. This may be the traditional 'Saints of God . . .' or one of the alternatives, 'I know that my Redeemer lives . . .' which appears in the rite at this point. This is put into metrical form and can be easily sung to any Long Measure tune.

After the prayer of commendation there is the procession when the body is carried out of church. During this (and a possible procession to a surrounding graveyard) the chant 'May the angels lead you into paradise' may be sung as an antiphon to Psalm 24(25) and the rest of this ancient chant is to be sung in the same manner.[4]

(It is possible, e.g. on days when Mass is prohibited, to have a funeral liturgy consisting of a liturgy of the word (holy communion) and the final commendation. See nos. 188–217.)

The rite of committal

'The rite of committal, the conclusion of the funeral rites, is the final act of the community of faith in caring for the body of its deceased member' (219). It is also often a moment of great emotion and the minister may have to do what he can to comfort mourners before proceeding to the service.

This begins with a 'sentence' from holy scripture, four in number from which the minister recites one. There are five prayers (to be used at choice) to be said 'Over the Place of Committal' and this is followed by the act of committal during which the minister may say one of two prayers. The second (taken with permission from the Book of Common Prayer) begins with the familiar words 'In sure and certain hope . . .' and includes the words, known to most Christians in this country, 'we commit his/her body to the ground, earth to earth, ashes to ashes, dust to dust'. There follow the intercessions (three sets given), the Lord's Prayer, a concluding prayer and a blessing.

When this rite takes place after the funeral liturgy it is very difficult to understand why intercessions and the Lord's Prayer are included. They are both palpably duplications of the prayers in the Mass, and duplications were banished from our liturgy by Vatican II. On such occasions as when there is no previous service this material is needed but otherwise not.

There are in fact six forms of committal, including of course two for cremation. There is also a brief rite for the burial of the ashes which was badly needed. In the forms of committal on the occasion of cremation too much seems to be demanded. In England at any rate cremation services are usually restricted to twenty minutes and the placing of pall and other symbols is contra-indicated. Suggestions for adaptation would have been helpful.

Funeral rites for children

Few will remember the meagre rite for the burial of children of the old Roman Ritual: a couple of Latin psalms and a prayer. Now the Order of Christian Funerals has made generous provision for this occasion which is usually one of great emotional stress. To understand the spirit of the rites it is necessary to read the texts of prayers and sentences which are marked by a moving tenderness. The rites envisage everything from the funeral of a child of school age to the burial of unbaptized infants, the stillborn and even miscarriage. Here by rite, symbol and word the church shows an immense compassion for her people who suffer greatly when these events occur.

The general sense of the rites is summarized thus: 'In the celebration of the funeral of a child the Church offers worship to God, the author of life, commends the child to God's love, and prays for the consolation of the family and close friends' (332). The Order also sees the local community as exercising a ministry of support and consolation and makes suggestions for the participation of that community and especially of children if the deceased child is of school age (339–also with reference to the *Directory for Masses with Children*).

The rites follow the pattern of those for adults, reception of the body (Vigil), funeral liturgy, commendation, and committal in its various forms. But the language of the prayers and other texts is adapted to the circumstances. The prayer for an unbaptized child is notable: 'Tender Shepherd of the flock, *N. now lies cradled in your love* . . .' which is a far cry from limbo and the ghostly existence that the unbaptized were supposed to live there. The Order however is careful to point out that baptismal symbols, white pall for instance, shall be excluded.

Funerals for catechumens: guidelines and texts (510–528)

Since catechumens 'belong to the household of Christ' they may receive Christian burial though certain symbols, holy water (a reminder of baptism) and the pall are to be excluded. The prayers and texts may be used 'in the various rites of Parts I, II, and IV' (i.e. funeral rites and Mass, funeral rites for children (of school age) and the Office for the Dead).

Office for the Dead (529-578)

It may seem surprising that the offices of Morning and Evening Prayer should be included among the rites. Is there not a Vigil? The General Introduction envisages a situation, for instance, when a funeral liturgy has been celebrated in the evening and Morning Prayer can be recited (sung) before the procession to the place of committal. Another possibility is that where parishes have the custom of reciting Morning or Evening Prayer, during the days before the funeral liturgy the people could gather together for one of these offices, the texts for which are given in the Order of Christian Funerals.[5]

Pastoral reflections

If the new Order of Christian Funerals is admirable in almost every respect it yet undeniably places a heavy responsibility on the pastoral clergy. Desirable as the many rites may be, in the circumstances of a large parish (with too few clergy) it is not easy to perform them all. The first the clergy hear of the death of a parishioner is often from the funeral director and preliminary arrangements may already have been made. Even in more propitious circumstances it is difficult to assemble members of the local community, difficult to get an organist or servers. In these circumstances one has to do the best and, unless the relatives of the deceased have good reasons for acting otherwise, at least the following should be done: the reception of the body with Vigil, the funeral liturgy and the committal. For long in this country these have been regarded as the essentials of Christian burial and if, as is reported, people are having recourse to the cemetery chapel or the crematorium in preference to the church it would seem that a considerable process of catechesis on Christian death and Christian burial with all they mean should be initiated as soon as possible. It may also be necessary to enquire into the reasons for 'chapel' burial. Is one of them financial? If so, should not church authorities approach the funeral directors and see if a certain simplification might not be possible. Is it necessary for instance to have vast coffins made of expensive wood which is only going to rot in the ground or be burned in the furnace? If relatives can carry the coffin is it necessary to have bearers as well? One can think of other questions. In conclusion it seems necessary that not only Catholics but funeral directors as well should be informed of the meaning of Christian funeral rites and all that they imply.

If there is one criticism of the rites it is that which has been referred to above. When there has been a Vigil with reception, a funeral Mass celebrated as well as possible, it seems quite unnecessary to have further intercessions and the Lord's Prayer at the side of the grave or in the cremation chapel. It is usually also a moment of emotional stress which should not be unnecessarily prolonged. Permission to omit those texts should be obtained as soon as possible.

Notes
~

[1] Michael Simpson, SJ, **Death and Eternal Life** (Theology Today Series, no. 42; Cork, 1971), p. 9.

[2] John 12:24. The words that follow give the teaching of dying to life so that we may come to a richer one: 'He who loves his life, loses it, and he who hates his life **in this world** will keep it for eternal life'.

[3] **Ordo Exsequiarum** (Vatican Press), promulgated 15 August 1969. Cf. **Notitiae**, 49 (1969), pp. 423–30, for the Latin text of the Introduction or **Praenotanda** which is the one used here.

[4] Suitable and very acceptable settings of texts to be sung can be found in **Order of Christian Funerals: Funeral Mass and Vigil Service: People's Book**, ed. Stephen Dean, Joan McCrimmon and Michael Shaw (McCrimmon, Great Wakering, 1990).

[5] For a brief commentary on the Order of Christian Funerals see **The Parish Funeral: A Guide to the Order of Christian Funerals**, ed. Stephen Dean; contributors J. D. Crichton, E. Sands, Ann Tomalak, Tony Rogers, S. Dean, M. Marchal, M. Cooley (McCrimmon, Great Wakering, 1991).

The Sacrament of Penance

~~~~~~

IN THE COURSE of this book I have tried to relate the sacraments and their liturgy first to ordinary human living and then to the Christian life. When I came to consider the new Order of Penance in *The Ministry of Reconciliation* (London, 1974) it seemed unlikely that this formula would work. Some reflection and reference to other documents and articles showed however that it was possible to relate penance to the religious experience of non-Christian religions and so to the life of those who make no profession of the Christian faith.

A link between the practices of non-Christian religions and Christian penance is established by Pope Paul VI in his letter *Paenitemini* (ET *Penitence*, published by CTS, London). He addressed it to men of goodwill and says that the church has noted that 'almost everywhere and at all times penitence has held a place of great importance in non-Christian religions and is closely linked with the intimate sense of religion which pervades the life of most ancient peoples as well as with the more advanced expressions of the great religions connected with the progress of culture' (p. 5). Judaism and Islam are examples that spring to mind. The final teaching of the Old Testament on repentance is so profound and important that it has been taken over almost wholly by the church. But in its earlier stages sin was often seen as the breaking of a taboo and 'repentance' was thought of as a ritual cleansing. The externalism of this phase had to be rejected by the prophets and they and the psalmists came to a deep understanding of the holiness of God and of the need for a total conversion if God was to forgive the sin. In non-Judaic religions, expiation – again perhaps for an external, ritual fault – seems to have played a great part and if it is unsatisfactory in that it leaves the personality unchanged, it is at least testimony of the sacredness of life presided over by the Supreme Being. Such an understanding of things brought with it the penitential practices of prayer and fasting which can be seen as medicinal in that they deliver man from slavery to his instincts and from the domination of material forces over his life. There is

~

something beyond it, Someone whom man acknowledges, Someone whom he can offend and whom therefore he must placate.

If all this seems very 'primitive' it provides some release from the anguish that man experiences in the face of wrong-doing, whether his own or someone else's. Modern man has denied himself this way out and yet he experiences the agony of right-doing in conflict with wrong-doing which St Paul described in Romans 7:14–25. Though writing in the context of law and sin, Paul is witnessing to the drama that goes on in every human being, a drama which he himself experienced: 'I do not understand my own actions. For I do not do what I want, but I do the very thing I hate. . . . I do not do the good I want, but the evil I do not want is what I do. . . . Who will deliver me from this body of death?' And the answer is 'Jesus Christ our Lord', 'who was put to death for our trespasses and raised for our justification' (Romans 4:25).

This teaching of course brings us right within the Christian context where sin is an ever-present reality and repentance a necessary accompaniment of the Christian life. This theme, too, Pope Paul took up in his Letter: ' "Repent and believe in the Gospel" . . . constitutes, in a way, a compendium of the whole Christian life' (p. 5), and since it is the mission and vocation of the church to preach the gospel to every creature, in that proclamation it must also announce the gospel of repentance for otherwise it would be unfaithful to its mission. But further, since all the members of the church bear the burden of that mission, there must be a penitential element in their lives, rejection of all that is evil and adherence to all that is good, restraint and abstinence even in those things that are good. In all this Christians may well experience in their own lives that drama of which St Paul wrote. Yet it is but a beginning. The Stoic could reject evil and adhere to the good but he was far from the kingdom of heaven. The whole process must be lifted into the sphere of the redeeming work of Christ. In him alone is salvation and through him alone can come forgiveness of sins. The living out of the passion, death and resurrection is central to the life of the church and to that of the individual Christian and it was to this that Paul VI pointed when he said that we are committed to the living out of the paschal mystery in our own experience: 'The sacrament of baptism configures him [the Christian] to the passion, death and resurrection of the Lord and places the whole future life of the baptised under the seal of the mystery' (p. 7). But this can come only through a constant turning in repentance to Christ, i.e. by conversion, *metanoia*. The Order of Penance (2) carries the matter further and shows the relationship between baptism and penance, thus returning to currency a notion that was prominent in the early liturgy and in the teaching of the Fathers: 'The first victory over sin is shown in baptism when we are crucified with Christ that "this sinful body" may be destroyed and we may be delivered from slavery to sin (Rom 6:6). Risen however with Christ, we can henceforth live for God. . . . But further, Christ committed a ministry of penance to his church, so that Christians who have fallen into sin after baptism may be renewed in grace and be reconciled with God.' As St Ambrose put it, 'The church has water and tears, the water of baptism and the tears of repentance', a theme that is expressed magnificently though in a more liturgical way in the great Maundy Thursday text for the reconciliation of penitents that is to be found in the Gelasian Sacramentary: 'Now has arrived, Venerable Pontiff, the accepted time, the day of divine propitiation and the salvation of mankind when death was destroyed and eternal life had its beginning, the day when a new plantation is to be made and all that is old cleansed and healed. . . . Our number is increased by the accession of those to be re-born and *we grow by the return of the repentant.* Water washes, tears wash, whence comes joy over the accession of those who have been called and rejoicing over the penitent who are absolved. . . .'[1] These few phrases formed part of the public liturgy of reconciliation of penitent sinners which was a sacrament-sign of the repentant church. As the Second Vatican Council said, the church is *semper purificanda* and the other face of purification is repentance.

Reconciliation

Both the texts cited above, and the Order, use the term reconciliation and this is a notion that dominates throughout. The term is used again and again and quite deliberately. If there had not been a pastoral need to maintain a certain continuity with past usage one suspects that the document might well have been called 'The Order of Reconciliation'.[2] It is necessary then to give some attention to this term.

Reconciliation means the reunion of two persons or two communities by the removal of whatever has separated them. Thus in Matthew 5:23, dissension between two members of the Christian community is a barrier to making an acceptable offering to God. Their differences must be resolved, the two must be reconciled before the offering can be made. In Ephesians 2:14–18, Jesus is spoken of as 'the peace' that has thrown down the barrier between Jew and Gentile, and this truth is driven home in a series of powerful phrases: by the blood of the cross Jesus has made peace, has created one single new Man in himself, and in his own person has killed hostility, so that both communities have the one Spirit through whom we have access to the Father. In penance the barrier we have set up by sin is removed by the reconciling power of the cross. But if this is to take place we must first respond to the word of God who indeed takes the initiative, who calls us and who by his grace makes our repentance possible. Nevertheless, the term repentance (and *a fortiori* 'penance') emphasizes the human response. If the sinner is to be re-united to God, the barrier of sin must be removed and repentance alone cannot do this. When we were in sin, God made us alive with him (Christ), forgiving our trespasses, cancelling the bond (*cheirographon*) that stood against us, setting it aside and nailing it to the cross (Colossians 2:14). Thus was the barrier removed and the sinner reconciled to God. In reconciliation there is not only the divine initiative to repentance, there is the second intervention through Christ through whom and in the Holy Spirit we are united to God. Reconciliation then emphasizes both man's approach to God and God's to man and the reunion effected by the passion, death and resurrection of Christ.

But the ministry of reconciliation is not separated from, nor merely exists alongside, the church or community that is the people of God—no more than the eucharistic memorial or *anamnesis* of the passion, death and resurrection of the Lord can be divorced from the church that celebrates it. As the new Order says (2), echoing St Paul, Christ committed the ministry of penance to his church: 'God was in Christ reconciling the world to himself . . . entrusting to us the message of reconciliation. So we are ambassadors for Christ, God making his appeal through us.' Therefore, continues St Paul, 'We beseech you on behalf of Christ, be reconciled to God. For our sake he made him to be sin who knew no sin, so that in him we might become the righteousness of God' (2 Corinthians 5:19–21). No doubt Paul had in mind the divisions of the church at Corinth but his teaching is applicable to the whole church. And as the church is the repentant church, the assembly of sinners who have repented, so it must be the church of reconciliation first among its own members and then as the instrument of the reconciliation of the world with God and of man with man. The eucharist is the sacrament-sign of the church that came into existence by the passion, death and resurrection of Christ and is sustained in its unity by the continual celebration of the paschal mystery. The sacrament of penance in all its breadth and depth is the sacrament-sign of the reconciliation effected on the cross and made present by the proclamation of the gospel of repentance, by the prayer of the church and above all in the continual celebration of the ministry of reconciliation in the sacrament of penance.

In this teaching will be found the fundamental reason why the church has turned the sacrament from being a purely private transaction (or so it seemed) into a public ministry in which the church in the name of Christ can call all men to repentance and through the power of the reconciling Christ bring all into union with God. Not surprisingly therefore the whole of the new Order is built on the two foundations of repentance and reconciliation and these two themes are expressed throughout the three forms that the celebration of the sacrament may take. If this 'reform' seems to be an innovation a brief glance at the history of penance will show that it is a return to tradition though that return is not a mere piece of archaism.

Penance in the past

Like many other parts of the liturgy penance has undergone considerable changes in the past and it could be said that from being one of the most public rites of the early centuries of the church it became the most private. Once a public acknowledgement of sin on the part of both the sinner and the church, it became the private avowal of personal sin in the darkness of a confessional.

The church began its life on the day of Pentecost with the proclamation of the gospel of repentance: 'Repent and be baptised every one of you in the name of Jesus Christ for the forgiveness of sins' (Acts 2:38) and we may observe *en passant* that this is the faithful echo of our Lord's own ministry, 'Repent and believe the gospel', words with which he opened his mission (Mark 1:15). Although in New Testament times the converted were not expected to sin, some undoubtedly did. There was the public sinner of 1 Corinthians 5 whom the local church was required to reject though the rejection was not definitive (cf. 2 Corinthians 2:5–11). St Paul tells the community to receive back the sinner, to

~

forgive him and comfort him lest he 'be overwhelmed by excessive sorrow'. For St John there was always prayer, if the sin was not 'deadly', and the powerful advocacy of Jesus Christ the righteous (1 John 2:1 and 5:16–17).[3] Above and beyond all this was the figure of the merciful Saviour who was a vivid reality to the first Christians and not a person in a book.

It seemed necessary to recall, however briefly, the spirit of New Testament repentance, forgiveness and reconciliation since in the second century a period of rigorism set in whose ultimate effects were not always happy.

Canonical penance

By the end of the second century the discipline called canonical penance was in full force and was very rigorous – though less so than, in the opinion of some writers, in the early part of the century (e.g. Hermas). The question was asked: Could great sins, that is, public sins, be forgiven? Some said no but others (and this was the Roman practice) said that after a long period of penance, usually lasting a lifetime, such sinners could be reconciled and re-integrated into the full life of the church. Reconciliation, however, could only take place once. A second sin meant exclusion for ever from the sacramental life of the church.

The pattern of the 'sacrament' was approximately this. There was one who had committed a public sin, either apostasy (frequent enough in times of persecution), homicide or adultery and in the small communities of the time such sins would be known. Through the church's preaching of repentance he was invited to repent and if he did repent this meant that he voluntarily submitted himself to public penance. By the time of St Augustine he approached the bishop and from him received the *correptio*, i.e. the bishop confronted him with the demands of the gospel and urged him to take upon himself the discipline of penance. This involved many years of fasting, abstinence from the use of marriage and in fact the living of the life of an ascetic or monk. Although the penance was rigorous it was not thought of simply as 'punishment' for sins committed, but rather as medicinal, a means by which the sinner could renew his spiritual life.

This can be understood the more readily when we see that along with the penance went the prayer of the church for sinners which formed a regular element of the intercessions or 'prayers of the faithful' at every celebration of the eucharist. This was regarded as of the highest importance, for it was by the prayer of the church that the ultimate and complete conversion of the sinner would be obtained.

By the sixth century in Rome (if the Gelasian Sacramentary reflects the practice of that time) the sinner, after penance, was reconciled in the public service of reconciliation that took place on Maundy Thursday. The rite in the Gelasian Sacramentary envisages several penitents. They are led into church by the archdeacon who bids them prostrate on the floor of the church. He then addresses the Pope, who presides, in very moving terms, one or two of which we have quoted above. In reply the Pope pronounces in a long prayer the reconciliation of the penitents, their re-integration into the life of the church and their re-admission to holy communion. As the texts indicate the church is renewed and made whole again by the return of the penitents who can now begin a new life.

Whatever may have been the disadvantages of the discipline of penance it kept before the people the great themes of repentance, of prayer, of reconciliation and of the ministry of reconciliation committed to the church by Christ. Moreover the whole process remained profoundly ecclesial: the sense of the church both in respect of sin and in respect of the reconciliation was acute. As St Ambrose wrote, 'by us the church is wounded (*in nobis ecclesia vulneratur*)' and again 'Let us take care lest our falls wound the church'.[4] Without slavish imitation of earlier models of penance, the church has now restored the ecclesial dimension to the sacrament.

Tariffed penance

Whatever mitigations the system of penance underwent it remained too severe for the generality of Christians many of whom (including Ambrose and Augustine) preferred to remain catechumens in all the stormy days of their youth. Others who had sinned put off reconciliation until their deathbeds with the result that they would go without communion for most of their lives.

For the daily faults of the Christian and no doubt for bigger ones that were not public the means of forgiveness were prayer (the Lord's Prayer was especially important in this regard), fasting and almsgiving: in the sermons of Leo the Great for Lent and the Ember days these can be clearly seen as reparatory. Whatever is to be said about this system, it did at least keep before the people the notion that penitence is a normal part of the Christian life.

Whether or not the people of Northern Europe found this system unsatisfactory or whether they acquired a deeper sense of sin is a matter for further investigation; for it was from there–from Ireland in particular–that a change came. There the church was organized on a monastic basis. The abbot was the all-important man and if there was a bishop in the community he was not necessarily its head. The rule was rigorous, the chapter of faults occurred frequently and the monks had to declare their faults to the abbot. No doubt they did not make much distinction between faults of breaking the rule and more serious faults that we should call sins. It is out of this situation that the notion of frequent confession came. In addition, what was regarded as an appropriate penance was allocated for the faults committed. As one writer has put it, 'ten years on bread and water for homicide and six blows for coughing during a psalm'.[5] The notion was that the punishment should fit the crime and when the system was transferred to the secular sphere, as it was very quickly, tariffs were drawn up that were conceived to meet the needs of the often violent society of the time. Then they were published in Penitentials of which examples remain from Ireland, England (the Penitential of Theodore of Canterbury), from Gaul and Spain, and whether with or without interacting influences, there were very similar penitentials in the Eastern church.[6]

How this system worked for ordinary Christians who never committed any sin of great consequence must remain a matter of speculation. If 'tariffed penance' opened the door to more frequent confession, it would be some time before it affected general practice. Penances in any case remained severe and the custom of postponing reconciliation to the end of one's life continued. Meanwhile the whole of social life was affected by tribal and feudal customs which are clearly marked in the Penitentials. Lords and other great people did indeed submit themselves to penance after a notable crime or sin but the tendency grew to get others to perform the very heavy penances. Sometimes the priest employed on their lands was made to do penance in their stead and many were the monasteries founded to pray for and make expiation for the sins of their founders. Again, penances were commuted; a long period of penance was replaced by a short sharp one, e.g. severe fasting for a number of days, or a payment, i.e. charitable alms, was substituted. All this led to obvious abuses and was undesirable in itself. Tariffed penance did however lead to the practice of more frequent confession.

There was however a further development. In tariffed penance the old order of events was kept: presentation to the bishop (or priest), some form of confession, the acceptance of penance, its performance (however done), reconciliation and finally re-admission to holy communion. But gradually this order was changed: reconciliation (now called more and more frequently absolution) was granted immediately after the confession and *before* the penance had been performed. Except for notorious sins, when something of the old discipline was retained, the penitent was immediately admitted to communion.

Private penance

This form of penance, which we have come to regard as typical, was little used before the Fourth Lateran Council (1215) which decreed that all should go to confession at least once a year before making their Easter communion. This is not to be seen as penal legislation; its intent was pastoral. The council desired that people should approach communion worthily and that the custom of infrequent communions (once or twice in a lifetime!) should cease. From the thirteenth century onwards the custom of frequent confession and communion became customary, at least among the devout. For most, however, annual confession and communion remained the norm.

It was this tradition that the Council of Trent took up and sought to improve. It urged more frequent communion and, again to ensure worthiness, laid down that normally it should be preceded by confession. When in the last decades of the nineteenth century, and especially after the decree on frequent communion of Pius X in this century, great numbers went to communion at least once a week, they felt a certain obligation to go to confession as often. This led to a situation that we can see now was more than a little odd: considerable numbers of devout souls with little if anything to confess besieging confessionals every Saturday evening. What had happened is that church legislation, which had quite different circumstances in view, was transferred unthinkingly to a new situation. The same thing happened, I believe, in the matter of children's first confession and as one views the past it is difficult to see that there was any worked-out theology underpinning this practice. There was indeed an ideal of spiritual perfection that the church authorities wished to put before the people but this hardly adds up to a theology and one has to ask whether what was intended by the use of the sacrament of penance could not have been achieved by spiritual counsel.

In any case the people themselves have seen that there is no essential connection between confession and holy communion and current practice is that people go to confession more rarely but very often make a better use of the sacrament. Its celebration is more relaxed, more human, the 'confession' is often more like a dialogue than the mere listing of sins and the existence of 'confessional rooms' (replacing the 'box') witnesses to the desire of many for spiritual counsel.

This, in very general terms, is the situation in which the new Order of Penance has appeared, and if it is in some sense a restoration of the past, only the exploitation of its *whole* content will show whether it meets the needs of people today and of future generations. Since the Order came into force two trends are noticeable: (1) most of the Catholics who use the sacrament of reconciliation do so about twice a year when the second rite (i.e. with individual confessions and absolution) is celebrated; (2) in some places where there are many confessors (e.g. a religious house in a town) many make use of the first rite (i.e. private confession) which in effect is often a counselling session. What however is disturbing is that great numbers of people, especially the young, never go to confession at all, whatever the opportunities offered them. How this situation is to be corrected is indeed a problem and the solution must lie along the lines of a general and much improved catechesis. Meanwhile a small minority appreciate the corporate emphasis in the revised liturgy and find the public service of penance helpful. Even so, the private confession and absolution that go with the second rite seem anomalous. As things are, a new understanding of the sacrament of reconciliation is necessary. If this is to be achieved three things would seem to be necessary:

1. The importance of the proclamation of the word of God calling Christians to repentance must be appreciated.

2. In no sacrament are the acts of the participant so important as in this. They are part of its very substance and a deeper understanding is necessary of all three elements, contrition, confession and satisfaction.

3. There is a need to understand the communal or corporate nature of the sacrament. It is an act of the church, involving the whole church both in its awareness of sin, in the corporate nature of reparation for sin and in the reconciliation it effects.

These points will now be taken up in the context of what the Order calls 'The Parts of the Sacrament' (6, 7).

The parts of the sacrament
~

As we have indicated above, these include the acts of the penitent, which have a special importance in this sacrament. Negatively the matter can be put in this way: without repentance there is no sacrament and, in the present discipline of the church, confession or avowal of sin committed is an integral part of the sacrament. Positively, with the absolution of the confessor they constitute the sacrament and if we look for the sign of the sacrament it is here that we shall find it. In other words, when the penitent declares his sorrow, confesses his sins and accepts the 'penance' imposed by the confessor he is making the sacrament. As Karl Rahner has put it somewhat bluntly, 'The confessing sinner celebrates a part of the Church's liturgy and does not receive the effect of someone else's liturgy'.[7]

Contrition

The Order retains the term and the definition of the Council of Trent:[8] 'Contrition is heartfelt sorrow for sin committed and detestation of it, together with the resolve not to sin in the future'. But, taking a lead from Pope Paul VI's Letter (p. 6), the Order broadens and deepens its meaning. The wider perspective sets it in the context of the Christian life as a whole: 'We may only approach the kingdom of Christ by *metanoia*, that is, by an inner change of the whole human personality (*totius hominis mutatione*), and in repentance we begin to examine and judge our lives and seek to put them in order'. This is undoubtedly the meaning of the gospel term and it might seem to make very great demands on us. This is true, but it is not for us to water down the truth of the gospel. Perhaps if we had been confronted with it earlier in life we should have taken 'conversion' more seriously: repentance in this sense would have been a more profound and permanent element in our lives. But precisely because repentance is so far-reaching it must be the matter of a lifetime and one of the purposes of the *sacrament* of penance is to maintain and make effective the spirit of repentance. The sacrament can be seen – and it is one of the great virtues of the Order that it so sees it – as part of the

~
224

continuing process of being or becoming a Christian. 'Conversion', says the Order, 'must affect man interiorly if he is to be progressively enlightened and become more and more like Christ.'

The Order continues with the traditional doctrine that sorrow for sin must be prompted by the love of God but the way it expresses it is more in accord with modern biblical considerations than the old formulation of it. The penitent is to be moved by the *holiness of God* and *his love as revealed in Jesus Christ*, in whom the fullness of God dwelt and through whom God reconciled to himself all things whether on earth or in heaven, making peace by the blood of the cross. Reference is made to Colossians 1:19, to the general teaching of the first part of that epistle and to the parallel passages in Ephesians. Thus the reconciling power of Christ is seen as the supreme motive of repentance. It would not be too much to say that the whole paschal mystery, concretely the passion, death and resurrection of Christ, is to be the motive of repentance: '[Give thanks to the Father] who has qualified us to share in the inheritance of the saints in light. He has delivered us from the dominion of darkness and transferred us to the kingdom of his beloved Son, in whom we have redemption, the forgiveness of sins' (Colossians 1:13–14). The paschal mystery is celebrated in the rite but it must be a reality in the interior life of each repentant Christian. As the Order says, on this heartfelt contrition depends the reality of the sacrament.

No doubt it is not the intention of a liturgical document to decide disputes between theologians – in this case that concerning contrition and attrition – but it must be said that attrition does not enter into the thinking of the Order. This may be because the Order regards repentance as a continuing process. At the beginning it may indeed be imperfect but, according to the mind of the Order, it should be deepened and grow towards 'perfect' contrition day by day. It would not seem however to be the implication that the confessor should make exorbitant demands of the penitent. He must meet him where he is and, by presenting to him the love of God as revealed in the passion, death and resurrection of Christ, seek to vitalize his repentance to the point where there is a response of love, however imperfectly formulated, to the love of God. On the other hand, all preaching and instruction about the sacrament of penance should put before people the whole doctrine of the Order in this respect, a doctrine that can be said to be that of the church. In this context services of penance have a very important role to perform.

Confession

In the time of Tertullian the avowal of faults was known as *exomologesis* which meant a great deal more than a detailing of sins. The word, a noun coming from the same verb used in some of the praising psalms (e.g. *Confitemini Domino*, 135), implied an act of worship, a recognition of the holiness of God and of what he demands of us. The Order seems to look back to this tradition rather than to the more recent one: 'examination of conscience and the verbal declaration are to be done in the light of the God of mercy'. Confession is the expression of what we *are* before God as well as of the contrition we have conceived in our hearts. Indeed as almost all penitents know (though they may not reflect on the matter), confession is a mode of contrition; it is penitential and sometimes painful because humiliating. If then we see confession as a humble avowal of what we are and of the faults that indicate what we are, then we shall see it not so much as a strict accounting of sins but as a way of putting ourselves before God as sinners seeking his forgiveness. If justification is sought for auricular confession of sins, it is to be found along these lines rather than in the sphere of providing 'matter' for judgement.

But, as we have seen above, confession is part of the sacramental sign and that is not just a theological statement. It expresses a profound human need. We can and do conceive sorrow for sin in our hearts but we also feel the need to express it in words or in some external action. An apology that is never externalized is simply not an apology. As many have borne witness, the need to confess, especially to one who, as the Order says, acts *in persona Christi*, is deeply rooted in human nature and releases many from what would be an intolerable burden. The apparent indifference of many modern Christians to this aspect of the sacrament is disturbing and may well be a symptom of the loss of the sense of sin which in turn may mean a loss of the sense of God.

The penitent, then, submits his sin to the 'spiritual judgement' of the confessor for absolution—or not, as the case (very rarely) may be. The Order is repeating the well-known doctrine of the Council of Trent but, as we shall see, when we come to consider the role of the confessor, the emphasis is a little different from what has been common in manuals of theology. He acts *in persona Christi* and the compassion of Christ must condition his 'judgement'; he shares in 'the power of the keys' but this is rather to authenticate his role as representative of the church than as some secular judge pronouncing sentence. The whole process is

~

different. Karl Rahner has noted that from the beginning the church has bound only that she may loose: 'Binding and loosing are not two sides of an alternative, but two phases of the one reaction whereby the Holy Church answers the sin of one of her members'. The purpose of the binding is to uncover the anomalous situation of the sinner *vis-à-vis* the church which is holy and of which he is an unholy member. His belonging to the church is a contradiction of her holiness and 'this has to be brought to light on the visible plane of the church' and only then can the guilt towards God and the church be lifted or 'loosed, again on the same plane, i.e. on the sacramental plane'. As Rahner goes on to say, this is how the early church always understood the matter. The 'binding' is essentially an act of mercy, not a condemnation with punishment attached.[9]

How the examination of conscience and subsequent confession are to be made will be considered later but meanwhile we may take into account some considerations of L. Monden.[10] The confession of the penitent is much more a sign of his repentance than a piece of criminal accounting. In practice, he often confesses more than he expresses in words and, on the other hand, sometimes and unwittingly less. As for the priest's judgement, 'his human meeting with sinfulness is only (again) a *sign*—often a very imperfect and shadowy sign—of the merciful salvific judgement of God'. The priest is the *minister* (servant) of Christ, not his substitute.

Satisfaction

'Satisfaction' is not a happy term. The human being can never make 'satisfaction' to God whom he has offended by sin. If satisfaction was to be made there was need of a Redeemer to make it. Moreover, it is difficult to find in the New Testament any basis for the distinction between sin and 'the punishment due to sin'. When God forgives, he forgives all. The *word* is first found in Tertullian (*De Paenitentia*, 8) and, according to A. Blaise, it refers there to the avowal of sin that in itself indicates an intention to do penance.[11] According to the same author, it means generally an action to make satisfaction to God by *penitence* or, more generally still, amendment of life by contrition, prayer and mortification. This puts us on the right way to an understanding of the term and the action as they existed in the time of public penitence. The time of penitence was not so much for the making of satisfaction—even to the church—but a time for the deepening of repentance and the acceptance of a whole way of life that would restore the sinner to his former condition. Perhaps it would be an over-simplification to say that for the Fathers and the Christian writers of the time the purpose of the penance was medicinal rather than punitive but that is the general impression one takes away from them. This view is supported by the continual prayer that was made for the penitents in the liturgy: to repeat what has been said above, the ban, the 'binding', was essentially an act of mercy for it is not an act of mercy to allow a sinner to continue in his sin or in the notion that what he has done is not sinful.

Broadly speaking, this is the view of the new Order. It is both reserved and positive on the subject. It nowhere uses the phrase 'temporal punishment due to sin' and is content to speak of 'reparation for the damage caused by sin' (which of course in cases of theft or calumny is a kind of satisfaction), of 'the order injured by sin' and of the 'disease' (*morbus*) which is to be cured by the appropriate remedy. In this paragraph the Order speaks of 'restoration', 'cure' and 'renewal of life', all of which it sees as the positive values of 'penance' (satisfaction) in the narrower sense. There is no suggestion of legalism anywhere, and in one sentence the Order goes to the heart of the matter. The penance is to be a remedy for sin and a means for the renewal of life so that the penitent 'forgetting those things that are behind' (Philippians 3:13) may *once more be inserted into the mystery of salvation*. That indeed is the whole purpose of the sacrament: re-integration into the saving mystery of Christ's passion, death and resurrection. We naturally think of the insertion of the individual into the mystery of Christ first through baptism and then in the eucharist. But if Christ came to take away 'the sin of the world' (John 1:29), it is here in the sacrament of penance that the penitent meets the saving, forgiving Christ, is reconciled with him so that he may take up the 'following of Christ' which, in Pauline terms (referred to in the Order), means sharing in his death and resurrection: 'All I want is to know Christ and the power of his resurrection and to share his sufferings by reproducing the pattern of his death . . .' (Philippians 3:10–11).

On this view 'penance' is the bridge between the sacrament and daily living, and it is the intention of the Order that it should be seen as such. It is also wholly in accord with the teaching of Paul VI in his letter *Paenitemini* (ET, p. 7): 'Following the Master, every Christian must renounce himself, take up his cross, and participate in the sufferings of Christ. Thus, transformed into the image of Christ's death, he is capable of meditating on the glory of the resurrection. Furthermore, following the Master, he can live no longer for himself but must live for him who loves him and gave himself up for him. He will have to live for his brethren. . . .'[12] The question of 'penance' is thus opened out to Christian living. It will consist first in the faithful performance of the duties of one's daily life and acceptance of the difficulties of one's daily work and existence. But 'living for the brethren' in current terms means serving one's neighbour and in this light 'penance' takes on a wholly new dimension which indeed is a main concern of the Order: sin, reparation, re-integration into the life of the church and a concern for others. It is what the Order calls the 'social dimension of the sacrament of penance'.

Absolution (6d)

Faithful to the sacramental theology of the Constitution on the Liturgy (7) the revisers describe absolution 'as the sign by which God grants pardon to the sinner who manifests his conversion to a minister of the church and thus the sacrament is brought to completion'. But as we have said above, the acts of the penitent are parts of the sacramental sign and with the absolution constitute the sacrament. We need to be aware that there is here a process (which in the earlier ages of the church took quite a long time) and absolution is the definitive moment when the whole process is brought to completion by the power of Christ working through the church and his minister. But the Order is not content with this; it goes on: 'By the divine economy, as God willed that the kindness and love (*philanthropia*, in the Greek) of God our Saviour appeared visibly to mankind (Titus 3:4–5), so it was his will to grant us salvation by visible signs and thus to renew the covenant broken by sin'. This puts the whole sacrament in the context of the history of salvation which reached its culmination in the passion, death and resurrection of Christ by which we are reconciled.

The profoundly scriptural teaching of the Order is reinforced by its own commentary on the meaning of absolution which in itself seems so cold a word: 'By the sacrament of penance, therefore, the Father welcomes the repentant son who comes back to him, Christ puts the lost sheep on his shoulder and brings him back to the fold, and the Holy Spirit sanctifies once more the one who is the temple of the Holy Spirit. . . . Finally, all this is manifested (one might almost say, "celebrated") through a renewed and more fervent participation in the table of the Lord's eucharist in which, now that the son has returned from a distant land, there is great joy in the banquet of the church of God.' This passage, perhaps more than any other, gives the church's view of this sacrament, reminding us as it does of the formula of absolution. There is the saving mercy of God, Father, Son and Holy Spirit, who are each active in the return of the sinner, and the eucharist is revealed as the culmination of pardon and absolution, as it is of all the sacraments. The way to it has been barred by sin but now the barrier is removed, pardon and reconciliation are achieved by encounter with the redeeming Christ.

The role of the confessor (9, 10)

In the mind of the Order the confessor is not just someone who 'hears confessions' or 'judges' the condition of his penitents in human fashion. Whether bishop or priest, he is a minister of *conversion*. Nor does he exercise this ministry simply in the sacrament. He 'preaches conversion and calls people to repentance'. This echoes the Constitution on the Liturgy (9): 'To believers also the Church must ever preach faith and penance' and it is especially in services of penitence, organized from time to time, that the church is able to preach the gospel of repentance. In the administration of the sacrament 'in the name of Christ and by the power of the Holy Spirit', confessors 'bear witness to the remission of sins and impart it'. The constant recalling in the Order of the operation of the Holy Spirit is quite remarkable and puts us in touch both with the thinking of the Eastern churches and with the practice of the early church when the laying-on of hands was the symbol of the communication of the Holy Spirit in the reconciliation of the sinner to the church.[13] Against such a background are set the qualities and function of the confessor. He is to have the necessary knowledge, acquired by study, which he will use with prudence 'under the guidance of the church' and he must pray for further guidance. But, given this, he will be able to discern the illnesses of the soul, provide apt remedies and 'exercise the function of judge'. But this power of judgement is of a quite special kind, as the Order makes clear: judgement in the sacrament of penance is an exercise of the 'discernment of spirits which is a gift of the Holy Spirit giving an intimate knowledge of the workings of God in the human heart and in itself the fruit of charity' (10). It is a teaching that once again emphasizes the work of the Holy Spirit in the sacrament of penance and reflects at once John 20:22–23 and the formula of absolution. Moreover, it extends what has been for long a traditional notion. 'Discernment of spirits' has usually been thought of as a special gift of special people who can guide those in the higher reaches of the spiritual life – or alternatively those who could discern diabolical from benign spirits at work in the heart. Now it is said that every confessor who has prepared himself by study and prayer has this gift and in the administration of the sacrament he is exercising it. He is not *just* a spiritual psychiatrist (though a knowledge of psychiatry is helpful), much less is he merely an earthly judge handing out sentence according to some code of law. He is a spiritual man – in the old medieval term, a 'ghostly fader' – who is operating under the influence of the Holy Spirit and bringing to birth in a soul the effects of repentance and amendment of life.

As if this were not enough, the Order adds that in the sacrament he is essentially 'father', bearing in himself the image of Christ and revealing to the penitent whom he welcomes 'the heart of the Father' who is ever ready to forgive. In himself he is a sign of the Father's love shown forth in the Son and by consequence he is exercising a function of Christ himself 'who in mercy effected the work of redemption and by his power is present in the sacraments' (cf. CL 7).

All this represents a high doctrine of the role of the confessor and if this role may be difficult always to live up to, it is as well to be aware that this is what a confessor is. The work of preparation for this ministry by study and prayer is seen to be all the more important.

Before speaking of the role of the confessor, the Order (8) has dealt with an aspect of the ministry of penance which has rarely been seen in modern times. 'The *whole* church as the priestly people', it says, is involved in different ways in this ministry of reconciliation. The church, the local community for instance, does this by calling sinners to repentance through the proclamation of God's word, by praying for them and by showing a maternal care and concern for them and by coming to their aid.

There is much that could be said about this. Few parishes seem to have any great concern for those who are called lapsed or the indifferent and all of us are a little self-conscious about calling other people 'sinners' since we are so conscious that we are sinners ourselves. But evidently there is here a whole pastoral policy to be thought out for the reclamation of those members of our communities who for one reason or another have fallen away. The phrase 'the priestly people' is very striking and since the Christian people are such they share in some way in the more strictly priestly ministry of reconciliation. Perhaps 'reconciliation' is the key-word. There is much that the laity can do in parish communities to reconcile those who are divided or to draw them back gently to the church from which they have become alienated. In any case, there is the whole ministry of *prayer* for 'sinners' which the early church practised with such vigour and conviction. At least in Lent, then, there should be constant and discreetly worded petitions for sinners and if a portion of the Divine Office is celebrated in parishes there is room there for the same intention.

The penitent (11)

Little enough is said here about the role of the penitent because the matter has already been dealt with (6a, b, c) and because there is more to be said in a practical way later on (17–20). What the Order does do is to emphasize the importance of the acts of the penitent and in doing so it echoes the teaching of Rahner given above. Through his acts the penitent is playing his (necessary) part in the celebration of the sacrament: 'Thus the Christian, while experiencing God's mercy and proclaiming it by his life, celebrates with the priest the liturgy of the church which constantly renews itself. The renewal of the penitent is part of the constant renewal of the church itself.'

Practical matters

Section 9a, b is concerned with the canonical aspect of ministry. The ordinary ministers of the sacrament are *bishops* and priests 'who are in communion with their bishop and act by his authority'. Priests must be willing to hear people's confessions whenever they reasonably ask. Lent is a particularly favourable time for the celebration of the sacrament and communal services of penitence should be celebrated at this time to give opportunities to the faithful 'to be reconciled with God and their neighbours so that, spiritually renewed, they may celebrate the paschal mystery at the end of Lent'. This is but one of the many touches that relate penance to the paschal mystery.

The place of confession

Since the sixteenth century confession has been made in a structure called the confessional and the Code of Canon Law (1918) laid down that it must be in a conspicuous place and that there must be a grille between the confessor and the penitent. Local conferences of bishops may now make other arrangements (38b). Two considerations come into play here.

1. For some time now many people have made known their desire to have what they call a more human situation for confession. To kneel in front of a veiled grille and to speak to an unseen person the other side of it some find inhibiting. Accordingly in many churches 'confessional rooms' have been provided where penitent and priest can sit facing each other and enter into a dialogue. There is also the problem of what to do when there is a service of penitence and many confessors are engaged to hear confessions. 'Boxes' cannot be provided for them all. Clearly different arrangements in different situations are necessary and it would be detrimental to the celebration of this sacrament if hard and fast rules were laid down, *ne varientur*. Provided that the secrecy of the confession can be preserved there would seem to be no reason why confessions should not be heard on the sanctuary (as in the Middle Ages) or in a side chapel.

2. This is all the more necessary as the one symbolic gesture of this sacrament is the laying-on of hands, which should be seen by the penitent and others. This gesture, in somewhat vestigial form, has been preserved throughout the centuries and the new Order insists on it: 'After the prayer (act of sorrow) of the penitent the priest extends his hands over his head (or at least his right hand) and pronounces the essential words of absolution' (19). The importance of this gesture is that in all the early practice of penance and reconciliation it was seen as the sign of re-integration into the church of the sinner effected by the power of the Holy Spirit. Since it is a sign or symbol it should be seen. But that is usually impossible in the conventional confessional. Other arrangements, then, need to be made if this symbol is to retain its importance and since this sacrament is weak in symbolism, there is all the more reason to see that it is made visible.

Likewise, conferences of bishops are to suggest appropriate gesture or gestures to be used in services of public reconciliation on the part of those who wish to receive the general absolution (35). This may be either a bowing of the head or kneeling down. Since this part of the service follows on the homily, the people will be sitting and it will be for the

~

celebrant to invite those who wish to be absolved to kneel. There is no difficulty about this since the whole assembly usually wish to receive the absolution. In other cultures than our own there may well be other signs of repentance that will be appropriate.

The three liturgies of penance

1. The reconciliation of individual penitents (41–47)

Since the Order has been in use for some long time now there is no need to give any elaborate account of this liturgy. There is the welcome by the confessor, the words he addresses to the penitent to stimulate trust in God's goodness, the proclamation of God's word (read either by the penitent or the confessor), the confession and the giving of spiritual counsel, the prayer of repentance, the absolution, a brief thanksgiving and the dismissal. Commentary on one or two of these points may be useful.

Before confessing the penitent is encouraged to make known to the confessor the conditions and circumstances of his life, the difficulties he may find in leading the Christian life 'and whatever may be useful for the confessor to know for the exercise of his ministry' (16). This is not laid down as an obligation and it is for the penitent to take the initiative but it does suggest that confession is to be seen as at least partly a dialogue and not just a listing of sins.

The reading of a passage of scripture is an expression of the axiom that we are saved by faith and the sacraments of faith but here in particular it is intended to confront the penitent with the demands of God that are made known in his word. Unhappily, it seems already to have become a formality and many if not most penitents seem quite happy to have it omitted. Old habits die hard. After confession the confessor exhorts the penitent to true repentance and will provide appropriate counsel for the living of the Christian life. If necessary he will instruct the penitent in the duties of Christian living and in the case of damage whether material (theft) or spiritual (calumny), he will 'lead the penitent to make fitting restitution'.

Closely connected with the counsel is the 'penance'. This is to be thought of not merely as expiation for past sins but as a remedy for weakness and a help towards amendment of life. It may consist of prayers, acts of self-denial but especially of 'service of neighbour and works of mercy which will throw light on *the social nature of sin and its remission*' (18). In a word, the new way of life that the penitent now undertakes is the real 'penance' and it will be seen that it is the link between the sacrament and life. It also extends the vision of the penitent far beyond his own private concerns and reminds him that he is part of a living body which is injured by his sins and which can be enriched by the quality of his Christian life.

Of the prayer, or 'act of contrition', which the penitent recites after receiving the 'penance', the Order says that it should be largely in scriptural terms. However, this is hardly verified in the formula it gives and the reader should note the many alternatives to be found under nos. 85–92. The shortest is one of the most effective: 'Lord Jesus, Son of God, have mercy on me a sinner' (cf. Luke 18:13).

Something has been said already about the formula of absolution but a few further remarks will be in place here since, apart from the public form of penitence, it is always used.

It should be noted first that, apart from the last sentence 'I absolve you . . .', it is in deprecatory form: i.e. it is a prayer, a fact that is disguised by the exigencies of English translation. In Latin it is in the subjunctive mood and is a petition to God the Father that through the paschal mystery of his Son who reconciled the world, and through the Holy Spirit who was sent for the forgiveness of sins, the penitent sinner may receive pardon and peace, which are the effects of reconciliation. This form reflects the church's usage of the time before the twelfth century when absolution and reconciliation were wholly in the form of prayer (cf. the Gelasian Sacramentary referred to above). The last sentence, in the indicative mood, comes from that same century when the canonists, who greatly influenced the theologians of their time as of subsequent ages, thought that the indicative was the appropriate mood for sacramental formulas.[14] The whole formula in English is this:

God, Father of mercies,
through the death and resurrection of his Son,
has reconciled the world to himself
and sent the Holy Spirit among us
for the forgiveness of sins:
through the ministry of the church
may God give you pardon and peace,

~

and I absolve you from your sins
in the name of the Father, and of the Son,
and of the Holy Spirit.
℟. Amen.

The prayer 'The passion of our Lord Jesus Christ . . .' which always
concluded the old rite of penance has been retained as an alternative text
but it may be noted that whereas the old edition spoke of the penitential
deeds of the penitent as 'taking away the sins', the revised version is
altered to 'for a remedy for sin'. This confirms the view of the 'penance'
given above.[15]

Pastoral considerations

After nearly twenty years' experience it must be said that this rite is not
working as it should. In spite of instruction and the provision of books
and cards setting out the rite, almost all make their confession in the old
fashion and so many seem to be in a hurry to get it over. The reading
of the scripture passage, however brief, seems to them an irrelevancy and
the old lists of sins make it difficult for the confessor to give that counsel
which not only the Order recommends but every book on the subject
recommended long before it. In addition, some priests find the whole
procedure tedious and go on much as before. And it must be admitted
that when there are great numbers of people to be confessed it is a very
fatiguing business. An enquiry into the stress and fatigue symptoms
of confessors would produce interesting results, among others perhaps
that no one should be *allowed* to hear more than a given number of
confessions.

The remedy for this unhappy state of affairs can only be a determined
and intelligent catechesis. This is particularly important in schools of all
kinds for it is only there that the young can be initiated into new ways
of using the sacrament and indeed into a whole new vision of its meaning
and what it could do for them. It is widely known that the young, in the
majority, do not in fact use this sacrament any more and if the necessary
effort is not made now the danger is that a whole generation of Catholics
will grow up without any knowledge or experience of the sacrament of
penance. This would mean a very considerable spiritual impoverishment
and eventually some very acute crises of conscience.

2. The reconciliation of several penitents with individual absolution (48–59)

In this service and in the one that follows the church has met the often-repeated request for a public liturgy of penance.

The case for it can be summed up like this:

1. All sacramental celebrations, by the terms of the Constitution on the Liturgy, demand a proclamation of God's word.

2. For penance it is particularly important that we should hear the urgent message of the Bible to repent.

3. The Order recognizes explicitly that penance is an ecclesial and communal sacrament, that sin has effects on the community and that the sinner's reparation must be assisted by the community. We sin not simply as individuals but as members of a community and indeed as a community: some expression of that common sinfulness is demanded by the nature of the sacrament.

4. Prayer once formed a very important element of the sacrament and in this rite the Order provides for common prayer for our own sins and those of others.

5. Confrontation with the word of God and in particular with the demands of the gospel assists 'examination of conscience', deepening our understanding of sin and widening our horizons about what is sinful and what is not. Psychologically this is of particular help to those who find reflection on themselves difficult.

6. The making of 'satisfaction' will be more realistic, for the whole community can be invited to take up 'the works of mercy' the Order refers to.

The rite

1. Entrance chant, greeting, brief address and collect.
2. The proclamation of the word of God with psalm.
3. The homily.
4. Examination of conscience.
5. The general confession (as in Penitential Rite I of the Order of Mass).
6. Prayer in litanic form always ending with the Lord's Prayer.
7. Private confession and absolution.
8. Thanksgiving, blessing and dismissal.

~

The form of the service is the now conventional one for Bible Services and does not call for extended commentary.

We may note that in the reading of the scriptures we are hearing *God's* word (cf. CL 7), in this case calling us to repentance and amendment of life. But, as the Order also says, the readings show forth the mystery of reconciliation effected by the death and resurrection of Christ and by the giving of the Holy Spirit. Finally, they give the message of divine judgement on good and evil in the life of mankind and thus enlighten the conscience.

As elsewhere in the new liturgy the homily is to be based on the readings (they are not meant to be vague moralizing extravaganzas). The preacher is to remember that the readings convey the voice of God calling to repentance, conversion and renewal of life. He is to remind his hearers that sin is committed against God, the community, their neighbours and themselves and he is to recall to them that God's mercy is infinite and exhort them to true, interior repentance, such that they will make reparation for any harm they have caused to others: the *social aspect* of sin is to be brought to their attention. They will have to practise love of neighbour if their satisfaction is to be adequate (24, 52). Naturally it will not be necessary to include all these considerations every time and what the preacher says will of course be conditioned by the nature of his audience.

The homily is part of, and leads into, the examination of conscience: if these two things are done well they are two of the most valuable parts of this rite. Most of us are very limited in our outlook on what sin is and what sins we ourselves have committed. The 'social aspect of sin', so heavily emphasized by the Order, is often completely overlooked. How far, for instance, are we responsible for at least some of the evils of our society? Do we accept evil situations simply because everyone else does and because if you lift up your voice you will get disliked? The texts and the homily can also help us to deepen our understanding of sin. Have we lost a sense of sin as something opposed to the holiness of God and the dignity of human beings? In the more private sector of morals is there not a need to point out that reconciliation between individuals, however effected, is a central requirement of the gospel? People can get all steamed up about sexual sins while at the same time failing to realize that their lives are full of bitterness and hatred. Within families it is sometimes necessary for their members to realize that forgiveness and reconciliation are the very condition of their lives as Christians.

These are some of the questions prompted by the scripture texts and the words of the homilist and while the shaping of such questions is a matter of some delicacy, they need to be presented. Knowledge of the laity on the part of the preacher will help him to frame the questions and during Lent, for instance, a consultation with them on the sins of the society in which they are immersed will be very profitable to both. As the community becomes aware or more aware of the evils of their society, the greater is the likelihood that they will be able to do something about them. This again relates the sacrament and the 'penance' to ordinary human living, for the community as such can be asked to correct those evils within the limits of its power.

(It should be noted that the scheme for the examination of conscience in Appendix III of the Order is optional and need not be used. It is no more than an up-dated version of the forms to be found in old-fashioned prayer books. It is better to 'search the scriptures' and find passages that meet particular occasions; there is general provision made for this in the Order itself. It means more work but the results are more profitable.)

The next section, significantly called 'the rite of reconciliation', consists entirely of prayer. First, there is a litany of intercession and then the Lord's Prayer which must always be included and said at this point. A study of the two samples given (and they are only samples) shows that the whole range of the new vision of the sacrament is conveyed by them, but the most important point to note here is that this is the prayer of the church for sinners and represents that element of the life of the church in the early centuries when sinners were conceived to be converted by prayer. One of the purposes of the long periods of canonical penance was that the penitent sinners might be converted by the prayer of the church and, as we have noted above, the Lord's Prayer was regarded as peculiarly effective in the remission of sins of the ordinary Christian. Private confession and absolution follow and the rite concludes with the thanksgiving and dismissal. The text leaves open wide possibilities: 'The celebrant surrounded by the other priests who have heard confessions invites the people to make a thanksgiving and exhorts them to good works *whereby the grace of penance may be manifested in the life of each of them and in the life of the community*' (56). This gives scope for the appointing of tasks to the whole community, which might be invited to accept them as visible signs of their repentance and thus relate the sacrament to life, the life of the society in which the community exists.

Pastoral considerations

This form of the celebration of penance is undoubtedly rich in content and can be effective in practice, as least as far as the awakening of conscience is concerned. Experience shows that if the service is carefully prepared and if the homilist is adequate to his task, subsequent confessions do benefit from it. There are two difficulties. Several priests are necessary for the private confessions and these are not always easy to come by. Even so, the confessions tend to take up a good deal of time (and that is as it should be) but the final act of thanksgiving can hardly take place because people are not willing to stay for it. The circumstances in which the rite is best used is a day or half-day of recollection for a parish or other community. A time can be appointed for the conclusion of the service, and if there are grounds or any other suitable place, the people can go there and await the concluding prayers for which they will return to the church. But after the very communal nature of the service the private confessions and absolutions do seem to be something of an anomaly and people have remarked on this.

As to how often these services are held, experience also shows that they are profitable in Advent and Lent though these seasons do not exhaust the possibilities. Parish 'missions' are somewhat rare events nowadays but if they do occur, this form of service could very properly be used though it is to be hoped that those responsible will respect the spirit of the Order and draw on its considerable resources. Another occasion is the dedication of a church, which used to be preceded by a day of fasting. Its sense, in the new Order of Dedication (1977), is that it is a sign of the spiritual renewal of the whole parish or community. A day of penitence could be appointed some convenient time before the dedication.

3. The Order for the reconciliation of penitents with general confession and absolution (31–35; 60–63)

From a liturgical viewpoint, the third rite of penance is the type or exemplar on which the other two may be said to be based. It is visibly a public service of the church, it involves the community, there is a public proclamation of God's word, there is a general confession of sin and the absolution and reconciliation are also public. But as everyone knows there are theological and what I would call administrative difficulties about which something will be said below.

First then let us look at the rite (60–66).

Let us consider the language with which it is introduced. As one writer has observed, the thought behind this rite is very different from what we have conventionally understood as a 'general absolution'.[16] It is a service of reconciliation with God and the church, it is a liturgical service and not just the utterance of a formula, and by its very texts and structure demands the repentance and conversion of the participants. Moreover, it retains all the features of classical penance (whether ancient or modern) with the sole exception of the *private* confession of sins for the occasion. The service differs but little from the second rite and may be summarized like this:

1. There is the usual introduction and the reading of the scriptures.

2. The homily.

3. The general confession made by all those who wish to receive absolution, according to the formulas used in other services or at Mass.

4. There is prayer, as above in the previous service, always ending with the Lord's Prayer.

5. Finally, there is absolution in very solemn form.

(The conclusion of the service is the same as in the second rite.)

Commentary

The fact that the reconciliation/absolution is embedded in a service of the word and prayer gives it a different complexion. Confrontation with the word of God and prayer provide the context for the whole service and they lead naturally and one would say inevitably into the reconciliation and absolution that follow. First, confrontation with the word of God enables the participants to realize more clearly the evil of sin. This is carried forward by the homily that leads into examination of conscience and repentance, on which the Order so strongly insists. The general confession here acquires its full force: the whole gathered community expresses its sinfulness *with a view to* reconciliation and absolution that appear as the climax of the service. There is no break: proclamation of the word, prayer, confession and reconciliation follow one after another. This, one feels, is as it should be and the hiatus of the second rite is no longer apparent.

The formula of absolution is in itself a remarkable piece of writing.

~

It invokes the Father, the Son and the Holy Spirit. The Father, who desires not the death but the life of the sinner and who first loved us and sent his Son to save us, is asked to show his mercy to us. The Son who was delivered up on account of our sins to make us righteous, gave the Holy Spirit to the apostles to forgive sins. The prayer continues: 'May he (Christ) through our ministry free you from sin and fill you with the Holy Spirit'. In the Holy Spirit, given for the remission of sins, we have access to the Father and he is asked to purify our hearts, to shed his radiance on us that we may proclaim the saving deeds of him who has called us out of darkness into light. The usual formula: 'I absolve you . . .' concludes the form of reconciliation.

We note that, apart from the last sentence, the whole text is a *prayer* that by means of a catena of scripture quotations expresses the great effect of the sacrament, reconciliation with God and his church. Secondly, the emphasis on the work of the Holy Spirit is strong. He is operative in all the work of reconciliation, he 'fills' the penitent, purifies his heart and radiates his whole being. Thirdly, while the formula of reconciliation is being pronounced the celebrant holds his hands over the penitents and the meaning of that ancient rite is made clear: the Holy Spirit is being given *for* reconciliation with the church, as it was in the early centuries of the church when the lapsed, the heretic and schismatic were regarded as having put themselves outside the ambit of the Holy Spirit's operation. For if he is the Spirit of Christ he is also the Spirit of his body which is the church.

The conditions of its use

All Catholics are aware of the practice in times of danger of death, e.g. shipwreck or fire, of absolving a number of people at once and after exhorting them to repentance. The Order takes this for granted as a permissible practice but it extends the occasions when such absolution may be given and lays down the conditions when it may be given. They can be summarized as follows:

1. There is a large number of penitents.
2. There is not a sufficient number of confessors to hear and absolve them.
3. Without their fault they would be deprived of the grace of the sacrament or of holy communion for some long time (*diu*).

4. This can happen in missionary territories but also elsewhere when there is a gathering of people and it can be established (*constat*) that the necessity (for confession and communion) exists (31).

All this seems clear enough and these conditions are found in a vast number of parish churches in Holy Week and at Christmas. There are large numbers of people to be confessed, and it is now in most places morally impossible to find a sufficient number of confessors, and the people have to wait an inordinate length of time. True, they are not sent away, but the quality of the celebration of the sacrament suffers considerably. After a certain number of penitents the confessor inevitably tires and the penitents themselves, feeling the pressure of all who are waiting, wish to get their confessions over as quickly as possible. In other words, all the evils of the old way of doing the sacrament remain, yet the Order is concerned that these should not continue! There is in fact a limiting clause in the Order: 'This (the use of general absolution) is not lawful simply on account of a large number of penitents since confessors can be made available (*cum confessores praesto esse possunt*)'. This is a statement of fact and a very extraordinary one. How can the authorities in Rome know when and where confessors can be made available? Not only in missionary territories but in vast areas of the so-called civilized world confessors in sufficient numbers simply cannot be obtained at times like Christmas and Easter. Almost all the parish clergy have had experience of the lack of confessors even for the second rite and all of them know what a burden is put on themselves and the people by the great number of confessions at the great seasons of the year. The Roman authorities have however insisted on the letter of the Order, greatly to the detriment of its operation and to the good of the people.

It is for diocesan bishops, in consultation with the conference of bishops, to determine when the rite may be used but some at least have been rebuked for giving what seemed to Rome over-liberal permissions. Even so, it is difficult to imagine that bishops can know the circumstances of all their parishes and so the Order gives permission to the local priest to decide if there is a necessity for this rite either after consulting his bishop, or if that is impossible, informing him afterwards.

Further clarification of this whole matter is necessary. One can only speculate on the reasons for the rigidity hitherto shown but the reason for it may be the fear that the practice of private and individual confession will disappear. But it may also be that the ruling of the Council of

Trent that all mortal sins must be confessed in number, kind and circumstances is regarded as absolutely binding. Certainly much of the
underlying theology of the Instruction is based on the teaching of that
council. There arises then the question of the confessing of mortal sins
and the further question of what is mortal sin.

As to the reception of general absolution it should be noted that the
Instruction incorporates the 'norms' of an Instruction issued by the Congregation for the Doctrine of the Faith issued eighteen months before the
Order.[17] The general view is that the Order in this place is to be interpreted by that document. The Order (33) gives the conditions required
for a fruitful reception of the general absolution:

1. The penitent must be truly repentant and have a true sorrow for
sins committed.

2. He must have the intention to refrain from sin.

3. He must be willing to make reparation for any scandal or injury
he has done.

4. He must have the intention to confess all mortal sins privately 'in
due time (*debito tempore*)' and in any case before benefiting from another
general absolution. Short of moral impossibility, he is to make a private
confession within the year, for the obligation of confessing all sins,
especially mortal sins once a year, still stands (34).

At the end of paragraph 33 the Order says that these conditions are
necessary *ad valorem sacramenti*. There has been some debate about this
last phrase.[18] What does this term mean? It has been argued that it does
not necessarily mean 'for validity' yet on the other hand the ICEL
translators have 'for validity'. If the whole paragraph is taken together
it can be seen as simply stating traditional teaching and therefore 'for
validity' is probably correct. But the crux of the matter is the confessing
of mortal sins and in the context of the rite of general absolution, within
a reasonable length of time, a year at most. The question then arises: is
the penitent absolved? Is the absolution effective (i.e. valid)? Probably the
answer to the question turns on the *intention* of the penitent to confess
in due time. If that were lacking, he would be putting an obstacle (*obex*)
in the way of the effect of the sacrament. On the other hand, if he has
the intention, but for one reason or another does not confess his mortal
sins privately, the absolution is probably valid. A deliberate intention not
to confess would, in the present discipline, invalidate the sacrament for
the penitent. That would seem to be the sense of the Order.

So we come to the second question which concerns first the obligation of confessing mortal sins. It is noteworthy that the terms of the Order are not on the whole restrictive. It simply says that the obligation to confess all sins, including mortal sins, once a year to a confessor is still in force. It does indeed refer in a footnote to the document of the Congregation for the Doctrine of the Faith which states that auricular confession is of 'divine precept'. But the meaning of this term is not beyond dispute. Thus Louis Monden states that though confession of mortal sins is said by the Council of Trent to be *iure divino*, this term 'had not yet acquired the meaning we assign to it today and was often used for ecclesiastical or even for civil law'.[19] This chimes with what Père Tillard has to say about a long debate at the Council of Trent. The debate was in fact inconclusive and Tillard goes on to say that the Council of Trent in its declaration *Statuit et declarat* was merely affirming '*the customary law of the church*'. He also cites the opinion of a modern moralist that confession before communion and after mortal sin is to be regarded rather as an ecclesiastical precept.[20]

The question may seem to be of not much more than academic interest and we must take into account that a Roman document of 1972 may well be interpreting earlier statements. Auricular confession has certainly been the custom for a very long time though it is a long step from 'custom' to 'divine law'. In any case, there remains the problem of reconciling this teaching with the practice of all the early centuries when people received communion at every eucharist they attended and, apart from the notorious and public sinners, never 'went to confession'. However, there is no doubt about the present discipline of the church, and there can be no question here of inviting people to ignore it. On the other hand, theologians might well turn their attention to the matter for in the long run it is the good of the people that is at stake.

This question is obviously connected with another: what is mortal sin? In recent years there has been a great deal of discussion about it.[21] Theologians are distinguishing between sin that is a complete turning away from God and the sort of sin that is by no means a rejection of God but rather a falling short of the dominant direction of a life which is towards God. This has been called the 'fundamental option'. People whether consciously or not have chosen God and his demands but from time to time fall away. There is a failure of response to the demands of God whom they wish with all their hearts to serve and, it is argued, the

relationship with God is not broken. The notion that anyone after breaking the law of God on a single occasion could be 'sent to hell' for all eternity is no longer acceptable and is indeed regarded as bizarre. What sort
of God would that be? The new notion (if it is new) also contains a fundamental psychological truth: the whole personality is rarely involved in
one single act and yet we find it quite conceivable that a long series of
wrong acts do produce a state that can be said to result in an alienation
from God.

All is not clear in this theology but it does seem to get nearer the truth
of human actions than the old quasi-automatic notion which has weighed
on the consciences of people for too long. No doubt, too, much more
needs to be said and further theological reflection is necessary. Conclusions in the direction indicated above would make the operation of the
third rite all the easier.

Pastoral considerations

Confusion over the conditions when the third rite may be used and what
seems to have been a genuine misunderstanding on the part of several
bishops in different parts of the world have rendered the use of this rite
very difficult. This is the greatest of pities because it has affected the
whole presentation of the new Order of penance. It is hardly honest to
present the new Order to people while holding back on the third rite.
And it is absurd to tell them about it and then say (more or less) 'but of
course it cannot be used in our circumstances'.

In the Order there is a progression from 'private penance' to the
second rite of which only a part is public and on to the third rite where
all is. As the Order itself lays out the pattern the third rite seems to be
what I have called the exemplar of the others. In practice there is a
reverse tendency. It is a matter of experience that, where people have
been able to benefit from a celebration of the third rite, after being
long away from the sacraments, they have readily confessed their sins
privately some few days later. It is a fact of psychology, known to most
of the pastoral clergy (though hidden apparently from the wise and prudent), that when the weight of *guilt* is lifted people feel able to confess
their sins in the confessional. The service itself leads them to a true
repentance unlikely to be attained if left to themselves. The experience
of being part of a congregation that as a whole confesses its sinfulness

helps them to repent and amend their lives. And this is the plain teaching of the Order, namely that we all share a solidarity in sin and all can contribute to its reparation.

The fear has been expressed that the third rite might eventually eliminate private confession. This fear is exaggerated, to say the least. The Order envisages that its celebration will be infrequent in the course of a year and it maintains the obligation to confess mortal sins afterwards. What still needs doing is that the whole of the Order, doctrine and practice, should be put before the people so that they know what is available to them and what is required of them. A vast catechetical programme is needed if this is to be achieved and it is particularly important that this should be done in schools at all levels. It is to be feared that this has hardly begun though where permission has been granted for the use of the third rite in secondary and comprehensive schools the result has been spiritually very satisfactory. The need in parishes is equally great and now that discussion and prayer groups are a normal part of parish life it is here that the teaching should be given, but for this people need a well-planned programme that will cover the whole of the Order. Given in an atmosphere of prayer, such teaching would be peculiarly effective for the spiritual doctrine of the Order is deep and rich.

Notes

[1] Gelasian Sacramentary, nos. 353-9.

[2] See Austin Flannery, OP, **Doctrine and Life**, 24 (April 1974), who refers to an issue of the **Osservatore Romano** (8 February 1974) in which it is said that the terms 'reconcile' and 'reconciliation' were deliberately chosen instead of 'absolve', 'absolution' and 'confession'.

[3] The 'deadly' or 'mortal' sin seems to have been apostasy, for which an intervention of the church was necessary (see JB **in loco**).

[4] See H. de Lubac, **Méditations sur l'Eglise** (Paris, 1953), p. 99.

[5] K. Donovan, **Music and Liturgy**, 1 (Autumn 1974), p. 11, to which article this section owes a good deal.

[6] See B. Dunne, OSB, 'The Sacrament of Penance in the Eastern Churches', **Doctrine and Life** (Supp. for January–February 1977).

[7] Karl Rahner, **Theological Investigations**, 2 (London, 1963), p. 160. Elsewhere (p.156) he says that 'within the totality of the sign (and only then) the priestly absolution is for St Thomas the decisive element as the causal effect'.

[8] Denz.-Schön. 1676 (as given in the **Ordo**).

[9] Rahner, **op. cit.**, p. 142.

[10] L. Monden, **Sin, Liberty and Law** (New York, 1965), p. 47.

[11] A. Blaise, **Dictionnaire Latin-Français des Auteurs Chrétiens** (Strasbourg/Paris,1954), **s.v.** 'satisfactio'.

[12] The number of texts given shows that the pope's teaching is wholly biblical: Phil 3:10–11; Rom 6:10; Gal 2:20; Col 1:24, though this last citation has a rather different sense from that given by spiritual writers. The 'sufferings of Christ' are intimately connected with the completion of **the preaching of the gospel**, so they would be the apostolic sufferings endured as the gospel is continually brought to new places until a certain quota is reached. Thus Maurya P. Horgan in **The New Jerome Biblical Commentary**, ed. R. E. Brown, J. A. Fitzmyer and R. E. Murphy (London, 1989), p. 880, **in loco**.

[13] This emphasis on the work of the Holy Spirit in the new Order seems to be quite deliberate. Père Ligier, who was a member of the first commission on the rite of penance, wrote in **LMD**, 90 (1967), p. 161: 'In the eastern perspective the administration of this sacrament requires not simply the **power** of the Holy Spirit but also a familiarity with divine things which is possessed by those who live in the Spirit and know the things of God and the secrets of hearts'. He refers to Origen, **De Oratione**, 28. The whole article seems to have influenced the redaction of the Order.

[14] Though they overlooked the formulas of the anointing of the sick which were always in the subjunctive. The same could be said of the sacrament of ordination, though the formulas here were overlaid with the more peremptory phrases accompanying the 'tradition of the instruments'.

[15] For further information about this prayer and its meaning see my book, **The Ministry of Reconciliation**, pp. 40–1.

[16] Austin Flannery, **art. cit.**, p. 206n.

[17] **Normae pastorales circa absolutionem sacramentalem generali modo impertiendam** (dated 16 June 1972), **AAS** 64 (1972), p. 511.

[18] See **Clergy Review**, 60 (May 1975), p. 334; **The Month**, 236 (July 1975), p. 218; **Clergy Review**, 60 (August 1975), p. 542, and the preliminary note to the second edition of **The Ministry of Reconciliation** (1976).

[19] Monden, **op. cit.**, pp. 47–8.

[20] **LMD**, 90 (1967), pp. 117–24. For a summary account of the debate, see **Penance: Virtue and Sacrament**, ed. J. Fitzsimons (London, 1969), pp. 45–6.

[21] See, for instance, D. O'Callaghan, 'What is Mortal Sin?', **The Furrow**, 25 (February 1974), p. 82, and L. Orsy, 'Common Sense about Sin', **The Tablet** (9 February 1974), pp. 125–8.

TWELVE

Pastoral Opportunities

PROLONGED STUDY of the new liturgical documents on the sacraments prompts certain reflections. In spite of the fact that the new rites are basically traditional, they have opened up a whole new world. The meaning of sacramental actions has been greatly clarified and for the Christian at any rate they are easy enough to understand. Pastorally speaking, this is of immense importance and in this the revisers have been completely faithful to the Constitution on the Liturgy. In addition they have clarified sacramental theology in many respects, notably in holy order and the anointing of the sick. The old organic system of the sacraments of Christian Initiation has, at least in principle, been restored. The non-sacramental rite of funerals breathes the air of the early church. But there are other aspects of this considerable work of reform that deserve attention.

One dominant impression left by a study of these rites is that they are so much more *personal* than those they have replaced. For centuries priests poured streams of Latin over half-comprehending people and the words were inevitably directed to no one in particular. But the change has not come from merely translating Latin texts into the vernacular. While translated texts would have been more understandable, they would still have lacked that personal emphasis that is to be found throughout the new rites. Words now are always directed to real people who are present and they in turn are required to be actively involved. If there is one calculable effect of the reform it is that people do feel so involved. This is a gain whose value can hardly be estimated and it does mean that the liturgy is doing that for which it was devised: to convey God's redeeming power to the people in a way that is in accordance with their nature and to enable them to respond with the whole of their personalities. No doubt something still remains to be done by way of adaptation to make the rites even more effective. There is too the still troublesome business of symbolism which may or may not be viable in the world of today. No doubt many of the clergy need to learn that liturgy is personal and not formal. They too must feel involved. It none the less remains true that the church has put into the hands of clergy and laity alike an invaluable means of approaching God and of being united with him.

Another inescapable impression is that the new rites are essentially *communal*. Their celebration demands the presence and co-operation of the local community and often their help before and afterwards. *Normally*, there is no such thing as a private celebration of the sacraments and in this too the revisers have been very faithful to the Constitution (26). This does not mean that we have to agonize over the notion of 'community', and ask whether parishes are or are not communities. Wherever two or three are gathered in the name of Christ, he is in the midst of them. The important thing is that the principle is stated and again that normally a community will be present. Often, as in the case of confirmation and ordination, the absence of community is hardly conceivable and would make nonsense of a good deal of the rites. Here too a change of mentality is required, especially among those laity who seem to think that *their* baptisms, weddings and funerals are purely private affairs. This principle of community is in fact carried so far that no one in 1963 would have thought that there could ever be such a celebration as a public anointing of the sick. And this has come from the rediscovery of an ancient truth that that sacrament is primarily a sacrament of healing.

As we have observed in the first chapter, the sacraments have once again been firmly set in the context of *life*. They are no longer isolated bits of ritual. This, it seems to me, has vast consequences for the pastoral life. Over forty years ago the French began discussing the possibilities of a *liturgie pastorale*. In more recent years they have been talking about a *pastorale liturgique*, a term almost impossible to translate into English. By it they mean at least that pastoral action should be centred on the liturgy and especially on the sacraments. For far too long pastoral life and practice have moved parallel with the liturgy when they did not cut across it (as in the case of those famous 'mission' services) or ignore it altogether. The new rites have now opened the door to a pastoral action that will be on the one hand rooted in the liturgy and on the other leading people to it. Here the emphasis on *faith* in all the new orders is the key factor. We proceed from faith to sacrament. We believe and then we are baptized. From baptism we move to the eucharist by which we live and from the eucharist we go to the world to carry to it the message of Christ.

Once we have got used to the new rites, it would seem that there should be a complete re-thinking of pastoral practice. This becomes more and more difficult year by year. There are all sorts of factors in play here which it would be impossible to deal with adequately. We may mention one only: the intense mobility of population. The pastoral clergy are constantly exhorted to 'instruct' their people; they are asked to do this or that with them or for them and yet as far as the people are concerned, it is often a case of 'here today and gone tomorrow'. The chances of any consecutive work are slim. Yet, most of these people require the sacraments at one time or another. They want their children baptized, they wish them to be confirmed. They want them to receive their first communion and so on. The young want to get married (distressingly young sometimes) and people fall ill and all die—even the clergy. All these are crucial moments of *life*, people's lives are patterned by these events, it is at times like these that they are most open to the word of God and it is of these occasions that the greatest possible use should be made. The clergy may or may not be able to visit house-to-house, they may or may not be able to organize parish councils, bazaars and/or football pools, but one thing they have to do by professional and vocational commitment is to celebrate the sacraments with and for their people.

Perhaps however it is not a case of either/or. It *is* a case of putting the liturgical–sacramental element, which is central to the Christian life, in the centre of the picture. If we look at the matter from a coldly practical point of view, it will be seen that once you refuse to accept sacraments as merely pieces of ritual, you are inevitably involved in people and their life.

Let us start at the beginning of the life-cycle with marriage. Nowadays and for some years past it has been common practice to see prospective couples several times before marriage. This is pastorally speaking a *tempus opportunum*. Almost invariably they want to make a good marriage. Often enough they feel that the event offers them an opportunity to deepen their spiritual life. They are interested in marriage! Here the priest has a golden opportunity to deepen their faith, to help them to see the implications of Christian marriage and often to change their whole outlook. Through these meetings he usually builds up a friendship with them and if they stay in his district afterwards, he has a ready *entrée* to their home. But even if they do not, in due course they will have a child whom they will want baptized and, according to the new Order of baptism, the clergy are required to see them, to talk about the meaning of the sacrament and to show them what their commitments are. Without anyone realizing it, their faith is being deepened. As the sacramental events go by there will be further contact with the parents in e.g. the matter of first communion and it is a reasonable estimate that for about ten years people will be in contact with the clergy and one may suppose growing as Christians. This is quite a long time in the life of anyone and if in that time the clergy have not managed to inculcate the essentials of Christian faith and practice, then there is something wrong with the presentation.[1]

In addition, there is all the care of the sick that is so constant a feature of the pastoral life, the ministry to the dying and all the attention that must be given to the bereaved on the occasion of death. Whatever may be the difficulties – and one is that it is often difficult to give as *much* time to the dying as one would like – all these events require constant contact with people who are in great need of help. It may be thought that there is a large time gap between the age of ten or twelve when there are no special sacraments to give and that of old age when illness and all its handicapping consequences set in. But parents and grandparents get involved in the younger members of the family and they too benefit from what is done for them. Baptism, confirmation and first communion are all or can be truly *family* events and have the great advantage of assembling the family around a sacramental celebration. It is in this way that worship becomes embedded in life, their life.

The above is no more than a sketch of possibilities. The contention that lies behind it is that the sacramental–liturgical system offers a framework for pastoral action. Life, instruction and liturgy will move together and it may be said that if the clergy were exploiting this situation for all it was worth, they would be exercising a pastoral ministry that would touch a very large proportion of the people committed to their charge. Nearly all these events require house visitation and on these terms it proves to be profitable. Without any beating about the bush, it is possible to approach people directly and talk to them about God and the things of God. It is a manner of 'preaching the gospel', unobtrusive if you will, but none the less fundamental.

No doubt there are other people with other needs. There are the lapsed to be regained, there are the non-Christians to be converted and for these other methods need to be worked out. One could wish that more thought was being given to the enormous problem that lies before us: hardly 10 per cent of the population attached to any church. There is in addition the problem of the young who are receding from worship and church-membership and who are completely allergic to injunctions and commands even of the highest authority. We must take account too of the increasing number of people in this country who are not baptized and even among Roman Catholics this number is likely to increase if the requirements of infant baptism are to be met. Whatever may be thought of the details of the Order for the Christian Initiation of Adults, it is important as showing a way by which the non-baptized, when once they approach the church, may be gradually incorporated into it. The day may not be far distant when there will be, as in the fourth century, a large section of the Christian community who are in one sense or another 'catechumens', people drawn to Christianity, full of good will and desirous of associating with Christians, but who are not yet ready to commit themselves to the whole of the Christian life. Many of the semi-lapsed are really in this position: unfortunately they have the *dis*advantage of being baptized!

But study of these documents prompts other reflections. In spite of all their flexibility, of the alternatives offered and the suggestions for adaptation, they seem a little rigid, perhaps because they bear a certain stamp. True, they have been drawn up by international groups of experts but the texts have a certain European and indeed Latin flavour. It is true that the needs of missionary territories with other cultures are constantly in the background and at least *opportunities* are given to adapt the rites as and where necessary. But still, the rites often say and require us to do things that we should have said and done rather differently. The question is then whether these rites are to be regarded as definitive or whether they can and should be used as points of departure for the construction of other rites that will more adequately express the needs of other peoples and cultures. Such long-range adaptation, which seems to be in accordance with the Constitution on the Liturgy (40), would seem to be on the horizon. The events covered by these rites are the great life-moments of ordinary people and if they are to become part of their lives, they will have to be so adapted as to express *their* way of life, *their* sentiments and *their* needs. How this is to be done is another matter and there is no need to be in any great hurry about it. With the use of the rites people will begin to discover their needs and since liturgy at its best is a matter of natural growth rather than authoritative dictation, it will be best to allow people to discover their needs. What is necessary is to see the rites as 'open-ended', offering opportunities of quite radical adaptation, for such adaptation is the very condition of their continued effectiveness.

When I wrote this book in 1972–73 most of the new rites had been issued though the anointing of the sick which came in 1971 had not come into use and the Order of Penance had not been issued at all. By the end of 1972 most people were familiar enough with the new rite of the Mass though some did not like it and moaned and complained in the Catholic press at great length. The new rites of baptism and marriage were in use by 1970 and have generally been pronounced a success. Although the anointing of the sick with its attendant rites has had a shorter life this too has proved to be very acceptable to the people. Of the Order of Penance I have spoken above. In a sense, then, the new liturgy has been absorbed into the current life of the church without too much difficulty and this must be said to be great gain. But in a sense only. What has become apparent in the last twenty-five years or so is that *celebration*, the meaning of celebration and the manner of celebration is a key issue.[2] Even good rites cannot wholly mitigate bad celebration though the worst features of the old way of doing things are a thing of the past. One does indeed hear of Masses said 'at speed' and of administrations of infant baptism that are scrambled affairs. On the part of some of the clergy there seems to be an indifference to the importance of symbolic actions like the sign of the cross, genuflexions, the laying-on of hands and one's general bearing during liturgical celebration. What is more important is a disregard for the *word* whether that is the word of God in the Bible or the words of the liturgy. The truth that we are saved by faith and by the sacraments of faith (and faith comes by hearing, said St Paul) does not seem to have sunk in. All the new rites insist on the proclamation of the word before the sacramental action itself takes place though theologically speaking it is difficult to separate the one from the other. No doubt it is difficult to achieve a balance between the formal utterance that the liturgy demands and that personal dimension which makes it possible for the ministry of the word to appear as a message from person to person. But it is not impossible and the remedy is to be found in a respect for the word and in a conviction that the word in the liturgy is not simply man's word but God's (cf. CL 33).

On the part of the laity, too, there seems to be an impatience about the word. Lay-readers often read too quickly as if the point of the exercise was to get it over as quickly as possible, or they mumble and so make an absurdity of the whole procedure. These defects can be cured by training but what is more difficult to cure is their indifference to the word as it is proclaimed to them in the course of various rites.[3] Here the need seems to be an educational one: a better initiation into the Bible and an ability to attend to words whether they are those of the scriptures or the liturgy. We seem to be moving into an un-literate age in which noises are taking the place of words, i.e. sounds that have meaning. If this is so, it is vital that the church should keep alive the importance of the word for without it the church cannot exist.

Another reason for this unhappy state of affairs is *haste*. Both laity and clergy, or large numbers of them, seem to want to get their worship done as quickly as possible. Why this should be so it is difficult to understand though it is probably the result, at least in part, of those quick 'silent' Masses of half-an-hour and those rapid administrations of sacraments to which so many were accustomed for so long. Here again, education in the meaning of worship would seem to be the remedy. But 'education' does not mean simply 'instruction' of the academic kind. People need to be initiated into the ways of worship largely through participating in liturgies well done. Then the *personal* dimension of the new rites, mentioned above, will be able to make its full impact.

As the experience of recent years has shown, this has become ever more important. It is this that many, perhaps most, are seeking, and oddly enough it is connected with the matter of community. This has been a bogey to some who still wish to preserve their splendid isolation in worship. What many are seeking, and not only in Great Britain, is a truly communal worship that is at the same time personal, one in which they feel personally engaged and in which the celebrant is someone who cares for them and is a great deal more than a hieratic figure. In the course of these years, then, the desire for *smaller* worshipping communities has made itself felt. The smaller parish with a living community is attracting many and the large church without any visible community is less and less popular. This would seem to bear out what I have written elsewhere in a rather different context.[4]

What can be done about this at the practical level is another matter: large parishes exist and large churches exist and they cannot just be wished away. One of the striking features of the Catholic Church is that vast numbers of people still go to Mass in spite of all that has been said about the dwindling faith and feeble practice of modern Catholics. This situation does pose problems but they are not insuperable. There are ways of creating community both within and outside the liturgy. If a parish, even a large one, has a genuine community life, this will show in worship and there are simple and unpretentious ways of making this apparent. If there is a welcome, the provision of the necessary book or books and a general sense of caring among the more active members of the congregation, the impersonality of so much worship in large churches would be removed. In fact, it is now a matter of experience that the new liturgy has done much to foster the sense of community in the church. The many 'good works' of the modern church, both intra- and extra-mural, witness to it.

It has been said above that 'the sacraments have once again been firmly set in the context of life', though whether the potentialities of the new rites have been exploited in parish life is not clear. Parishes seem to go on much as before: sacraments are 'administered', social events are organized and people are visited (though less and less). Prayer and discussion groups have indeed appeared and are doing valuable work. But all this activity still lacks a centre. It is still not seen as proceeding from the liturgy and leading back to it. In other words we still lack a *pastorale liturgique*. Although new problems are already on the horizon, e.g. the continuing shortage of priests, no effort at serious pastoral planning is being made—or if there is, it is local and perhaps temporary. The hesitation and even reluctance in some places to institute lay ministers of holy communion or to ordain married men to the permanent diaconate are symptoms of a deep-rooted refusal to change, whatever the situation in which the church has now to live and act. Too many are content to go on doing what they have always done with just a top dressing of 'new liturgy'.

Nor are these simply domestic matters. The Roman Catholic Church in Great Britain has moved into a position where it is seen to be an important element, perhaps an irreplaceable element, in the national life. This is not a position of honour but one of responsibility but we need to show more effectively than we do that we have responsibilities to the whole country. All that we do and say has repercussions far outside our own community with the consequence that we need constantly to weigh our words and examine our modes of action. We need to realize more vividly that we are under scrutiny by vast numbers of people, many of whom are 'searching for God'. As far as liturgy is concerned, this situation raises two questions, that of adaptation and that of evangelization.

To take the second first. Evangelization, though having one overriding aim, namely to proclaim the Good News of Salvation and to bring men and women into contact with Christ, is specified by the situation in which the word has to be proclaimed. This for us is Great Britain and even within that area there are considerable differences between England and Scotland, between England and Wales and between England and Northern Ireland. Even more specifically, localities differ from one another and what can be done in a small town cannot (often) be done in a large industrialized city. This is no more than a long way round of speaking of those 'basic communities' which are given such emphasis in *Evangelii nu. 'iandi* of Paul VI. Communities that belong to a given district, tha' reflect the concerns of the district and that know or come to know what are the needs of the district, are the places where in one way or another the Good News is going to be made known. It is in these communities, where people know each other as persons, that the word of God can be effectively proclaimed and where people can be brought to Christ.

This is of course an enormous question that cannot be dealt with adequately here. I cannot, even were I competent, suggest ways and means although I believe that the vitalization of 'basic communities' is fundamental to the whole matter. But one or two more questions may help towards finding the right answers. What is the stance of the church in this country to the community in which we live and by which we live? Or have we any stance at all? Are we content simply to preserve (and more and more precariously, some would say) what we have got and so conduct our diocesan and parish affairs, including the liturgy, as if we had nothing to say to the world and the world had nothing to say to us? Do not some parishes seem to exist in what I would call a sociological void? To give one example: in most places the arrival of a new parish priest arouses a certain interest. People, and not only Catholics, wish to meet him and, among other things, want to know if he is the sort of man who will have a concern for the community in which he is going to work.

~

And yet his induction is often a purely domestic affair. Only Catholics are invited and the ceremony usually takes place in the context of the eucharist. Implicitly the local community is excluded and even if they are invited, they cannot take part in the eucharist by receiving holy communion. Here a change of attitude brings with it a realization that there must be a certain adaptation (the organization of a non-eucharistic service) to meet the needs of those whom we call our brothers and sisters in Christ even if they do not belong to our church.

Again, many parishes have a potential in manpower, buildings and sometimes money, not to mention the undoubted *devotion* of many of the laity within their parishes. Could not some of this potential be actualized for the good of the surrounding community? Ought not this to be regarded as the normal and necessary use of parish resources? The church does not exist for itself, we do not exist for ourselves—or, to put the matter in the positive terms of Vatican II, the church is essentially missionary and all its members everywhere are responsible for that mission. Perhaps we are victims of conventional expressions. When we say 'mission' we think of preaching the gospel to 'natives' of other countries. Perhaps we think we have to 'talk religion', that we have to expound the Bible or instruct others in the doctrines of the church. We must *convert* them or all our work is in vain. In spite of Vatican II, which spoke of the servant church, we do not seem to have realized that the gospel can be preached, and very effectively, by *service*—and *that* is pretty close to the heart of the gospel. The simple, humble, psychological truth that you cannot reach anyone, even with God's word, unless you have won his or her confidence and perhaps affection, still seems to be largely unknown. Service is a mode of loving and only when we love, whether as individuals or communities, can we reach others.

This attitude, too, affects the tonality of our worship. Nowadays there are many who have no formal attachment to our church but who come to attend services. If the local assembly is welcoming, they will at least feel that we are trying to be Christians, loving our neighbours even when they are anonymous. This of course is particularly important for baptisms, confirmations (when non-Catholic parents are happy to attend), marriages and funerals. On all these occasions nowadays there are considerable numbers of those we call loosely non-Catholics, and through the liturgy, through the way we celebrate it, we are—or are not—serving them, trying to convey to them something of the gospel truth, the saving word of God that is made known to people in the ordinary circumstances of life of which these events are an inevitable part. Surely it does not need to be repeated that the celebration of marriage is one of the most effective ways of 'preaching' the Christian doctrine of marriage and the care and attention that the parish clergy take over preparation for baptism is usually a lesson in itself to the family. The bearing and the words of the bishop at confirmations and his willingness to meet the parents afterwards and talk with them are what is now expected and everyone knows that such encounters can be very fruitful. Likewise, the attentive care of the sick and dying which the Order so greatly facilitates, and the celebration of the funeral rites for the dead, coupled with comfort for the bereaved, are so many sermons in words and action that reach the hearts of many. Viewed in this light the revised liturgy has been of immense *pastoral* benefit to great numbers of people. In this sense a *pastorale liturgique* is in existence, at least where the possibilities of the new liturgy are being realized.

For that is the point. As I have said above, the new liturgy is open-ended but it is so in two senses. It is open-ended first for those with the necessary understanding and imagination to arrange a service for a particular occasion or a particular group of people. The rubrics of the revised liturgy are not blueprints or working drawings that dictate every word and action to be done. They are directives or guidelines that make it possible for a celebrant, in consultation with the laity (who are also celebrants), to produce a liturgy that over the whole range of its action will communicate the message of Christ. Some few years ago there was a good deal of discussion about 'creativity' in liturgical matters and too many thought that this meant creating new liturgies but it was made clear that quite apart from such (unlawful) procedure there was considerable room for 'creativity' in the manner of arranging, organizing and celebrating the liturgy.[5] The *same* rite celebrated with the requisite qualities of knowledge, understanding and imagination can appear to be very different from one where those qualities are lacking. As Cardinal Schuster said more than seventy years ago, the written liturgy as found in the books is no more than a libretto. It has to be brought to life and that happens only in celebration. It has to be clothed with sound (music – of the right sort), light and movement, and it is only then that it begins to make an impact or, more importantly, communicate the divine message of which it is the medium. This is as true of the sacraments as it is of the Mass. The baptism and confirmation of an unbaptized convert within the celebration of the Easter Vigil is a very different thing from a private event which can hardly be called a celebration at all. No doubt there are occasions when a more domestic kind of treatment is appropriate. Some baptisms have to be celebrated with the minimum of ceremonial and when there is great grief it is often a kindness to the bereaved to make the funeral as simple as possible. Public anointings of the sick, too, call for a previous psychological preparation and an initiation into the meaning of the sacrament. But granted that, such a celebration can bring comfort to the sick and show the sacrament for what it is. It is strange that there has been no official encouragement in this country of public celebrations of the anointing of the sick.

Much, then, still remains to be done within the limits of the existing liturgy if its potential is to be realized.

Those however who have done their best to 'make the most of the liturgy' have come up against problems and difficulties and they as well as others have come to realize that the new rites are sometimes defective. I have remarked above that the texts have a European and inevitably, since they were drawn up in the language of the Western church, a Latin flavour. They in turn have been translated into what someone has unkindly called 'mid-Atlantic' English. Yet, while granting that it was hardly possible to achieve perfection (if it ever can be achieved) in rites and language, it is necessary to say that those committed to the use of the Roman rite are now very numerous in many countries and continents that know little or nothing of European culture. Thus the question of *adaptation* is raised, adaptation that goes far beyond the permitted adaptations that are available in the official books to conferences of bishops and pastors. It is highly likely that this will be the great question of the future. Fortunately both the Constitution (37–40) and the official books, in numerous places, allow of such development.

What then will happen? No one, I imagine, would be so rash as to predict anything in detail but it may well be that in India, in the very different countries of Africa and perhaps (who knows?) in China, Christians will examine the traditions of their own cultures and will find in them insights and ways of doing things that are consonant with the liturgy but which are expressive of *their* culture, their ways of thinking and their ways of acting. As a recent writer has pointed out, in the early formative period of the liturgy there was not only adaptation but there were two ways of doing it: by assimilation and by substitution.[6] The Roman liturgy in the course of centuries took over certain cultural elements and added them to the rites, sometimes to their detriment. But the church also *replaced* certain symbols with others. Thus the rite of anointing the forehead in confirmation has ousted what was almost certainly the primitive rite of the laying-on of the hand. Both procedures are fraught with danger, for the first can clutter up a liturgy and the second can obscure its original features as did the anointings in ordination. Historically speaking, then, adaptation has sometimes been a mixed blessing, and in our own time, when there is often a misunderstanding of or a disregard for the meaning of symbols, we should be duly cautious. The new and unwarranted breaking of the bread at the words of institution distorts the shape of the eucharist as we have known it from the beginning. Both assimilation, then, and substitution need to be carefully watched in the process of adaptation that will certainly go ahead in years to come.

None the less there is a strong case for adaptation. The church is Catholic and it must be able to incorporate into its life and worship as many elements as are necessary to show that it is. Already and for centuries there are the Eastern liturgies which differ widely not only from the Roman liturgy but also often from each other. There is no reason why Africa, Asia and India should not gradually evolve liturgies that are comparable to the Eastern rites but that also express their cultures. One can see three areas where such adaptation might take place.

1. Symbols

Though there is a strong case for the retention of the basic symbols of the liturgy that derive from the Bible, bread and wine, anointings with oil and the laying-on of hands, there are others that could be changed though even the use of oil has not quite the same importance as the others. It does indeed seem to be a pretty universal symbol of abundance though apart from the anointing of the sick (where it need no longer be olive oil) and in the present discipline of confirmation, its use is no longer necessary for the validity of any sacrament. In regions then where it has no significance—perhaps in the far North—it might be dispensed with. Again, the rigid system of liturgical colours which in the West is not attested before the thirteenth century (Innocent III) is no longer imposed. In China (and apparently in sixteenth-century France, if we are to trust the portrait of Mary, Queen of Scots, *en deuil* for the death of her young husband, François II) white is the colour of mourning.

2. Gestures

The ancient Christian and indeed Jewish gesture of holding the hands raised with the palms upturned as a sign of supplication may not be expressive to some peoples and even in the West it has been largely replaced by the gesture of holding the hands joined. This derived from feudal custom in the Middle Ages and for the laity it has to all intents and purposes ousted the more ancient custom. The Indian gesture of joining the hands together as a sign of welcome is already in use in the liturgy of that country. In the West the genuflexion, a Byzantine gesture apparently, largely replaced the bow as an act of obeisance (except in secular ceremonial). No doubt in different parts of the world there are other ways of expressing the same thing. One would ask also whether kneeling, which is really a sign of repentance and to which Western Christians are so much attached, has the same or any significance in other parts of the world. In many cultures it would seem the dance plays an important role in worship; if that is so, there would seem to be no reason why it should not be introduced into Christian worship. The Constitution (37) speaks of 'the genius and talents' and 'the way of life' (i.e. cultures) of different peoples and these are very various, perhaps more so than the Fathers of the Council knew. Different peoples express their sentiments and emotions in different ways and these, with the precautions laid down by the Constitution, may be allowed to have a formative influence on worship. There is really nothing new in this. A liturgy according to the Byzantine rite which gradually received its form from the culture of the Byzantine empire *looks* very different from a celebration of the Roman rite but its content is exactly the same. It is simply a different way of doing the eucharist that the church received from Christ. Yet it can reach the hearts of its participants and speak to them in a way that the Roman rite cannot. In years to come we should expect that the peoples of Africa, India, Asia and elsewhere should construct liturgies that are as eloquent as those of the Eastern churches and as authentic.

3. Language

As everyone knows, the Roman liturgy since the Council has been translated into dozens of vernaculars of almost all the peoples of the world. What has not been sufficiently noticed is that this has been the first and major adaptation that has taken place in the last thirty years or so. For translation, if it is to be authentic, is an attempt to transfer the *thought* of one language into the thought of another. It was and remains a major task and the opinion is widespread that, with some exceptions, the English translations have not been very successful. Perhaps it is significant that the French and Italian translations are generally judged to have been more successful, though the French has been criticized.[7] The reason for it may be that they are more closely related to Latin than English is. However that may be, what English-speaking peoples have yet to learn is how to express in a language that is really their own what needs to be expressed in the different rites of a liturgy that is Roman but not necessarily Latin. As has been observed above, some texts of the marriage rite are very unhappy and could without much difficulty be improved. Other unfortunate translations have been mentioned in the course of this book and there is no need to repeat them here.

Another development that we can look for is more important. It should be possible for different regions and even different countries to re-shape the rites according to native genius. English people do think and express themselves differently from Americans and what might seem starchy or over-dignified to the latter may well be the natural way of expression for the former. What may seem to be to English people a proper and natural way to handle the marriage rite may be unacceptable to Americans. This has to some extent been done. The marriage rite is proper to England but a writer in *Liturgy* (the organ of the English National Liturgical Commission) has expressed the view that more might have been done and could still be done to exploit the English tradition stemming from the old Sarum rite.[8] He wishes to retain the archaic sentences 'With this ring I thee wed; this gold and silver I thee give; with my body I thee worship; and with all my worldly goods I thee endow'. He finds this more expressive than the current formula. And one agrees with the writer that 'the Introduction to the *Ordo Celebrandi Matrimonium* (OCM) gave ample encouragement to individual bishops' conferences to adapt or even omit elements of the rite provided in

OCM and to substitute other elements which would fit in better with the practice of the people'. This is in fact to say little more than the Ritual of 1614, which envisaged the use of local rites, very numerous at the time, and wished to insist only on what was essential, namely, the exchange of consent before an authorized priest.

What is more important is that the recommendations of the OCM could be more widely applied. It is not only 'missionary' countries (which are rapidly becoming the mainstay of the church) that have cultures and usages apt for incorporation into the liturgy. Other, older countries have them also, and it should be possible for them to adapt, re-shape and reform rites so that they are expressive of their ways of thinking and their cultures. If the fear were expressed that there would be a vast diversity that would be either disturbing or intolerable it has to be said that unity of faith with diversity of rite has been a mark of the church for centuries. A wedding according to the Byzantine rite is very different from one according to the Roman rite but they both celebrate the same sacrament. The same can be said of the sacraments of initiation and ordination.

Nor would this be diversity for its own sake. The great task—and opportunity—for the church today is to insert the saving message of the gospel into the lives of ordinary people. Every time we seem to distance them by rites that seem 'foreign' or difficult to lay hold of, we are making that insertion of the gospel message less likely. At this point liturgical adaptation joins mission for if liturgy is not of itself a missionary device it is largely through a liturgy that speaks to a particular people that the gospel message is communicated. Mission and liturgy march together and it is to be hoped that the days are long past when it was thought that you could 'instruct' people in the faith and then let them make their way in worship as best they could. Liturgy incarnates faith, arouses faith and communicates faith and it does so at the level of life. If the liturgy is apt, the right instrument for a given people, they will believe, live and act as Christians through their experience and celebration of it.

Whether or not such adaptation goes ahead in the years to come is a question that no one can answer at the moment. Much will depend on a real and realistic decentralization of the church, but meanwhile it can be said that our current liturgy remains open-ended and allows of a development that can only be for the good of the people of God.[9]

Notes

[1] It is my personal view that there is. One straw in the wind is that even now people still seem to be 'instructed' in the sacraments without any reference to the liturgical texts. And yet these are supposed to teach!

[2] See *Christian Celebration: Understanding the Mass*, chapters 10 and 11.

[3] Cf. *The Lector's Handbook* (CTS, London, 1978).

[4] *The Once and the Future Liturgy* (Dublin, 1977), pp. 75ff.

[5] See (among other places) *Notitiae*, 73 (May 1972), pp. 151ff. and 157ff.

[6] A. J. Chapungco, 'Greco-Roman Culture and Liturgical Adaptation', *Notitiae*, 153 (April 1979), pp. 202ff.

[7] The change of opinion of Julien Green, however, is interesting. In his *Journal 1966-1972* he was critical of the first attempts, but later, when the official translation had appeared, he finds in it a certain dignity and his reservations have largely disappeared (see *Ce qui reste du jour*, 1972, the title of this volume of his *Journal*).

[8] See editorial of *Liturgy*, 3 (August/September 1979) by A. A. B(oylan). This has now been done in the proposed English rite. Alternatives have been provided.

[9] The most thorough example of adaptation or inculturation known to the author is that of Zaire.

Name Index

Subject Index

This index covers the main text, but excludes the end-notes. Major references within a sequence are indicated by **bold type**.